UNIX for
Super-Users

INTERNATIONAL COMPUTER SCIENCE SERIES

Consulting editors   **A D McGettrick**
University of Strathclyde

J van Leeuwen
University of Utrecht

UNIX for Super-Users

ERIC FOXLEY

ADDISON-WESLEY PUBLISHING COMPANY

Wokingham, England · Reading, Massachusetts · Menlo Park, California
Don Mills, Ontario · Amsterdam · Sydney · Singapore · Tokyo
Mexico City · Bogota · Santiago · San Juan

Printed in Finland by Werner Söderström Osakeyhtiö.

First printed in 1985. Reprinted 1986 and 1987.

Cover computer graphic courtesy of Dicomed.

British Library Cataloguing in Publication Data

Foxley, E.
 Unix for super-users, — (International computer science series).
 1. UNIX (Computer operating systems)
 I. Title   II. Series
 001.64'25   QA76.76.063
 ISBN 0–201–14228–7

Library of Congress Cataloging-in-Publication Data

Foxley, Eric.
 UNIX for super-users.

 (International computer science series)
 Includes index.
 1. UNIX (Computer operating system)   I. Title.
 II. Series.
 QA76.76.063F69   1985   005.4'3   85-15841
 ISBN 0-201-14228-7

To my Mum and Dad

Preface

The need for a wide-ranging introductory text on the administration of Unix systems became apparent at a very early stage of the author's experience of Unix. Although all the necessary information was in the documentation somewhere, it was not collected together in a convenient way. Talking to an experienced Unix user was often the best way of sorting out problems, and of gaining a better understanding of the system. People who attended some of the early Unix courses run in the UK asked for particular emphasis to be placed on problems of systems administration, and the notes for those courses formed the basis of this book.

The book attempts to cover a wide range of user needs, over a wide variety of sizes and styles of computer system, running a wide variety of variants of Unix. This is a daunting task. The author owes a debt of gratitude to a large number of people, since the breadth of coverage which has been achieved would have been impossible without their help. The ideas covered in the book reflect experience arising from a variety of computer systems, from some which are small and informal, to others larger and more security conscious.

In chronological order, the first to thank are the people who attended the early Unix courses on which this material was developed; they suffered the original experimental versions of the notes which eventually became the basis for this book. Their questioning showed the need for a text on the administration of Unix systems.

As far as the content of the book is concerned, particular thanks to my colleague Julian Onions for extensive original contributions; each time I asked him for a few ideas on a given area, the electronic mail system soon carried from him to me an outline for a fairly full text for that area. Thanks must also go both to William Armitage and to Julian Onions for checks on points of detail and for answering endless questions from the author.

Many people from other computer installations have helped in the development of the content of the book. A number of them have spent a considerable amount of time commenting on the draft text; their efforts have been very much appreciated and have resulted in a text improved almost beyond recognition. Of course, the responsibility for accuracy still rests with the author! A major contribution came from Peter Collinson at the University of Kent at Canterbury, whose experienced advice has always been particularly appreciated. I would also like to include in my thanks Steve Bourne, Selwyn Castleden, Jan van Leeuwen, Andrew McGettrick, John Quarterman and Steven Simmons; all of these gave generously of their time and their many detailed comments and helpful criticisms have broadened the value of the book considerably. It was interesting to observe the difference in the pattern of comments from different sources. There were significant differences between the comments from those concerned with the relevance of the book for users of small Unix systems (perhaps those growing out of single-user machines) and those whose experience was mainly in the running of large multi-user systems; and between hardened administrators who were concerned to restrain a large community of users and those much more concerned for the provision of a helpful user environment. It is to be hoped that the final version of the text balances their two sides of the scene in a satisfactory way. It was also interesting to see how many people used locally developed commands and assumed that they were part of standard releases!

Thanks must also go to Eddie Bleasdale, who through his company (Bleasdale Computer Systems PLC) organised the original Unix courses which showed a need for the type of information covered by this book.

The book has been produced on a Unix system; the fact that this was a pleasure and convenience is due to the excellent design and implementation of Unix, which, although not perfect by any means, far outstrips all other systems to which the author has access in these two respects. The author is greatly indebted to the designers and implementors of all the relevant software on the machine, including the general Unix system software itself, the software used in the generation of the text, and that used in the production of the final copy. For the Unix system, thanks must go to the original trio of Brian Kernighan, Dennis Ritchie and Ken Thompson who set up a basis on which many others could add small but significant enhancements.

As far as the text preparation goes, the main item was a superb general-purpose editor by Andy Walker of this department, modified and extended by John Haxby. For the production of the final copy, the standard *troff* and related software has been much modified (and improved) locally by Douglas Woodall and Julian Onions. George Paechter is the local wizard at typesetting macros who sorted out the final photo-typesetting to conform both to the publisher's house style and to his own very high standards, and who undertook the preparation of the final copy. Betty Hickling, who looks after the photo-typesetter, was calm and unruffled throughout the exercise. Thanks again to Andy Walker who has improved a number of our Unix text-processing tools (such as those for speeling ckeching) and general author support considerably. Thanks to Ali Haddara for the multi-window environment which helps poor users who have only one terminal on one serial line to pretend that they have several. All those named in the above paragraph are colleagues with whom I continue to work: such tolerance! I also use with much appreciation an on-line *Roget's Thesaurus* supplied by Longmans, which makes writing even more of a pleasure; the programs to access it have been augmented by Dave Allsopp.

The final copy was produced using the *titroff* program and related software, locally modified, run on a DEC PDP 11/44 computer into a Linotron 202 photo-typesetter.

In spite of the above help, all failures in accuracy remain squarely the responsibility of the author; he would be happy to hear about them and to be told of any other improvements which would make the book more readable, more generally applicable to different versions of Unix, and thence more useful. This is an area where as much experience of different situations as possible should be combined, and contributions would be very welcome.

Last, but not least, thanks go to my wife Joy and the rest of the family, who have survived without me for many hours during the preparation of this text; apologies for all the missed and late meals, but, I am glad to say, never a missed music performance.

Eric Foxley
Mathematics Department
Nottingham University
June 1985

Contents

Chapter 1 Introduction

Many books have been written about the Unix system. Some are aimed at enlightening users new to computers, some are for users new to Unix, some describe the more complex commands for more advanced users, some are for the writers of applications programs, and yet others have in mind the interests of systems programmers.

This book is aimed at the person who has been given the job of supervising a Unix-based facility. Such a person is likely to be already familiar with the basic features of the Unix system. They may have previously been a user of that system, and have now been given administrative responsibility for it. Alternatively, it may be a newly installed system, in which case the person chosen as administrator will probably be a potential user of it, and will learn the basic operations straight away. The company may already use other time-sharing mainframes, so that the ideas of Unix are not totally new, or the company may be moving up from single-user machines, in which case many of the basic ideas of providing a shared multi-user service need careful consideration. The person put in administrative charge will thus either already be a Unix user, or will soon become one, but not just an ordinary user. In addition to knowing the techniques for the general use of Unix by ordinary users, they will have the additional responsibility of maintaining its security, obtaining the best possible response time for users, creating new login names, being required to restore old copies of files which the user has accidentally deleted, and so on. Such information as this person requires is, of course, in the Unix manuals and documentation. However, in that form it is not necessarily easy for a beginner to understand, and is not collected together in a logical way. In particular, users coming from a single-user microcomputer system to Unix will find a number of the concepts of security and filestore maintenance new. Those coming from large mainframe systems may be surprised by other aspects of Unix management.

In this book we describe those aspects of the Unix operating system (and some related to its associated implementation language C) which are the particular concern of someone who has the responsibility of managing a Unix system. Among the topics included are descriptions of management functions such as

>the creation of new login names;
>the maintenance of filestore security;

1

the monitoring of user resource usage;
the maintenance of documentation;
machine performance considerations.

In each of these areas, we discuss how Unix works, the basic principles, the relevant commands available under Unix and the significance of the possible responses from those commands. General principles to ensure good security and performance, and all operations normally requiring 'super-user' privilege are included. Shell scripts and C programs for various system management functions are outlined both to illustrate the Unix style of programming and to show that the Unix system can be understood by any system manager and can be 'tailored' to any particular user community's needs.

1.1 Background assumed

We assume that the reader has a knowledge of using Unix as an ordinary user, including features such as the following.

- The functions of the common Unix commands, such as *ls*, *cat*, *grep*, and most of those in section 1 of the standard Unix manual. The commands relating more closely to Unix management rather than ordinary user applications are described in detail at the appropriate point in the book, and are summarised in Appendix 3.
- The simpler additional features of the shell syntax, including output redirection to files (the '>' symbol in the shell, for example, to redirect output from the screen to a file), the concept of pipes (the '|' symbol, to redirect output from one process to another process), and the use of forked-off processes (the '&' symbol). The fundamental difference between ordinary data files and directories is also assumed. Examples of shell scripts given later will use the Bourne shell. The two major shells, the Bourne shell and the C shell, are summarised in Appendices 1 and 2 respectively.
- Elementary C programming at a user (application) level. This is not necessary for the major part of the book, but some of the illustrations of how new system commands could be written use simple C programs as illustrations. The C preprocessor (which contains useful features of which many users are not aware, and which are not generally documented) is summarised in Appendix 4.

The following areas relate more closely to Unix system management, and are explained more fully in the text.

- The Unix management commands in section 8 of the standard Unix manual, which are intended for use by system managers. In Version 7 Unix, there are certain additional commands classified as '1M' in section 1, which are mainly for managers, but may be of interest to users. These include commands to dump the filestore for security reasons, to check on the machine performance, and to execute other management functions.
- The principles of operation of the Unix filestore, which are described in sufficient detail for the user to appreciate the reason for the

recommended filestore activities such as dumping, and security considerations.

- The standards which should be adhered to when adding new commands to an existing Unix system. A proposed standard to be adopted when designing new commands is summarised in Appendix 5.

We further assume that the user has a Unix system available to them and has access through the supplier to the full Unix manuals. These contain more precise details of the commands and systems calls and are *essential* for checking accurate details of the implementation of any particular command on their machine. When a particular aspect of a given command is described, it will be assumed without further mention that full details can be checked as required in the Unix manuals (which may be available on paper, or on-line using the *man* command). This book is not a duplicate of the Unix manual – the areas in which administrators may be involved are often the areas where there are significant differences between different implementations of Unix.

The user should be aware of the distinction between what is referred to here as the Unix manual (containing short summaries of every command, system call, library subroutine and so on, usually about a page for each entry) and the Unix documents (longer documents of up to 20 pages or more, describing in detail an area of Unix or a complicated program).

Many of the operations described below, being those for system management, require that the user have the special privilege which in Unix is obtained by being logged in as 'root', or by using the *su* ('super-user') command to obtain a root-owned shell. However, in view of the awesome powers it offers, the use of super-user privilege should be avoided whenever possible. This reduces the possibility of catastrophe being caused by an accidental error. For example, to inspect the access permissions on system files and directories as recommended in Chapter 3, super-user privilege may not (indeed, should not) be necessary; it *would* however be necessary if you wished to change the information in a system file.

For further details, the reader is referred to books by Steve Bourne[1] (a comprehensive summary of all aspects of Unix), Peter Brown[2] (a text primarily aimed at beginners), David Barron and Mike Rees[3] (covering the text processing facilities of Unix), and Andy Walker[4] (a general description for potential programmers under Unix). In addition, there have been two special issues of *The Bell System Technical Journal* devoted to aspects of Unix, one from 1978[5] and a more recent issue in 1984[6].

1.2 Warnings

A number of the features described in the book may occur in slightly different forms on some of the many different versions of Unix which are now available. While some of these differences are comparatively insignificant, others are major, and not all changes by suppliers retain the Unix conventions in spirit or detail. Where feasible, we will try to specify these differences, but since the target being aimed at (the set of all available Unix systems and look-alikes) is a moving one, some slight discrepancies are inevitable.

The text at some points may contain a condition such as 'If you have the Writer's Workbench package ...'. The files and programs discussed at that point will not be on your machine unless you have the named package in addition to the standard Unix system. Such items are included since, even if you do not possess the package, it is always useful to be made aware of such packages and their facilities.

At other points, possible features that could be added to Unix are mentioned. It is not the intention of the book to be parochial, but one of the major features of Unix is the ease with which the user interface (the details of the commands, for example) can be changed. A number of modifications and additions have therefore been mentioned, as examples of simple changes which can result in significant improvements in particular situations. These may encourage administrators to tailor their system to suit their own institution's needs.

1.3 Variations in Unix systems

It must be emphasised that there will be many variations between the different Unix systems available on different machines, and later chapters must be read with this in mind. Differences between different versions of Unix will be specified where possible, but there will still be occasions when the exact arrangements on your machine do not correspond with the details given here.

The variety of Unix systems arises from a number of causes. Firstly, from historical considerations, there have been a number of distinct Unix systems released by Bell Laboratories over the years. These include the oldest widely distributed version, 'Version 6' (now obsolete), the very widely distributed 'Version 7' (the standard older Unix for DEC PDP11 computers), and the newer releases 'System III', 'System V', and now 'System V.2'. In addition to these, there are Bell versions for 32-bit machines (Version '32V' is the 32-bit version of V7), and 'PWB Unix' (the 'Programmer's Workbench', an enhanced and more professional Version 6 Unix). Lastly, there are the widely available 'Berkeley Unix' distributions, distributed by the University of California at Berkeley (UCB) and referred to as Berkeley System Distributions or 'BSD'. These started off in life essentially as the '32V' version modified by UCB both to provide enhanced facilities for the user, and to enable it to run more efficiently on 32-bit virtual storage machines. There have been a number of BSD releases, of which the latest include both System III and System V enhancements. The BSD releases have always been very close to standard Bell distributions in respect of all conventions and standards.

In addition to the different 'vanilla Bell' and BSD versions of Unix mentioned in the preceding paragraph, there are now many implemented versions of Unix distributed by a number of software and hardware suppliers. Some of these have been generated under licence from Bell Laboratories and are based on Bell provided source code, while others are written with no acknowledgement. These versions (even the licensed ones) may differ from the standard Bell issues in a number of ways. In particular, there are variations in the area of compilers and loaders, where different hardware (the processor or memory management system) requires a major rewrite of the software.

As if the above variations did not provide enough problems, it is unfortunately often the case that those suppliers who market their own versions of Unix under a variety of names (and even those who do so with full acknowledgement to Bell Laboratories) often decide for crude marketing reasons to release an 'improved version', hoping to try and trap customers into that supplier's particular system. The word 'improvement' is often a misnomer to the unbiased observer, and should be translated as 'incompatible change'. These changes result in yet more variations. Many of these 'improvements' are not really improvements at all, and many added commands do not conform to existing Unix standards.† A further, and often more serious, aspect of these actions is that such suppliers often (quite deliberately) do not make clear to the user which of the features are 'real Unix' and which are (dubious) 'improvements to Unix'. If they did, the user might notice that they were not really 'improvements', and might then take care to avoid using them, thus not becoming trapped into that supplier.

A third level of variation is that the local management of a Unix system again may add, for example, further commands tailored to the local environment. In some cases these (deliberately or otherwise) do not conform to the existing Unix standards, so that different rules may apply to the locally modified parts of the system. The author has taught Unix courses using many different varieties of Unix systems, and the variations are really very significant.

The licensing arrangements for Unix are far too complex, varied, and varying to be described in detail here; however, a little history of licensing does help to explain some of the features of the present Unix scene. Early releases by Bell were, because of anti-trust legislation, mostly just snapshots of the system running in their research section, and because of the requirement that there would be no support, source code was distributed. The main customers were academic institutions who were happy to do their own support work. An original tape would be distributed, but enhancements and bug-fixes would be entirely the responsibility of the user. The distribution of source code was essential in this case, when no manufacturer support was available. This resulted in two characteristics of Unix installations.

Firstly, it resulted in a wide variety of enhancements by different installations, and little collaboration occurred between users. Almost the only exception was the 'teletype driver' developed by the European Unix Systems User Group (EUUG), a set of enhancements to the part of the Unix kernel which drives terminals, which most European Unix sites implemented.

† Perhaps we should use the word 'conventions' rather than 'standards' here, since we are not talking of officially defined Unix standards. The conventions agreed among a number of Unix users are listed in Appendix 5.

Secondly, many parameters which might need to be changed by the system manager were built into the source code of the system. If the manager wished to, for example, reconfigure the system, the source code of the particular module defining the configuration was altered, that module recompiled, and a new kernel generated; this might take 15 minutes. The more modern releases such as Systems III and V come from a more marketing-oriented section of AT&T, and are generally distributed without source code. The earlier designs of Unix, the lack of source would severely restrict the possibilities for reconfiguring. The newer releases of Unix try to build as many system parameters as possible into data files which are read by the system as and when they are required. Reconfiguring is then a matter of editing the data files, and perhaps a minimal relinking and reboot.

The hope for the future is that the Bell 'System V.2' release will become much more of a standard than any of the previous versions of Unix. This cannot be achieved until Bell's new marketing arrangements have been finalised. These are now being co-ordinated with a number of manufacturers of processors. It is hoped that there will eventually be an arrangement for the validation of Unix systems in a similar way to the techniques by which, for example, COBOL compilers have for many years been validated by suites of test programs. It is the author's opinion that standardisation to this extent is unlikely to occur; apart from the fact that there are already so many variations to which different suppliers are committed, a fundamental characteristic of Unix is the ease with which new and modified commands can be installed. Different administrators will have different preferences, and systems will retain a wide variation in their details.

1.4 Notation

In the typesetting of this book, different fonts are used to distinguish command and file names. Command names are distinguished in the text by printing them in italic, typically as in the name *command*. File names are distinguished in the text by printing them in bold text, as in the name **file**.

1.5 Outline

The topics in this book are arranged as follows. Chapter 2 presents an overview of how computer operating systems work; this is aimed primarily at those readers whose previous experience has been mainly with microcomputers acting as single-user facilities.

This is followed in chapter 3 by a perusal of the contents of the Unix filestore; this briefly introduces most Unix topics, and encourages the user to explore a real Unix system. This chapter should be read with a Unix machine at hand if possible.

The way in which a number of fundamental system operations work is then described in order, from booting up the machine to taking it down, through the logging in and out processes. The understanding achieved from chapters such as these helps greatly in the understanding of why a Unix system behaves the way it does.

The chapters on the control of users, and file-systems, describe in detail a number of typical systems administrator tasks, such as the creation of new users on the system, the deletion of unwanted users, and the maintenance of the integrity of the filestore. These chapters contain very specific illustrations of certain administrative functions.

The chapter on devices (chapter 8) describes how devices in Unix function, in particular the filestore devices. This background is particularly useful in the understanding of why there are several different ways of dumping the filestore, for example, and the advantages and disadvantages of each.

Chapter 10 describes various aspects of monitoring the performance of a Unix system, and of the considerations involved in improving it. Any user whose system has a sluggish response should study this chapter carefully.

Chapter 11 collects together a number of details concerning the security of Unix systems, which may have been mentioned earlier in the book, but are gathered here for convenience. Users whose installation must be very security conscious will find a number of suggestions here, in which general user convenience and friendliness must be traded off against security considerations.

In response to a number of suggestions from friends who already administer Unix systems, chapter 12 summarises some of the major more complex Unix commands which are available to all users, but which are particularly relevant to system administrators. Only the official Unix documents can fully describe these commands, but there is enough in this chapter to get the user started, and administrators are encouraged to use such tools to simplify as many aspects of their job as possible.

Finally among the chapters, chapter 13 gives some examples of system commands written either as shell scripts or as C programs. It is hoped that these will help to take some of the mystique out of the system, and will encourage administrators not to be frightened by it. The examples have been chosen to support some of the descriptive chapters earlier in the book.

The first two appendices summarise the two major shells (command interpreters), while appendix 3 details the features of ordinary commands of particular interest to administrators. Appendix 4 gives features of the C preprocessor which appear not to be documented elsewhere, and appendix 5 summarises suggested standards to which any newly created Unix commands should conform.

1.6 References

1.   Stephen Bourne, *The Unix System,* Addison-Wesley, 1983.
2.   Peter Brown, *Starting with Unix,* Addison-Wesley, 1984.
3.   D W Barron and M J Rees, *Text Processing with Unix,* Addison-Wesley, 1987.
4.   A N Walker, *The Unix Environment,* John Wiley, 1984.
5.   *The Bell System Technical Journal,* Bell Laboratories, July-August 1978.
6.   *AT&T Bell Laboratories Technical Journal (Computer Science and Systems),* Bell Laboratories, October 1984.

Chapter 2 How do operating systems work?

2.1 Introduction

It is anticipated that readers of this book will fall into two categories. There will be those users who are already familiar with multiprogramming computer systems, who perhaps used mainframe machines before, but whose organisation is now basing at least some of its workload on smaller machines running Unix. Then there will be another group of users, whose organisations have previously used single-user microcomputers for word processing and accounting, and who are now moving towards shared and perhaps networked Unix systems. To these latter group many of the ideas of a multi-user system may be new, and this chapter summarises very briefly a few of these points. Experienced users of multi-programming systems may choose to skip it!

It is not our purpose to delve deep into the mysteries at the heart of Unix (i.e. in the *kernel* of Unix). To do this would require us to write another book entitled 'Unix for gurus' and would possibly involve us in litigation with AT&T who are understandably anxious that the detailed methods used within the Unix kernel should not become public. Indeed there are non-disclosure clauses in Unix source-licence agreements which prohibit the preparation of documents which describe the fine details of Unix operation.

Fortunately we can give a good qualitative picture of how Unix and the other operating systems work without trespassing into confidential areas. This knowledge is a worthwhile acquisition both for its own sake and, more particularly, for the insights it gives into those factors which cause performance degradation on a badly configured system.

In the next few sections we shall build up a model of operating system functions starting from very simple systems, which are much less powerful than Unix, and gradually adding functionality until we end up with multi-user multi-process operating systems of the Unix variety.

2.2 Simple operating systems

In an elementary one-board computer, such as the simplest personal micro-computers, or ones intended perhaps for on-line control of equipment, there will be some built-in software, usually called a 'monitor'. This will consist of the code for a number of standard subroutines, and these will be stored in read-only memory (ROM) so that the user cannot accidentally damage them. The subroutines may be for performing such functions as sending characters to a printer (involving timing considerations to ensure that the previous character has finished printing, and that the printer is now ready for the next character), or converting a character into a serial signal (eight or more pulses at correctly timed intervals) suitable for sending to a terminal. Such subroutines make the programmer's life easier, and can perhaps be augmented by the manufacturer if, for example, a new peripheral (with different driving requirements) is purchased. The programs for such a small system will often be written in Assembler and the monitor subroutines will be called perhaps by reference to a particular address, by a call such as 'jump to the subroutine at address so-and-so'. All the addresses and purposes of the subroutines will have to be known. The ROM itself will usually have a 'strange' address (perhaps at the top end of the machine's addressing capability), and the user's programs will be constructed to load and operate at address 0 of the machine.

The monitor or supervisor program will thus offer software routines which assist in performing the details of input and output to devices such as lineprinters and VDU terminals. In this way, although the user at the terminal is communicating with his or her own user program this transfer of information may well be taking place via input/output routines in the monitor program. All modern operating systems grew from the humble beginnings of monitor software of this type. The monitor relieves the user from the tedium of writing software to drive hardware devices such as terminals and lineprinters. Instead the user issues some form of *system call* to the monitor asking for a specific input/output action to be performed, and the monitor software takes over the job of issuing the correct sequence of low level operations to make the terminal or lineprinter perform the required action.

Two further points are to be noticed before we move to more complex operating systems. Firstly, the monitor software is not usually being asked to drive devices such as discs, only serial devices such as printers, cassette recorders, or a serial line to another machine. This limits the scope of our notional computer somewhat in that programs cannot be easily saved on disc files, and recalled at a later time. The second point to notice is that, although there are two areas of code (the user's program and the monitor) resident in memory the CPU can only execute one of them at any given instant.

2.3 Single-user systems

The next significant stage of development takes us to operating systems for microcomputers which include file systems on discs, and which are typified by operating systems such as CP/M.† The resident system code now includes subroutines for accessing the filing system (to refer to a file by name for

† CP/M is a trademark of Digital Research.

reading, for example), so that programs again call the system whenever they wish to perform an input or output function. Whereas in the simple case of the 'monitor' in ROM described in the previous section the address of each subroutine in ROM had to be known, there are now two distinctions. Firstly, the user doesn't want to have to remember the addresses of all of the monitor subroutines. Each function which the monitor can offer (i.e. each user requirement) is therefore numbered, and the user merely calls the system with an appropriate service number; for a *read* request the program may ask for 'service number 26' or some such. In different implementations of the system, the system code for a *read* might be at a different position; the user now doesn't need to know where it is, it is sufficient to give the number of the service required, and the service number for a *read* will be constant across all implementations of the system. Secondly, because an 'improved' or extended version of the system might become available, the system code is itself stored on a disc, and is written into memory at the start of a session; it is not normally in ROM, where it would be difficult and expensive to install an improved version. However, while the system is running, the co-existence of the system and the user program is as before; both will be resident in main memory. We will refer to the memory-resident system code as the 'kernel'.

A more major difference is now that the system code usually appears in memory at the 'bottom' of the machine, from address 0. A user program will no longer actually be stored at address 0, but at an address just beyond the end of the system code. The operating system will include code to enable user programs to be brought in from floppy disc and to be loaded into memory addresses from the top of the system code onwards. We presume, for the sake of simplicity, that the kernel occupies low memory addresses from 0 to K inclusive, and the 'user program' will then be loaded starting at address $K+1$. The term 'user program' covers the whole range of user software which may be an editor, a spread-sheet program or a game, and may either have been provided with the computer system or written by the user.

There is a need now for special hardware to enable a user program at any address to act as though it were at address 0, through a 'base address' or 'datum' register. When the user program is executing, the address which has been stored in the datum register is automatically added to every address used in the program, so that the program is unaware that it is not actually situated at address zero. In addition, there is often a second additional register specifying a maximum address beyond which the program may not refer, to protect system code or other special memory at the top of the machine. These additional registers form the basis of what is termed 'memory management'.

When the program makes a system call, perhaps requesting a disc read, the datum register is automatically disabled, or the system code (starting at real address zero) would be unable to operate. Such hardware thus operates in one of two modes; on the one hand, there is interrupt or executive mode (during which the datum register has no effect, and access to all addresses in memory are possible) and, on the other hand, user or program mode (during which time the datum register is added to all addresses, and access is prohibited outside a specified range). These two processor modes, and the datum and upper limit registers, form additional hardware essential for a multiprocessing system.

The simple memory-resident operating system we have just described is reliant on the fact that there is only one process other than itself in the machine. Moreover this process or program is located at a known address, and need not be shifted from that address until it has terminated. The processor will be active on the user program except

(a) when a system service has been requested (in which case the processor may be forced to wait for data to be input, for example);
(b) when the user program terminates.

At program termination control reverts to part of the system which offers a variety of commands for operations such as the deleting of a file or the loading of a new program. Once the program has been loaded from the floppy disc into memory there is usually no need for further disc interactions unless the program itself reads from a file of data on the disc; all the system code to support the system calls a running program may require is memory resident once the machine has been booted. It does not have to be called in from disc when required. In view of the rather poor performance (in terms of transfers per second) of floppy discs it can only be counted as a virtue that the system does not generate any additional disc traffic.

The kernel relieves the user of the detailed difficulties of loading programs and data from discs, and of detailed activity when reading files, but it still remains the case in many single-user systems that, once a user program is started, it remains firmly attached, in some sense, to the terminal. This can be particularly annoying when a process is running and has no further need for terminal interaction, such as a run to send to the printer a summary of the current warehouse stock. Under these circumstances the terminal 'seizes up' and the only further interaction that can be attempted is to abort the program completely. It would appear a reasonable request to ask to 'spin off' the program as a background process and to get on with something such as deleting or renaming files, or starting an edit session at the terminal which needs human interaction.

While the program runs it usually makes use of a terminal for input and output; there is no way in such a simple system to ask that a program should be run 'in the background' (in an 'unused' or 'spare' portion of memory perhaps) while an editor or other package executes 'in the foreground' and the user interacts with it via the terminal. To have more than one program executing in a computer we need an operating system that can support a *multi-process* (sometimes called *concurrent*) environment.

Now for certain specific, simple and frequent background tasks (a very common one is the slow process of printing a file of results to a line-printer, often referred to as 'spooling' output) it is possible to modify a simple single-user operating system to support concurrency in that special case. This is a long way from being a general multi-process capability. Even the simple addition of concurrent spooling to a system can significantly degrade performance, since both the current user program and the spooler will be competing for access to the floppy disc.

2.4 Multi-process and multi-user systems

Let us straight away place Unix in its correct context. The Unix kernel is firmly built around the idea of supporting a multi-process environment, so that the system can share the memory, the processor and the peripherals between a number of competing processes or programs. The Unix kernel acts at two levels. Firstly it services user requests for disc accesses and so on, just as simpler systems mentioned above did. The list of possible requests is exactly the set of entries in section 2 of the Unix manual; these include requests to open files, read data, and so on. Section 2 is derived straight from the full list of system calls, and each call has a number (for use when calling from Assembler) and a name (for use when calling from a higher-level language). Compared with the simpler systems described in the previous section, all the expected calls for reading and writing are there, but with in addition some more sophisticated requests concerned with multi-processing; for example a running program can ask for a new (and potentially independent) process to be started (by the call *fork*), or can ask for a signal to be sent to another process (by the call *kill*).

At a quite separate level, and not affecting the user's view of the system directly, the kernel has to organise such areas as security (ensuring that one user doesn't access another's files or main memory without permission), and the sharing of the processor between the different active processes (ensuring that one demanding user cannot monopolise the processor). The system obviously keeps a table of information concerning all running processes, with details of where they reside in main memory, their size, their owner, and so on. Each process has a number for its unique identification, the 'process identifier' or PID, which is that number shown when a process is set off into the background as in

```
pi | lpr &
```

Unix responds to this command by returning the process numbers of the *pi* and *lpr* processes that have been sent off into the background, followed almost immediately by the prompt from the shell to signal that the terminal can now be used for other tasks.

Once the mechanisms for a multi-process environment exist then a multi-user environment follows as a totally natural extension. The distinct logging-in or command interpreting processes for each terminal will co-exist in main memory. The principal additional feature of a multi-user environment is the increased need for security, in order to ensure privacy for users' processes and files if required.

2.5 Aspects of multi-user systems

We now have an idealised if rather static picture of how Unix might run multiple processes. Provided the active processes always stay at the same memory addresses (which are known to the kernel) then it appears to be a simple matter for the kernel to schedule the CPU, a few milliseconds at a time, between all the processes in turn. Eventually any given process will run to completion and its memory area can be given to some fresh user process which needs to be run. Would that things were this simple! In the following sections we shall examine just a few of the things that can cause problems.

2.5.1 Processor scheduling

Once Unix has handed over the CPU to a given user process how does control ever return to the Unix kernel? Like most other multi-process operating systems Unix expects that the majority of processes will need to perform frequent input/output operations particularly to and from filestore files. Such operations often appear as *read* or *write* in languages like C or Fortran 77. Although in the first instance the read and write routines are linked into the program from system libraries, it remains the case that, inside these library modules, it will be a low-level machine code instruction (it is often called a TRAP) which will have an immediate effect on the computer hardware. Specifically it causes the current process to be suspended, and the CPU then starts executing whatever instructions exist at a hardware pre-determined location. Unix has been careful, of course, to ensure, when it was booted up, that it is Unix kernel code which is squatting firmly at that location, so that Unix controls the actions that take place in response to the system call. So now we have the situation that the Unix kernel has been reawakened by an interrupt generated from within a user program. Such deliberate program generated interrupts are used by Unix as a means of implementing *system calls*.

Almost immediately the reawakened kernel can establish

(a) that it was reawakened by a system call from a user program;
(b) that the system call was requesting, say, that a certain number of bytes be read from a disc file.

A significant proportion of the kernel is taken up with the code necessary to enable it to satisfy requests such as this. It contains a number of 'device-drivers', which consist of the code for the low-level driving of exotic machinery such as discs and multiplexers. However, while the requested disc transfer is under way, the kernel will very probably take the attitude that there is little that the suspended process can usefully do until the read has been performed and that this is a golden opportunity to give some other process some attention from the CPU. The system knows where the chosen new program resides in main memory, and can resume its execution, carefully setting the datum and limit registers to the correct values before entering the program. Thus each system call provides an opportunity for a new decision on which process should be given the next share of the CPU, so that priority systems can be implemented.

Thus we can discern a scheme of scheduling (give each program a turn in using the CPU) which works well provided that most programs make frequent use of system calls, which most of them do for input/output purposes if not for any other reason.

Time interrupts

The scheme just described will not, of itself, cope with the occasional CPU intensive program which performs no input or output for an extensive period; it therefore makes no calls to the system, giving the system no chance to let another program have a share of the CPU. The hardware must therefore be extended to include a mechanism for interrupting the CPU (a time interrupt) after a given length of time if nothing else has happened. Thus no process can hog the CPU to the exclusion of other processes. The timer usually includes in addition the ability for the processor to monitor the amount of time being spent by the processor between interrupts, and the system can then perform accounting to work out the actual processor time being used by each process. This may be used just for accounting/charging purposes, but may also enable the processor, for example, to lower the priority of a process which is having an excessively large share of the processor.

2.5.2 Memory management

The memory overflows

Suppose the main memory is fully occupied by programs, and a user or program requests that yet another program be started up. There is no spare main memory, so the system must decide on a process which can be moved (temporarily) out of main memory to disc, to make way for the new program; the 'swapped out' program must be 'swapped in' at a later stage to allow it to continue. In a heavily overloaded system, where the number and size of programs requesting to be run far outstrips the amount of main memory actually available, the quantity of the swapping traffic and its administration will degrade the system performance drastically. With more memory, there would be less swapping, and the system may appear as though its processor had increased in power. The choice of which program is to be swapped out is yet another example of scheduling in the system; if possible, the system may well choose a process which is waiting for terminal input as its next victim, since such a process may wait for seconds or even minutes before being able to restart.

Fragmentation

When one active program finishes, its memory becomes available for a new program to be swapped in. A new program which is larger cannot be fitted into the same slot. If the new program is smaller than the old, a small area of memory will remain unused, and gradually the memory may come to have many small spare 'holes', whose total area is quite large, but with no hole big enough for a given new job to start. This problem is known as fragmentation, and to avoid it, the system may 'compact' programs already in memory by shifting them up or down to adjoin another program, thus combining several small available holes into one larger one. The system must keep careful note of the location and size of each program, to enable it to set the datum and limit registers correctly when resuming the program.

Virtual memory

On 'virtual memory' systems, programs do not have to be completely swapped in or out; each program's memory is divided in to units ('pages') which can be located independently, and can be swapped in and out one at a time. As long as the currently active part of a program is in main memory, it can proceed. This reduces swapping activity considerably, and reduces also the problem of fragmentation. The program's separate pages do not need to be contiguous in memory, so that separate small 'holes' at different places in the memory can be used to load one program. The program now needs effectively a number of datum registers, one for each page; yet more special hardware!

Shared code

On any system, two simultaneous activations of the same program (for example, two editors, or two Fortran compilers) will contain a lot of duplicate information in the memory; their 'code' will be the same, but their 'data' (the included variable values) will be different. Virtual systems (and some of the more sophisticated non-virtual ones) allow the code to be held once only in memory, but both programs access it, and have their own data segments. This is performed by allowing the two programs to have certain of their datum registers in common, pointing at the same section of memory.

2.5.3 Input/output management

Queueing disc requests

A number of programs may be suspended, awaiting information from a disc file; the system will hold a queue of requests for access to a given disc, and when one transfer is finished, can choose any of the requests from the waiting queue as the next one to act upon. Yet another scheduling area! The system may order requests in the order in which they were received, first in/first out style. Alternatively, since head movements form a significant part of disc access time, it may order the requests by their position on the disc, and execute them in order. This particular aspect of scheduling is very important under Unix, since disc activity is very extensive.

Input/output buffering

When a program requests a 16-byte disc read, for example, the system is interrupted for the request to be satisfied. Since most discs operate in larger units, it is normal for the system to read, say, 512 bytes, retain them in memory, and at the next read request from the program, deliver to the program the next bytes already read. Unix keeps a pool of such buffers for input and output, and if more than one process is read from or writing to a nearby point in a common file, will economise by using the same buffer for all the processes. Buffered output may mean that the new information resides for a while only in memory and that it has not yet been transferred to disc. This implies that the disc and memory must be synchronised occasionally; typically this will occur when a buffer is finished with (when the file with which it is associated has been closed), and must occur before any shutdown procedure.

2.6 Conclusion

It is hoped that the above summary, although brief and grossly over-simplified and attempting to compress what constitutes a huge subject into a few pages, gives newcomers to multi-programming systems a feel for the new problems which arise. The additional hardware mentioned is essential for a multi-programming system such as Unix, and all the points in this chapter are behind the characteristics of Unix when compared with single-programming systems. Both security and performance issues will be discussed extensively later, and will be easier to follow if the basic principles just described are understood.

Chapter 3 **A tour of the filestore**

As the first major discussion of Unix in this book, we will take a look at the standard filestore† locations in which certain information required on all Unix systems is stored, discussing the position, purpose and significance of most standard items. The term 'standard' is used above to indicate that the facts described below are common to all variants of the Unix system; where it is known that differences exist between different marketed systems, such differences are described as far as is feasible.

Some of the simpler operations involved in Unix management will be described as the relevant files are mentioned; this will include operations such as adding a new entry to the manual, or checking the names of the subroutines in a given library. More complicated operations (such as the sequence of events which takes place when a user logs in) are described in detail in later chapters. Some of these standard filestore conventions are absolutely compulsory so that, for example, a directory called **/tmp** is essential for the temporary files created by the *cc* compiler and other commands; the system could not function at all without that directory. The fact that temporary filenames start with the characters '/tmp/' is written into the C compiler source. However, some of the other 'standards' mentioned below could be changed if there were a good reason, so that for example, the location of the documentation could easily be changed providing only that the commands to access it were changed too; since the documentation commands are mainly in the form of shell scripts, this would be fairly straightforward. The documentation could even be removed completely without affecting the basic running of the system.

When comparing the layout of information in the filestore as described below with its layout on your own machine, note that there may well be local variations both in the location of certain items, and in the presence or absence of items. For example, the binary program for mounting external file-systems is called **mount**, and is located in the file **/etc/mount** on some

---

† The term 'filestore' will be used throughout this book to refer to the complete set of on-line file storage. The term 'file-system' will be used to refer to that part of the filestore treated as a unit by Unix (for example, one of the discs). The filestore will normally consist of a number of file-systems each forming part of the hierarchy.

systems, and in **/bin/mount** on others. If, for example, you do not have the 'Writer's Workbench' package, then those files associated with it (which are mentioned below in section 3.3.4) will not be present. The final complication in this varied landscape of Unix-like systems arises because some suppliers of Unix systems do not always themselves conform to Unix standards and conventions; it is to be hoped that one result of this book should be that customers will feel more free to demand completeness, improvement and conformity in suppliers' standards.

On most systems other than Unix, the basic system commands for listing the names of the files in a given directory, deleting files, and so on, are an integral part of the main system program or kernel. With Unix, all systems files (files containing the programs for commands and utilities, the documentation, the subroutine libraries, and so on) are stored in the standard filestore, and this chapter will undertake a tour of those parts of the filestore which are standard across Unix systems, and which contain information which is normally controlled by someone with a title such as 'system manager' or 'system administrator'. Such items include details of all author-ised users of the system, accounting information, subroutine libraries and packages, and so on, and will normally be readable (data files and shell command scripts) or executable (commands in the form of shell scripts and program files) by the users of a system, but will not be writable or removable by ordinary users.

The top directory is known as 'root' and written as /, and can, of course, be reached by the command

    cd /

Below it at the top level are a number of standard directories and files, which must be present on any Unix system. It may be useful for this chapter to be studied by the reader with a Unix machine present, so that you can actually move to the directories as they are discussed, using the *cd* command, and can inspect their contents using the *ls* command, or the variant

    ls −l

to obtain more details, and to compare them with the description given here. Familiarity with the use of the shell to issue simple commands is assumed, so that, for example, to list just the directories at a certain point, the reader would observe that directory entries in an 'ls −l' listing start with the letter 'd', and would then select them by using a piped command such as

    ls −l | grep "^d"

As an example of what is meant by Unix 'standards', the top level of the filestore must include directories named **/bin**, **/etc**, **/tmp**, **/lib**, **/usr** and **/dev**. We will look at each of the standard directories and files at all levels of the hierarchy in turn, and discuss their uses and restrictions.

As you explore the filestore, you may find in certain directories a file with a name such as **READ.ME** or something similar. If so, read it by a command such as

    cat READ.ME

It is a common (and good) practice to maintain such a file in many directories, and to put into it general information for anyone interested in using, amending or inserting items in that directory; typical information in the **READ.ME** file includes details of who wrote the original version, how it works, who modified it, and when, and why, how to create a new version of the command, and so on. Such files are very common on informal distributions, and help recipients insert new material into their system; they are not so common on standard distributions.

There may also be a file called **Makefile** or **makefile** concerned with the *make* command (see the section on *make* in chapter 8 for more details), or in some later versions, an equivalent file whose name ends '.mk'. There may also be a file named **run** containing a shell script which is intended to be run to regenerate certain information. Listing any of these files can give you some information about the contents of the directory, and its significance. It is however very dangerous to actually execute *run* or *make* unless you are absolutely sure that all the required information is present. The file is often intended mainly as documentation of how to regenerate the system, rather than for execution.

When listing files, it should be remembered that Unix allows any file to be listed; if it turns out to be a binary program, the result on the screen is garbage, and the non-printing characters may cause strange effects on 'intelligent' terminals. To check on the type of a file before listing it, use the *file* command, detailed in the following section.

When looking through the directories discussed below, no special privilege should be necessary. It should normally be possible for any user to look through the main directory structure. As a general principle, it is unwise to use special privileges (such as logging in as 'root', or using the *su* command) unless those privileges are really necessary; the power conferred on a 'super-user' under Unix is awesome, and accidental mis-typings of commands can have ruinous effects. As an example, consider the effect of intending to type

    rm *.o

and accidentally typing in error

    rm *>o

an easy error, since '.' and '>' are on the same key on many terminals. Another user intended to type rm *.o

and received the reply "file .o not found". He had actually inserted a space character, as in

rm * .o

again with catastrophic results.†

The descriptions below are discussed more or less in the order in which one might peruse the filestore; this does not necessarily form a logical subject order. All the major areas of activity for a system manager are discussed in later chapters by topic. There are therefore inevitably points where a forward reference can be filled in only on a second reading. The index at the end of the book should assist in locating all references in the text to a particular file.

Some of the explanations of the function of a particular item in the filestore are given as 'in-line code', that is to say, appear in the text at the point where the item of information is discussed. Others, where the explanation required is longer, are given as 'subroutine calls', that is to say, the user is referred to another chapter in which the process is more fully described.

3.1 /bin and /usr/bin; { commands }

Public commands are stored in these two directories, both of which are normally searched by the shell command interpreter when attempting to locate a named command. Commands may be either executable binary programs, or shell command files. Commands which are binary programs are just ordinary programs, and may be compiled from C or Fortran or Pascal or any language for which the compiler produces a loadable program in an **a.out** type of format. Files containing binary programs must be executable, but need not be readable. The removal of read permission stops the command being copied by unscrupulous users. For the Bourne shell, files containing commands in the form of shell scripts must be both readable and executable, so cannot be completely protected. This drawback has been overcome on some new versions of the kernel.

When a user types a command into the machine, the shell determines the first word of the line (that is to say, the text up to the first space, tab or newline character) and this is interpreted as a command name. With very few exceptions‡ this will be the name of a file containing either a binary program or a shell script; the shell must first find this file, and then execute it. After determining the name of the file, the shell searches various directories looking for a file of that name which has execute permission for the user trying to use it. The particular sequence of directories it searches was

---

† One motto of these examples is that you should always use explicit filenames when removing files as 'super-user', never use the asterisk.
‡ See chapter 6 on the shell for an explanation of why there are exceptions which cannot be handled in the normal way.

fixed in earlier versions of Unix (up to Version 6), but is now defined by a shell variable called 'PATH', so that it may be changed easily by the user, and the default changed by the system manager. The normal default for the Bourne shell (**/bin/sh**) is that it searches first the user's current directory, then **/bin**, then **/usr/bin** to find the file. For the C shell (**/bin/csh**) the directory **/usr/ucb** is usually searched too; for Perkin Elmer machines a further directory **/usr/woolagong** may be included in the list. Some managers have a system where by default each user has a local **bin** directory **$HOME/bin**.

The current value of 'PATH' can be found by typing

    echo $PATH

A typical value of 'PATH' for an ordinary user will be something like

    :$HOME/bin:/bin:/usr/bin

to cause the following sequence of directories to be searched:

(a) the current directory (indicated by the absence of any character before the first colon);
(b) the user's own **bin** directory (described as **$HOME/bin**, where 'HOME' is the shell variable which gives the user's home directory);
(c) the first system command directory **/bin**;
(d) the second system command directory **/usr/bin**.

See the chapter on security for reasons why the PATH for the user *root* should not start with the current directory.

If a file is found which has the correct name, but which does not have execute permission, it will be ignored, and the search continues in the other directories listed in 'PATH'.

3.1.1 Why two areas for commands?

The original reason for having two areas for the commands (and for other collections of files, see below) is historical, and relates to the size and cost of discs some time ago. When discs were small and expensive, and fast discs were significantly more expensive than slow ones, the concern was to minimise the requirement for fast disc space. The system was therefore arranged so that the more frequently used files were kept on a small fast device, and those which were less frequently accessed were kept on a slower, larger and cheaper one.

Having the commands in two distinct areas of filestore (**/bin** and **/usr/bin**) has advantages in that it may still enable the manager to put the more frequently used commands in **/bin** on a disc with faster access time. (See chapter 10 for more ramifications of mounting parts of the file-system on different discs.) In addition, the **/bin** directory will then be smaller, which will make it faster to search. (This is insignificant under the C shell, since on entry to the shell, all directories listed in 'PATH' are hashed to speed up searching. This slows down the logging in considerably.) Another consideration involved in deciding how to split the commands between **/bin** and **/usr/bin** is the fact that, on 'boot-up' (see chapter 4), only the root filestore may be available, and this will normally exclude the complete contents of the filestore below the directory **/usr** if, as is the usual case, it is mounted on a separate disc. If that is the case, any system commands which might be needed during the booting process, or during the single user shell which follows the initial boot-up, must be available before the separate **/usr** disc is mounted, and so must not be in a directory below **/usr**. They would typically be in the directory **/bin**, or perhaps **/etc** if the commands are of interest only to the system manager.

3.1.2 Checks on commands

It is easy to perform certain simple checks on the command directories. For example, it should be possible to determine from the output of the command

        ls −l

whether any of the commands has public write permission (there should not be any; it would be surely very dangerous!). Again, the user is encouraged to think in terms of writing commands which will pick out exactly the information required, and in this case the command

        ls −l | grep "^........w"

would print details of only those files with public write permission, or use of the *find* command with arguments such as

        find . −type d −print

or

        find . −type d −exec ls −ld {} ";"

would print the names of all directories below the current directory.

As well as checking the permissions set on the files in **/bin**, a check should also be made of the permissions on the **/bin** directory itself; the author has seen several installations where this check has been forgotten. The **/bin** directory itself should, of course, not have public write permission, unless for some strange reason it is the manager's wish that the public should be able to add their own new commands at any time, and, more seriously, should be able to remove existing commands.†

In a similar way, the root directory / should also be checked; it is surprising how often its permissions are overlooked.

All binary commands should be optimised (compiled with a '−O' flag to minimise the size of the program code and maximise the speed of execution),

---

† In Unix, write permission to a directory gives permission to create and remove filenames in that directory, since these are the operations which involve amending the directory file.

stripped (compiled or loaded with a '−s' flag to cause the relocation tables to be omitted, to reduce the size), and perhaps sharable. (See section 2.5.2 for the significance of the term 'sharable' in relation to multi-programming systems; the extent to which all programs should be sharable will be very system/processor dependent.) The command *file* can be used as in

    file *

to give more information about each file. The output gives details of the types of the data in the files, and for the directory **/bin** might include lines such as

adb:	separate executable not stripped
as:	pure executable
at:	executable
awk:	separate executable
bc:	pure executable
cal:	pure executable
calendar:	commands text
col:	executable
df:	pure executable
diff:	separate executable
diff3:	commands text
dir:	pure executable
dumpcheck:	pure executable not stripped
echo:	pure executable
ed:	separate executable
true:	empty
xsend:	pure executable
yacc:	separate executable

Note that on your machine, the distribution of command files between the directories **/bin** and **/usr/bin** and even **/etc** may be different from the system from which this table was generated; the command names illustrated may not therefore all appear. The various messages include

empty: The obvious meaning! It should perhaps be pointed out that zero length files are perfectly possible under Unix, and occupy an entry in the directory, but no data space. They are often used as flags.

executable: A compiled program; the prefixes 'separate' or 'pure' have their general meaning, and may not be present or applicable on certain hardware.

    The term 'separate' relates to 16-bit address machines, where programs were basically limited to a total size of 64 kbytes, but where this could be extended to 64 kbytes of program plus a separate 64 kbytes of data on certain hardware. The C compiler flag for separate code production is usually '−i'.

The term 'pure' is synonymous with 'sharable', and implies that several invocations of the program may be active on the machine, but that only one copy of the program code will be in main memory, the one copy being shared by all the invocations, hence the alternative term 'shared' code. Each invocation will, of course, need its own data segment. All Unix compilers should be able to produce pure code, using the flag '−n'.

The suffix 'not stripped' implies that the relocation tables produced by the loader for use in debugging (with the command *adb*, for example) are still present. This should not generally be the case with commands, which are presumably fully tested and debugged. Programs can be stripped either using the '−s' flag in the compiler (passed to the loader) or by the *strip* command after compilation as in

```
strip filename
```

ascii text: The *file* command has deduced that this is an editable file of ASCII characters.

commands text: A text file with execute permission is assumed by the *file* command to be a shell command script.

There are other types of file which the *file* command can detect (such as C program source) which will not appear in directories such as /**bin**, but may be found elsewhere. It should perhaps be mentioned that the *file* command does not always make a correct judgement; in particular, it may confuse Bourne shell scripts with C programs.

Try the commands

```
cd /bin; file *
```

to see some of the above features.

All commands should be owned by user 'bin' and group 'bin' except those requiring special SUID facilities (see chapter 9). If the command is a compiled program, the file should have public execute permission, but not for reading or writing; if it is a shell script, the file should have public permission for reading and execution, but not writing. These permissions can be checked by executing commands such as

```
cd /bin; ls −l; ls −lg
```

for both /**bin** and /**usr/bin**.

Special requirements concerned with SUID, SGID, and 'sticky' bits are discussed later in chapter 9.

3.1.3 To install a new command

As you develop special commands for your installation, you will want to make these available to all your users, and will need to install them carefully.

Recommendations for the design of the user interface to commands (the Unix conventions for option parameters such as '−1', for example) are given in appendix 5. Let us assume that the command has been written, and is to be called *new*. The exact sequence of operations will depend on the degree of formality of the installation, but would typically include the following:

(a) Create the file containing the required command either as a compiled program, or as a shell script, and test it to your installation standards.
(b) Create the necessary documentation, using one of the **/usr/man/man1** files as a model (see section 3.4.1 later in this chapter).
(c) Move the compiled program or shell script to the file **/bin/new** (if the command is likely to be heavily used) or to the file **/usr/bin/new** other-wise.
(d) Ensure that the owner of the new command is 'bin' (UID 1), and its group is your chosen system group, usually the group 'bin' (GID 1). This can be done by executing

    chown bin /bin/new; chgrp bin /bin/new

(e) Ensure that its modes are correct; there should be no public write per-mission; a typical requirement might be that all permissions should be available for the owner and group, but only read and execute permis-sions for the public. The command would then be

    chmod 775 /bin/new

If there is a need for SUID facilities, the SUID bit should be set, as in

    chmod u+s /bin/new

or with 'g+s' to set the SGID bit.
(f) Put the documentation you have prepared into the file **/usr/man/man1/new.1**. (See section 3.4.1 below for details of the on-line manual.)
(g) Put the source (if it is a program rather than a shell script) into the file **/usr/src/cmd/new.c** (or other suffix for languages other than C). This is the directory for all command sources in full source Unix distributions; see section 3.4.10 below for details. If you do not have a source distri-bution, it is still good practice to adhere to the convention of putting all your command sources in this directory.
(h) Put the appropriate details in the **makeall** or **cmake** file in the **/usr/src/cmd** directory.
(i) Update any *help* commands which your system may have, so that they offer help on the new command facilities; general purpose *help* com-mands are not part of the standard distributions.

   Some managers keep local modifications (both commands and documen-tation) completely separate from the standard distribution, and store local commands in a directory named **/usr/local**, for example, with recently added commands still under test stored under **/usr/new**, and recently deleted commands under **/usr/old**. Each user's shell variable PATH would have to be amended as appropriate.

3.2 /tmp and /usr/tmp; { temporary files }

All the complex commands such as editors and compilers need temporary files for working space. Such files last only for the duration of the one process. The standard area in Unix for such files is the directory /**tmp**, although for historical reasons there are again two areas, /**tmp** and /**usr/tmp**, and some programs may still use the latter. It is hoped that new software will gradually resolve this problem.

The access permissions on the /**tmp** directory should be checked, and must be read, write and execute in all categories.

The directory /**tmp** may also be used for lock files, which indicate whether a given single-user resource is free; this technique is discussed further in chapter 9.

Your reboot sequence should normally clear these directories. However, although rebooting would appear to be a sensible time to tidy up the /**tmp** directory, some 'recovery' files may need to be kept. Good editors maintain a file in which changes to the file being edited are logged, so that if the terminal line goes down during the edit, the results can be recovered. This is particularly useful if there is extensive dial-up use of a system. The recovery can also be useful if the system goes down unexpectedly; however, in this case, the recovery files should not be removed on rebooting. Some editors keep these files in /**tmp**, thus creating a problem when rebooting; other editors keep them in the directory of the file being edited. The penalty of the latter approach is the increased traffic on the user disc.

If a shell script requires the use of a temporary file, the usual convention is to use a name involving the process number, which makes the name unique to that particular process. The process number is available in a shell script as the parameter '$$' so that the file can be named, for example, /**tmp/ef$$**. All such files should be erased on both normal exit and interrupt exits from the shell script, so that it will be necessary to trap interrupts. In the Bourne shell this is done by having the command

```
TMPFILE=/tmp/ef$$
trap "rm $TMPFILE; exit" 0 1 2 3 15
```

at the start of the script.

There are also subroutine calls from C to find a suitable name for a temporary file, in which the user supplies a 'template' for the name in the form of a string with six trailing Xs. The subroutine then replaces the Xs by a letter followed by the process number, to provide a unique name in the /**tmp** directory. Again the file should be deleted by the user under all exit conditions.

3.3 /lib and /usr/lib; { system libraries }

These areas were originally intended for libraries of compiled subroutines, to be searched during the linking phase following the compilation of a program. In addition to their use for storing subroutine libraries, these directories have since become general depositories for miscellaneous items such as the programs invoked by commands but not seen by the user (for example the various passes of a compiler and the programs for the output spoolers) and datafiles referenced by commands (for example the font details for the programs driving photo-typesetters, and the conversion factors behind the *units* command).

There are again two areas, one directly under /, called **/lib**, and a second under **/usr**, called **/usr/lib**. The same considerations apply concerning the distinction between these two areas as with **/bin** and **/usr/bin**.

3.3.1 Subroutine libraries

The major items here are libraries associated with the loading phase of compiling commands such as *cc* or *f77*. Flags relating to libraries are for the loader program to interpret. Such flags can be given to a compiler, as in

        cc prog.c −lp

but in that case are passed directly to the loader after compilation. A flag such as '−lp' causes libraries **/lib/libp.a** and **/usr/lib/libp.a** to be searched by the loader. It will be seen that the letter or string in the flag argument following the '−l' flag causes a library to be searched whose name consists of the letters 'lib', then the string following the '−l' flag, then the terminating characters '.a'; thus the flag '−lp' implies a library name of 'libp.a'. (The '.a' stands for 'archive'.) The library **libc.a** is automatically searched by the C compiler, and the library **libF77.a** by the f77 compiler.

Libraries are searched in a serial fashion. This can cause problems if backward references occur. Thus if a particular subroutine is required by a program, the loader will search for it in the library; if, when it is found, it requires a subroutine which occurs earlier in the library, which has not been loaded, the loader will flag it as missing. The crude solution may be to search the library twice, as in

        cc .... −lm −lm

The problem is, however, more properly overcome by ordering the items in a library so that all references can be satisfied in a forward direction. Some items may have to occur twice to ensure this. To assist in ordering libraries automatically, the commands required are either a combination of *lorder* and *tsort*, or the single command *ranlib*, depending on the version of Unix.† The essential difference is that while *lorder* and *tsort* merely produce a reordered

† The *ranlib* command disappeared in System III, but re-appeared in System V.

library, *ranlib* produces special header information in the file which enables the relevant routines and unsatisfied references to be located. The latter can handle mutual recursion, which reordering the modules can never achieve. The *ranlib* command can be used on an existing library, as in

```
ranlib libname
```

which will index the named library. The other commands are used in setting up a new library, as in

```
ar −cr libname `lorder *.o | tsort`
```

which takes all the '.o' files in the current directory, orders them using *lorder* and *tsort*, and creates a new archive file using *ar* with the modules in the new and correct order. Note that the construction

```
... `command`
```

in a command causes the command between the '``' symbols to be executed, and its output substituted at that point in the command.

Libraries are standard archives of compiled code; the loader first determines which external modules are called from within the program, and extracts these from named libraries, extracting also those external modules called by the modules it has just extracted. These are then all combined, and the inter-relating addresses 'linked' to each other correctly. The use of libraries (which involves a searching process to select only those items required by the program being loaded) should not be confused with the inclusion in a loaded program of complete archives of compiled code.

To find the names of the modules which are in a library, for example the library **libc.a** in the directory **/usr/lib**, use the command

```
ar tv /usr/lib/libc.a
```

To find the names and addresses of specific entry points and internal identifiers involved in a routine, see the *nm* command.

Subroutine libraries in */lib* and */usr/lib*
The common libraries may divided between these two directories in different ways on different systems, the criteria being similar to those for the division of commands between the directories **/bin** and **/usr/bin**. The libraries on different systems will differ considerably depending on the Unix release, the processor on which it is running (there will be different compiler and hence libraries for different processors), and on other bought-in software, particularly for other languages. They may include

libc.a	the standard C compiler library, searched by default in the loading forming part of *cc*.
libf.a	the standard RATFOR library.
libfpsim.a	the floating fpoint simulation routines for use if the machine doesn't have floating point hardware.
libm.a	the library of mathematical routines.
libplot.a	plotting, Bell, general plotting procedures.
libt450.a	alternative, for a particular device.
libcurses.a	Berkeley terminal independent cursor and window handling subroutines.
libtermcap.a	library subroutines supporting the 'termcap' facilities.
liby.a	the routines associated with the YACC command.
libF77.a	the library for the f77 compiler.
libg.a	graphics routines.
libmon.a	routines for 'profiling' with the '−p' flag in C.
libmp.a	multi-precision arithmetic routines.
libsa.a	standalone routines for, for example, *boot*ing programs.
libtermlib.a	linked to libtermcap.a above.
llib−lc, etc	libraries for use by *lint*.

Inserting or amending a library subroutine

The subroutine will normally be in a file whose name ends '.o'. Let us assume a module **new.o** as an example. The operations necessary to add this item to the library **libz.a** (which would be included in a program loading process by the flag '−lz' to the loader or compiler) are now

(a) To append the new code to the end of library, the command is

      ar a libz.a new.o

where **new.o** is the compiled module to be added to the library **libz.a**.† If it is required to insert the new item at a particular point within the library, use

      ar −b old.o libz.a new.o

to insert the new item **new.o** immediately before (the '−b' flag) item **old.o** in the library (or a flag '−a' for after). If it is to replace an existing (older) version of the same module, use the command

      ar −r libz.a new.o

to replace the existing **new.o** in **libz.a**.

† Of course, it is dangerous to other users to perform updates such as this while the system is active; work on a copy and link the copy to the original name when complete.

(b) If there are likely to be any problems with back-referencing, the library should be ordered using the *ranlib* command as in

```
ranlib libname
```

if you have it; otherwise all the modules must be extracted with

```
ar −x libname
```

and the *lorder* and *tsort* commands used to generate a new correctly ordered library as described below.
(c) Put the documentation in **/usr/man/man3/new.3** or as appropriate (see section 3.4.1 below on **/usr/man**).
(d) Put the source code in **/usr/src/libz/new.c** (see section 3.4.10 below on **/usr/src**).
(e) If it is a standard library which you have altered, and a routine has been added or deleted, or the types of the parameters of an existing subroutine changed (not a good practice generally), the *lint* mode-checking libraries (**/usr/lib/llib−z** for example) should be kept in conformity.

Creating a complete new library
Let us assume that the library is to be accessed by the flag '−lnew'. The steps here are

(a) Generate the complete set of semicompiled modules, all in '.o' files.
(b) Archive them in the correct order using

```
ar −rc libnew.a `lorder *.o | tsort`
```

and run *ranlib* on the library if available.
(c) Move the library file to one of the directories **/lib** or **/usr/lib** as appropriate. Ensure that its owner and group are correct. Set its access permissions for owner, group and public.
(d) Document the separate routines, perhaps in section 3 of the manual.
(e) Create the directory **/usr/src/lib/libnew**, and put the source code modules under it.

3.3.2 /usr/lib/tmac { text formatting macros }
The directory **/usr/lib/tmac** is used for storing text formatting macro files for commands such as *nroff* and *troff*. The '−m' flag in *nroff* or *troff* commands such as

```
nroff −ms file*
```

causes the file **/usr/lib/tmac/tmac.s** to be read before other *nroff* input, where the letter(s) following the '−m' flag in the command follow the letters 'tmac.' in the filename. Macros defined in these files then become available to the user. (The same effect could be obtained either by typing the command

```
nroff /usr/lib/tmac/tmac.s file*
```

or by including at the top of the first file of *nroff* input the line

```
.so /usr/lib/tmac/tmac.s
```

Neither of these is convenient for general public macros.) Some of the files in that directory on the author's system are **tmac.AW**, **tmac.an**, **tmac.e**, **tmac.m** and **tmac.s**. The file **tmac.an** will be invoked by any command such as

```
nroff −man /usr/man/man1/ls.1
```

(which is itself invoked by the *man* command), and the file **tmac.s** by

```
nroff −ms file
```

The set of macros called by a '−ms' flag, stored in the file **tmac.s**, is known as the 'ms' macros. They include various standard document formats such as internal memoranda, released papers and technical reports, which can be edited to form a house-style for the institution using them. Some system managers amend the 'ms' macros in **tmac.s** to suit their particular organisation, so that, for example, the standard address which appears at the top of 'Internal Memorandums' (documents starting '.IM' using the 'ms' macros) is that of their organisation, not the default as supplied, which includes the address of the suppliers of the software! This introduces portability problems if documents starting '.IM' are sent to another machine in raw form. Such documents should probably be in a form such as '.RP' (released paper), in which the '.AI' facility (Author's Institution) is used to specify location, and no default is involved.

There are two other major sets of macros shown in the listing above, both of which are used extensively in Unix documentation, the 'mm' macros, and the 'me' macros. For full details, see the companion volume by David Barron and Mike Rees referenced at the end of chapter 1. The file ending 'AW' above is the file on the author's machine containing the Addison-Wesley house-style macros, based on those in an appendix to Steve Bourne's Unix book, and used in the preparation of this book.

Macro files are all straightforward (ASCII) text files, so can be edited using standard text editors.

3.3.3 /usr/lib/learn; { lessons for the *learn* command }
This is a forerunner of the system now marketed unbundled under the name 'Instructional Workbench'. For reasons of lack of filestore space, some distributions of Unix systems do not include the *learn* command, and some managers choose to remove it.

The *learn* command provides computer-assisted instruction on a number of topics. The *learn* command asks the user which of a number of courses of instruction is required. Each lesson is stored in a separate file, the lessons for a particular course being stored under a directory under **/usr/lib/learn**. The lessons for the 'files' course, for example, are stored in separate files under a directory **/usr/lib/learn/files**. For full details of how to create or amend the lessons in an existing *learn* script, or to create a complete new course, see the *learn* document under the directory **/usr/doc/learn** which comes with all Unix systems.

The lessons forming a *learn* course each specify possible successor lessons, the particular lesson chosen depending on the correctness of the candidate's answers. In the courses supplied as standard, there are certain lessons which cannot be reached, and so are redundant.

3.3.4 Other directories under /usr/lib
In addition to their use for storing libraries of subroutines for programming support, the directories **/lib** and **/usr/lib** are used to store assorted programs and data files not normally seen by the ordinary user. Where there are several items concerned with one command, those items are usually stored under a directory; where there is only one item, it is stored in a file. It must be emphasised again that the files and directories on a machine will depend on the type of machine, and on the particular compilers and packages installed on it. The lists below are merely typical examples.

The more common directories include the following:

edhelp   help information for the editor.

font   font details for photo-typesetting.

learn   lessons for the various courses in the *learn* command.

local   for any files which are peculiar to local requirements; it is good practice to keep them separate from more general files.

refer   the programs which form the *refer* command, which is a preprocessor to *nroff* for looking up references in documents.

struct   the programs which form part of the *struct* command whose purpose is to structure Fortran 4 programs into Ratfor.

style   programs and shell scripts for analysing English text stylistics, associated with the 'Writer's Workbench' commands. This is another unbundled package, and is not common at the present time.

term   *troff* terminal details.

uucp   *uucp* support programs.

3.3.5 Other files under /lib and /usr/lib

The files which may appear under the directories **/lib** and **/usr/lib** (and which may be divided between these two directories in any way, and which will vary from system to system) include files for the following purposes:

- Run-time support subroutines for the programs compiled by the standard C compiler (typically **crt0.o** and similar names). These will be completely different on non-DEC processor systems.

- Files containing programs comprising the passes of the assembler (typically names such as **as2**).

- Files containing programs comprising the various passes of the C compiler. If the C preprocessor (usually called *cpp*) can be found it can often be of considerable use as a separate program, since it supplies the '#include' and '#define' functions, which can be useful in quite different contexts. (See appendix 4 on the C preprocessor for details.)

- The programs for the passes of the Fortran 77 compiler.

- The program *atrun* (which is run at regular intervals as part of the *at* command).

- The program associated with the *calendar* command. The program generates an edit command to pick out lines of any file which contain today's or tomorrow's date. The main *calendar* command (which is a shell script) then uses this output to edit files of dates and events.

- The file **crontab** defines regularly occurring events to be scheduled by the *cron* program.

- A number of files concerned with 'Writer's Workbench', such as the data files for the *diction* and other commands.

- The file **lib.b** contains support routines for the *bc* command.

- There are programs and data associated with the *lint* command. The programs have names such as **lint1**. The data files contain declarations to enable type-checking to be performed relative to the main system libraries (whose source will not normally be available). A file such as **llib−lc** contains the mode declarations for the subroutines in the library **libc.a** (and should be kept up-to-date with any changes to that library).

- The 'line printer daemon' or spooler, *lpd*. This is a good example of a system program which the user does not call directly; it is called by the *lpr* command as appropriate.

- The program behind the *spell* command, *spell*. The command itself is a shell script (see also section 3.4.4 on **/usr/dict** below).

- The data for the (occasionally useful) *units* command is contained in the file **units**. The format can easily be found by inspection.

- Data files of words to be ignored by the cross-referencing program (either *cref* or *xref*). The program ignores different groups of words depending on whether it is producing an index for English text, C programs, etc. The files may have names such as **xref:ign.e** or **eign** for the words to be ignored when analysing English text, **xref:ign.c** or **cign** for the words to be ignored when analysing C programs.

- The YACC parsing tables are kept in a file such as **yaccpar**.

3.4 Other directories under /usr

3.4.1 /usr/man; { manual }

The complete documentation for Unix consists of the 'Manual' (containing short entries for every command, library subroutine etc.) and the 'Documents' (longer items such as the 'Beginner's Guide to Unix'). On full releases of Unix, the 'Manual' is stored under /usr/man, and the 'Documents' are under /usr/doc (see below). Once again, mainly because of space limitations, some distributions do not include all of this information.

The Manual

As much as possible of the 'Manual' should be kept on-line, for use by the *man* command. The manual is divided into eight sections. Each of the eight sections of the manual has a directory under /usr/man, the entries for section one being in separate files under the directory /usr/man/man1, and so on. The files under man1 generally have names ending in '.1', those under man2 end in '.2', etc. In addition, on pre-System V releases, commands concerned with management (but of interest to general users) end in '.1m', those concerned with communications in '.1c', and those with graphics in '.1g'. Presumably other special additional characters may appear before too long.

The sections are reserved as follows:

(1)   Section 1 contains entries for all the ordinary shell commands; thus all commands in /bin and /usr/bin should have an entry here. If you add a new public command, or provide an amended version of an existing one, be sure to add its document to this section.†

(2)   Section 2 contains details of the basic system calls possible to the Unix kernel, as made available to C and Assembler programs. These represent the basic properties of a Unix kernel, and it is highly unlikely that they will ever be changed, even by a user with a source licence. Some distributions (most notably XENIX by Microsoft) have, however, added new system calls, and their documentation does not make clear which are the non-standard ones.

(3)   Section 3 contains library subroutine calls; it may be necessary to add to or amend this section if you amend the entries in a existing library (see section 3.3 on /usr/lib above) or add a new library.

(4)   Section 4 contains for details of 'special files', in particular the devices on the system. It is therefore very configuration dependent, but should be kept up-to-date with the software by your supplier. Not all suppliers keep these compatible with the actual system.

(5)   Section 5 contains file formats; the entries describe the exact format of various files under Unix, so that programs which use the files can be written by the user. For full details, inspect your own system. The files typically described here could include those involved with accounting, terminal capabilities, etc.

† Some installation administrators believe that the standard manual should not be changed. Any local modifications should exist in a separate additional special section, e.g. section 9. This simplifies the purchase of standard manuals from external sources.

(6) Section 6 contains details of games; on some systems it is emptier than on others.

(7) Section 7 is officially headed 'Miscellaneous Useful Information Files'. It typically includes items related to word processing; details of character sets and *nroff* macros are included.

(8) Section 8 contains management commands, those commands that only a system manager should use. This includes such commands as filestore recovery, disc formatting, and rebooting details. In addition to this section, certain management commands which might be of interest (and are of no danger) to ordinary users are in section 1, and the filenames end '.1m'.

The entry for, for example, the command *ls* is in section one, and is in a file called **ls.1**, or, in full, **/usr/man/man1/ls.1**.

The reason for the section number being represented both in the directory name and the ending of the filename is partly so that, when software is distributed, the documentation with it can be put into the appropriate section. It also enables a system manager to have a separate section for local modifications (say section 9), in which the files end not in '.9', but in the number of the section to which that entry strictly belongs.

Some versions of the manual (later BSD releases and System V) are slightly reorganised relative to the above.

Speeding up the man command
The *man* command normally prints manual entries using the '−man' formatting macros, as in

    nroff −man

stored in **/usr/lib/tmac/tmac.an**. For full details of these see the entry in section 7 of the manual. This formatting takes time, and tends to make the *man* command slow. If a system has sufficient disc space to allow it†, it is worthwhile to keep pre-formatted copies of the documents in a parallel set of directories, (usually called **cat1**, **cat2**, etc), and alter the *man* command (which is just a shell script anyway) so that it searches first for a formatted copy; if one is found, it is simply listed by the *cat* command or a simple variant. If no formatted copy exists, *man* then searches for the ordinary entry, and formats it in the usual way. In this case, the use of the *man* command should obviously be monitored carefully, so that only the most commonly required commands are kept pre-formatted. The non-formatted versions must of course be kept, so that later amendments can be incorporated. The *man* command could be improved to compare the latest amendment date of the unformatted and the formatted files, and reformat if necessary.

Some administrators whose systems are limited by disc space keep the master copies of the manual off-line on, say, a floppy disc, and all the on-line

† On the author's system, the manual entries occupy 2000 blocks of disc space.

copies are pre-formatted, having been previously run through the *nroff −man* command. Any changes to the manual entries are performed on the floppy disc (plus any backup copies of it!), and the new version formatted into the on-line manual.

The space problem for storing documentation can also be eased by packing all such files in an optimal form. This can be done using the *pack* and *unpack* commands, which are standard on System V, but are also available on earlier versions. Packing files can save between 35 and 40 percent of the space required, and involves only minimal time overheads.

Creating or amending entries in the manual

To create a new entry for a newly created command, the rules for the '−man' macros should be followed. It is usually simplest to start from a copy of a similar entry, and work from there.

One particular point is worth further explanation. The heading (first line) of each document takes the form

```
.TH "COMMAND NAME" '1' "heading"
```

where the name of the command and the section number are followed by a heading. This will appear in the centre at the top of the page. This should be used to indicate the origin of the command, whether it is a local modification, or a totally new command obtained from a different organisation. It is bad practice to modify a command, and its manual entry, but to leave the appearance that it is still the standard Unix command. The comments at the end of a manual entry should further exlain the pedigree of the command.

The ptx (permuted index) command

The permuted index at the beginning of Volume 1 of the manual is generated using the *ptx* command. The index is produced by taking the summary line for each manual entry, of which a typical example is

```
ls - list contents of directories
```

The objective of *ptx* is to reproduce the above entry at several plances in an alphabetically sorted list, one position for each keyword in the phrase. For the above example, there would perhaps be four entries as in

```
            ls - list  <>  contents of directories
    ls - list contents of  <>  directories
                   ls -  <>  list contents of directories
                   <>  ls - list contents of directories
```

The lines are each the same, but the words lined up vertically halfway across the page are the keywords in alphabetical order. For the full index, the sets of entries for every manual entry are sorted together, so that any manual entry may be found from any of its keywords.

The *ptx* command produces the required information as a number of calls to an *nroff* macro *.xx*, as in

```
.xx "" "ls - list" "contents of directories" ""
.xx "" "ls - list contents of" "directories" ""
.xx "" "ls -" "list contents of directories" ""
.xx "" "" "ls - list contents of directories" ""
```

Each call has four parameters, and the *.xx* macro can defined in any way the user thinks fit. Again, see the manual for full details of *ptx*, and the companion volume by Barron and Rees for details of how to construct appropriate *.xx* macros.

A help command

One of the features lacking in Unix is a good user 'help' system. The *help* command available on some systems merely converts the error numbers (which are the only error reports given by some programs) into messages which explain the error; it is not a *help* command in the usual sense.

A possibly more helpful and therefore genuine *help* command can easily be devised, which offers help by assisting users in finding the manual entries relevant to their problem. It is based on the permuted index of the summary lines in the manual entries, similar to that printed at the beginning of the manual. The command is outlined in the chapter of example programs. A similar command, sometimes called *apropos*, has been added to some Berkeley distributions, and on other systems can be accessed by a '−k' flag to the *man* command.

3.4.2 /usr/doc; { documents }

The longer documents associated with Unix, such as the 'Tutorial Introduction to the Editor' and so on, are stored under **/usr/doc**. The smaller of these documents are each in a single file at this level (e.g. the 'Assembler' and 'Desk Calculator bc' documents are stored complete in a single file, the particular files being **/usr/doc/assembler** and **/usr/doc/bc** respectively). Documents which are too long to be stored sensibly in a single file are stored in a number of files under a directory in **/usr/doc** (e.g. the *adb* and 'Beginner's Guide' documents are stored in files under the directories **/usr/doc/adb** and **/usr/doc/beginners** respectively).

Most of these documents use the 'ms', 'mm' or 'me' macros, and a number of them need the additional *nroff* preprocessing programs *tbl* (for laying out tabular information) and *refer* (for automatically picking up journal and book references) as well.

The file **run** in **/usr/doc** should include details for the full production of each document, so that

```
run adb
```

should invoke the correct commands to produce the *adb* document. The **run** file allows for different formatters and associated programs to be used. A typical subset of the **run** file as a Bourne shell script is shown in figure 3.1.

```
pkg=-ms
name=$1
fmtr=nroff
eqn=neqn
shift

case $name in

impl*)
        refer -e /usr/doc/implement | $fmtr $pkg $*
        ;;
bc)
        $fmtr $pkg $* /usr/doc/bc
        ;;
eqnguide)
        $eqn /usr/doc/eqn/g* | $fmtr $pkg $*
        ;;
ms*)
        tbl /usr/doc/msmacros/ms | $fmtr $pkg $*
        tbl /usr/doc/msmacros/refcard | $eqn | $fmtr $*
        ;;
fsck)
        $fmtr $pkg /usr/doc/fsck/fsck.n $* 2> /tmp/fsck.toc
        : process and print the index page
        ed - /tmp/fsck.toc < /usr/doc/fsck/fsck.toc.ed > /dev/null
        $fmtr $pkg /usr/doc/fsck/fsck.toc.mac /tmp/fsck.stoc $*
        rm -f /tmp/fsck.*
        ;;
*)
        echo "what is" $name 1>&2
        ;;

esac
```

Fig. 3.1 Extract from a typical document run file

Note the use of shell variables to define the particular text formatters in use at the installation; such shell scripts are more easily ported than ones in which the formatter is specifically named at every occurrence. Note also the '$*' passed to each formatter command, to allow additional formatting parameters to be passed over.

If the documentation is on-line, it is a good encouragement to the system manager to keep it up-to-date. For example, it is usually necessary to alter the beginner's document to include details of your particular installation's arrangements for access to the terminals and the machine.

3.4.3 /usr/adm { administration }

Various files to do with administrative operations live in the directory **/usr/adm**. In particular, the file **/usr/adm/wtmp** maintains a record of all logins and logouts on the system, so that records of terminal time spent by users can be accumulated; for further details, see chapter 5 on logging-in, and the command *ac*. Further files exist here for shell command accounting; for further details see chapter 6 on the shell, and the command *sa*.

Both of these accounting files grow indefinitely until they are processed and summarised; some system administrators therefore choose to delete them completely, in which case the system keeps no details, and no regular accounting actions are necessary.

Error reporting (an essential part of administration) in earlier versions of Unix took the form of reports which appeared on the console. Thus if one of the system parameters was exceeded (the number of open files, or the filestore capacity, for example), or if there was a disc reading error, the error report was not passed to the users of the system. This technique is now being replaced by a special (pseudo-)device called **/dev/error**, on which error messages are generated, and which is read and acted upon by a daemon program. The daemon can be user-supplied if appropriate. Some users have amended their systems to send error messages to a file **/usr/adm/errfile**, but this is not very common.

Some installations maintain a file **/usr/adm/sulog** in which for reasons of security details of every call of the *su* command are kept; this file must be read and cleared out from time to time.

3.4.4 /usr/dict { word processing }

This directory contains various files concerned with text handling commands such as *spell*. The file **/usr/dict/words**, for example, is the list of words from which the command *spell* works; all words in the given text are compared (allowing for variations in endings, for example) with words in the file **/usr/dict/words**. Any words not found are flagged as suspect. Apart from the word endings part, this could be performed by the shell script shown in figure 3.2.

```
deroff −w | sort −fu | comm −23 − /usr/dict/words
```

Fig. 3.2 Possible *spell* shell script

Typical files in this directory are (depending on the packages installed):

hlista hlistb and hstop: These files contain hashed lists respectively of American-only words, British-only words, and 'stop-words' (words which the program may think acceptable, but which are not) for the *spell* command. The originals of the hashed wordlists are stored with the source of the command in the directory **/usr/src/cmd/spell**. The list of British-only words does not always appear to be correct.

papers: The directory **papers** contains files of references for the *nroff* preprocessor *refer* and its associated commands *lookbib* and *pubindex*. This is a system for enabling bibliographic references to be inserted automatically in technical reports. This information needs to be kept up-to-date with new publications as they appear if it is to be used seriously. The inverted indices are maintained using the command *runinv* or *indxbib*.

roget: The directory for files associated with the 'roget' thesaurus command for suggesting alternative words.

spellhist: A history of the use of **spell** (i.e. all the words it has rejected), so that new genuine words may be found and added to the dictionary if thought appropriate by the manager. The file **spellhist** grows steadily, and should be inspected and truncated from time to time. The *spell* command itself is a shell script, and can easily be changed to obviate the need for the **spellhist** file if it is not required.

words: This file contains the main **spell** list of words (dictionary).

3.4.5 /usr/games { games }

The game programs provided on Unix systems are stored here. On some systems the directory is empty, or has no access permissions during working hours (set on and off by the *cron* facility).

3.4.6 /usr/include

As part of the C compiler, the C preprocessor allows lines of the form

```
#include "myfile"
```

and

```
#include <passwd.h>
```

to be inserted in programs. The distinction between these two forms appears blurred, and varies between distributions and compilers (or, to be more accurate, compiler preprocessors). The first form (using '"' signs) originally caused the named file to be searched for in the current directory, and the second form (using '<' and '>' signs) searched in the **/usr/include** directory. More recent versions of both forms search first the local directory, and then (if the named file is not found) search the **/usr/include** directory. Assuming that the user does not use names such as **passwd.h** in their own directory, there is no confusion. When found, the file is inserted in the text at that point. The name is relative to the current directory. The second type of inclusion is not available under System III and V, but is in general covered by the first type.

On the Bell C compiler, there is a flag '−I' which enables the directory in which the included files are to be found to be specified at compile time, as in

    cc −I/usr/lib/include ...

This is one area where non-Bell software suppliers often omit significant features; the '−I' and '−D' flags to the *cc* command are not implemented on a number of other C compilers. Other portability problems may arise because some C compilers treat the '−I' flag as specifying a file to be included rather than the name of the directory to be searched. See the manual entry for the *cc* command for details.

A number of the files under **/usr/include** specify structure formats for reading particular Unix files, and hence have corresponding entries in section 5 of the Programmer's Manual. Others are simple '#defines' for simple functions, such as *isalpha* (a C function to test whether a given ASCII character corresponds to a letter, presented as a macro which will expand the call to the required conditional expression).† It is suggested that the reader study the **/usr/include** directory in conjunction with section 5 of the manual.

A second group of '#include' files lives under the directory **/usr/include/sys**, and are those concerned with communication with the kernel. Some give structures for entries in certain chosen kernel tables, whilst others define structures for receiving information delivered by system calls. These files are included by statements such as

    #include <sys/types.h>
    #include <sys/fstat.h>

Any file which is intended for inclusion by general programmers at your installation should normally be kept under **/usr/include** to make it readily available, or perhaps in a **/usr/include/local** directory if you wish to keep all local changes distinct.

The convention is that names of files involving no code generation end in '.h' (all those in **/usr/include** fall into this category), while names of those which will generate executable code end in, for example, '.c' for C text. The characters '.h' presumably indicate 'header' files. Thus files whose names end '.h' can be included with no overhead to the compiled program. The convention is not universally adhered to.

3.4.7 /usr/pub { various }

This directory contains various public files to do with special character sets. The file **ascii** contains all the ASCII characters, and can be useful in checking the peculiarities of a terminal or printer, or the characters on a particular printwheel on a daisywheel printer.

---

† Observe that functions defined as macros look like ordinary functions in a program, but do not actually exist as functions in the program. They therefore cannot be used, for example, as parameters in C programs.

3.4.8 /usr/mdec
This directory is for booting programs, usually containing the binaries of the first-stage boot (see the next chapter) which is loaded to block 0 of the boot device. The source code (for those with a source licence) for the initial boot programs may also be kept in this directory.

3.4.9 /usr/spool { areas for spooling }
The directory /**tmp** is essentially intended for those temporary files which last only for the duration of a particular running program (a process) such as a call of a compiler or editor. Any process requiring secure temporary files, to be retained across times when the system is taken down and rebooted, requires a more secure arrangement. This is provided by the directory /**usr/spool**. (This should therefore be subject to the same standards of security as the main parts of the filestore, and should be made secure by dumping copies regularly to another medium; see chapter 9 on file-systems.) Its standard sub-directories include the following:

/usr/spool/lpd
In a standard system there will typically be a directory /**usr/spool/lpd** for printer spooling. The user calls the program *lpr* (a standard command in /**bin** or /**usr/bin**), which stores the output in a temporary 'spool' file. The 'daemon' *lpd* then spools the stored output to the printer as convenient, and removes the spool files after printing. There is a further sub-directory here on some systems, /**usr/spool/lpd/tmp**, for storing output being piped into the *lpr* command. This has to be stored in a temporary area until the pipe is closed, at which point it is moved to the main spooling directory. Only at this stage is the complete file ready to be printed.

/usr/spool/uucp
There is a similar spooling area for the command *uucp*, which provides inter-machine spooled file transfer. Inter-machine mail also goes via this process, spooled by the program *uucico* (which operates for inter-machine files in a similar way to *lpd* on the printer). If a file is large, it may be wise to use the *uucp* flag to tell the command to use the named file directly at the time that the spooling has actually started, rather than to take a spool copy at the time the command is issued.

/usr/spool/mail
Most mail systems save stored mail below the directory /**usr/spool/mail**, but systems differ in whether each user's information is stored in a file below there, or in files below the home directory.

/usr/spool/at
The *at* command (which enables the user to issue a command which is to be executed at a given future date and time) stores a file in this directory for each command waiting to be executed. The name of each file indicates the time when it is to be executed. The command relies on the program *atrun*

being started regularly by *cron*, which looks to see whether there is a command ready for execution.† There is a sub-directory **/usr/spool/at/past** in which details of any currently running at-script is kept.

3.4.10 /usr/src; { commands, library and games source }

For systems licensed to have source code, the source code for the system is often stored under the directory **/usr/sys**, and the other source code under **/usr/src**, with the commands, the libraries and the games stored under the directories **/usr/src/cmd**, **/usr/src/lib*** and **/usr/src/games** respectively; a common alternative convention is to store all the source (including both the system source and the commands) under a common directory such as **/usr/src** or **/usr/sys**, so that it may be dismounted for security reasons when not required. Check your system for the exact conventions applicable to you. Even if you don't have a source licence, new source code for commands and libraries (and games if you insist) should follow the same conventions.

/usr/src/cmd { command source code }

New commands should be included here. Simple commands (such as *who* and *date*) have the source in a single file, more complex ones (such as *ed* and *cc*) have a directory, with a number of source files below it.

The command file for the directory is *makeall*, a simple shell command file. This compiles the source, moves the object file, changes ownership and sets permissions on each command as necessary. The **run** file is typically of the form shown in figure 3.3.

```
arg=−cp
case $1 in
        −cmp)  arg=−cmp ;;
esac

for i in *.[csy]; do cmake $arg $i; done

case $arg in
        −cmp)  arg=cmp ;;
        −cp)     arg=cp ;;
esac
(echo ==== plot =====; cd plot; make $arg)
(echo ==== prep =====; cd prep; make $arg)
(echo ==== tp =====; cd tp; make $arg)
(echo ==== xsend =====; cd xsend; make $arg)
```

Fig. 3.3 A typical **run** file

---

† It would be more efficient to sleep until the next command's execution time, subject to the need to be woken up whenever a new *at* command is issued, in case the new command is due before any of the existing ones.

In that example, the commands *plot, prep* and so on have their own directory, each of which contains the source files, and its own make-file. The special argument 'cmp' to the *run* command indicates that it is merely wished to compare the new command with the old. The argument 'cp' indicates that the new command is to be copied into the system directly.

The simpler commands, whose source code is stored in a single file, are made using *cmake*, a shell script whose code typically includes code such as is shown in figure 3.4. This gives the exact compilation parameters necessary for each command, and the name of the directory in which the program is to be placed. The use of *cmake* is being replaced by makefiles on later systems.

On the whole, the **run** file is used more as a documentation of the detailed arrangements necessary for recompiling each command, than for actually running to perform a complete recompilation of the whole set of commands. Complete recompilation is unlikely to be a wise decision in normal circumstances.

/usr/src/lib* { library source code }
Under the **/usr/src** directory, there is one directory for each library, each directory with its own source code and **Makefile**. The source for **libc.p** (invoked by the flag '−lp'), for example, is in files under the directory **/usr/src/libp**.

3.4.11 /usr/sys or /usr/src/sys; { kernel source }
For systems with a source licence, the system kernel source lives normally under one of the directories **/usr/src/sys** or **/usr/sys**, depending on the particular release. (Some managers keep it under **/usr/src/sys**, so that the complete system source can be unmounted and mounted through a single directory as and when required.) There are four main directories here.† The directory **/usr/sys/dev** (or **/usr/src/sys/dev**) is used for the code of device handlers (the disc drivers, tape drivers, etc), the directory **/usr/sys/sys** is used for the other kernel code (handling the file-system, the process table, the buffering system, etc), **/usr/sys/conf** is used for configuration details (detailing the particular devices, and numbers of devices on the system), and **/usr/sys/h** for the included header files required by the above.

3.5 /etc; { admin / management }

A wide variety of administrative files live here, many of which will be described more fully in other chapters where appropriate. Some are programs to be used as commands (these are either commands not intended for general access, such as the *mount* command, or programs which are initiated by the system itself, such as the *init* program), some are shell scripts, some are data files maintained by the system, while some are data files which the manager will need to edit. The list will vary greatly from system to system (some managers put all the commands under **/bin**, others move all management-related commands to **/etc**), but may include the following:

† Again, conventions differ between different releases.

```
C=
FP=
FPLIB=
SEPID=−i

Small Machine equivalent ie 11/34 and 11/23
: C=
: FP=−f
: FPLIB=−lfpsim
: SEPID="−n −DSMALLSYS"

for a
do
   s=.c
   case $a in
         *.y)     s=.y ;;
         *.s)     s=.s ;;
   esac
   b=`basename $a $s`
   D=/bin
   echo $a:
   case $b in
         −cmp)  C=cmp
                continue ;;
         −cp)   C=cp
                continue ;;
         ac)    cc $FP −n −s −O ac.c −o ac $FPLIB ;;
         ar)    cc −n −s −O ar.c −o ar ;;
         atrun) cc −n −s −O atrun.c −o atrun; D=/usr/lib ;;
         bc)    yacc bc.y && mv y.tab.c bc.c && \
                      cc −n −s −O bc.c −o bc && rm bc.c ;;
         dcheck) cc $SEPID −s −O dcheck.c −o dcheck ;;
         dd)    cc $SEPID −s −O dd.c −o dd ;;
         f77b)  f77 −l2 −i −s −w f77b.f −o f77b ;;
         *)     echo "cmake: don't know about $b"
                continue ;;
   esac || continue
   case $C in
         cmp)   cmp $b $D/$b && rm $b ;;
         cp)    cp $b $D/$b && rm $b ;;
   esac
done
```

Fig. 3.4 Typical *cmake* shell script

accton: The file for setting up shell accounting; see chapter 10 on performance.

cron: The program for process scheduling by timetable (always running); see chapter 12 on major commands.

ddate or dumpdate: The file containing the times and levels of recent dumps of the file-systems; it is maintained by the *dump* command; see section 1 of chapter 9 on dumping.

fsck: The program for file-system consistency checking.

getty: The program which forms a part of the logging-in process; see chapter 5 on logging in.

group: The file listing the login names of users permitted to use the *newgrp* command to change temporarily into a named group, to be edited by the system manager; see chapter 7 on the control of users.

init or inittab: The program controlling the multi-programming; see chapter 4 on bringing the machine up. This file is absolutely mandatory; you cannot boot up if it is absent or corrupted.

logmessage or ident: If such a file exists, it contains the configuration identification message listed before the 'login' request (to be edited by the system manager).

mkfs: The program for the make-file-system command. This is kept in **/bin** on some systems.

mknod: The program for the make-new-device command. This is kept in **/bin** on some systems.

motd: The 'message of the day' text file, listed during logging in (to be edited by the system manager).

mount: The program for the command both to mount a file-system, and to enquire the names of the currently mounted systems. This is kept in **/bin** on some systems.

mtab: The file containing the list of mounted file-systems, maintained by the *mount* command. It should be cleared at boot time, usually within the **rc** shell script.

passwd: The main file of user details (to be edited by the system manager).

rc: The shell script file to be executed when going multi-user at the end of the booting-up process (see chapter 4 on booting-up).

shutdown: The shell script for politely closing the system down; see the last section of chapter 4.

termcap: The text file of terminal capabilities, which needs editing when a new type of terminal is introduced. It is normally best to add local terminal types at the top of the file.

ttytype: The text file specifying the type of terminal attached to each active line. See section 4.3.3.

ttys: The text file specifying the active terminal lines, and their baud rate. See chapter 4 on booting-up.

umount: The program for the command to unmount a file-system. This is kept in **/bin** on some systems.

update: The program to flush the memory to disc regularly, which should be running whenever the system is active in multi-user mode.

utmp: The file containing a list of logged in users (used by commands such as *who*), maintained by the *login* and *init* processes.

wall: The program for the command to write to all users (in **/bin** on some systems).

3.6 /dev; { devices }

This directory by convention holds all the 'special' files representing devices on the system. It should contain a 'Makefile' like any other directory, to call the command *mknod* to make the devices. Chapter 8 on devices gives further details of the *mknod* command. Devices other than terminal lines should not, in general, have any public access.

3.7 /mnt

There is often a directory of this name at the top level, for the temporary mounting of file-systems on demountable devices such as floppy discs, so that the information on them becomes part of the filestore. Such devices can, of course, be mounted under any directory (see the *mount* command and the chapter on file-systems), but most managers use **/mnt** as a general purpose mounting directory for copying files out and in for users. The standard mounting command is then

        /etc/mount /dev/f2 /mnt

if the name of the disc to be mounted is **/dev/f2**, or

        /etc/mount −r /dev/f2 /mnt

to mount it (software) read-only.

3.7.1 lost+found

The significance of this directory relates to the file-system on which it appears; the file-system checking command *fsck* is detailed in chapter 4 on booting-up, and requires that each separate file-system have a directory at its head named **lost+found**, in which it stores files suspected of being corrupt.

3.8 Other files at the top level

3.8.1 unix

This file contains the main system kernel, and is loaded as the third stage of the booting process. It should not be stripped, since commands such as *ps* read their process information directly from the process tables in the kernel memory, and require the relocation tables to be available to determine the address at which the tables are stored. There may be more than one kernel for different configurations on a given system; if so, the files may be called **unix1**, **unix2** and so on, and the current one should then be linked to the name **unix** for the *ps* command.

3.8.2 boot

This is the second stage booting program, whose name is given as the first response after rebooting the system. It should not to be confused with the first stage booting program, which is stored on block 0 of the booting device, and is not actually in the file-system proper.

3.9 Conclusion

We have now completed an extensive tour of the whole Unix filestore and, in doing so, have encountered most features of the Unix system. In the following chapters we expand on the details of all of the major activities of a Unix system from a functional viewpoint.

Chapter 4   Bringing up the system and taking it down

The tour of the Unix filestore in the previous chapter has given an overview of many of the operations carried out on a Unix system. The ordering of the information in that chapter was determined by the location of the corresponding files in the filestore. A number of areas of Unix activity will now be described in more detail, to fill in aspects of their operation such as the files and programs involved. To start this set of more detailed descriptions, it seems logical to describe the first operation necessary on any system, namely that of bringing the system up. We immediately encounter the problem that the booting operation of a Unix system is unfortunately (but inevitably) one of the most system-dependent areas.

The booting sequence to be described first is the one considered by the author to be the 'standard'. This was developed for larger computer systems, and assumes that the machine is installed in a separate computer room, and that it will be rebooted by a qualified operator. It is rarely the sequence implemented on the smaller commercial Unix systems. One reason for the difference of approach is that the 'standard' system on booting comes up in 'super-user' mode on the console; this is obviously an unacceptable approach in an ordinary user context with a small machine in the same room as the users. If the machine is (accidentally or otherwise) switched off and on again, it will come up in 'super-user' mode, and any user present will have privileged access to the whole system. Many machines therefore adopt other approaches, which will be described in section 4.4 below.

It is normally recommended particularly for larger computer systems that the console should be a hard-copy device; this ensures that a log of all events such as rebooting is automatically kept.

4.1 Standard full booting sequence

On a standard system, the sequence of operations on switching-on is as follows.

(a) On 'power-on' and/or pressing the 'reboot' button (depending on the hardware) the system first reads block 0† from a default or specified

† On some systems, the hardware does not allow the reading of block 0, so that the Unix file-system then starts at block 1 or some other later block instead.

49

device, usually a disc of some sort. Variations include both hard and floppy discs, magnetic tape, and ROM. This program is known as the 'first stage' boot. The technique whereby a reboot causes block 0 of a particular device to be read is, of course, true of most hardware and operating systems. The block size will be 1024 bytes on System V and BSD systems, and 512 bytes on other systems. Note that if, for example, the default is an exchangeable device (a demountable disc, or a magnetic tape) this allows a variety of booting programs to be available; a number of discs or tapes can be held, with different characteristics represented by the systems on them, and with spare backup copies of each. If the normal booting device is not demountable, for example a Winchester disc, then it may be necessary on occasions to be able to come up off some other device such as a floppy disc or magnetic tape or cartridge for system recovery (after disc failure or corruption) or for initialisation of a new disc.

On Unix systems, block 0 is not part of the filestore on discs, and ordinary filestore commands cannot be used to access block 0. To put the initial boot program onto block 0 of a disc, the command *dd* is necessary. The boot program itself is not an ordinary Unix program (since it runs on a 'naked' machine, not under a Unix kernel) and has to be specially written and compiled. If the program is stored in the file **/usr/mdec/dboot**, the command necessary to transfer it to block 0 of the disc **/dev/rdisc** is

    dd if=/usr/mdec/dboot of=/dev/rdisc skip=0 count=1 bs=512

(or bs=1024 on System V or BSD). This should be done carefully, or any file-system on that disc (starting at the next block) may be overwritten if the file occupies more than one block. Since the *dd* command reads its information in a serial fashion, the disc device specified should be a 'raw' or character device; the significance of the raw devices is described more fully in chapter 8 on devices. The first stage boot program need not reside in the filestore during normal running, although of course it is necessary to generate a new copy if a new disc is to be initialised for booting.

(b) The first stage boot program then requests (usually without a prompt because of space restrictions on it) the name of a 'second stage' boot program from the filestore, usually in a file with a name such as **/boot**. (On some systems, a default name is built into the first stage boot program, and a return character is sufficient.) This second stage boot must normally exist in the outermost file-system on the device, although given the program source of the first stage boot, the latter could be re-compiled to pick up the second stage boot from elsewhere. One thus types

    boot

remembering that there are no facilities for correcting mis-typed characters at this stage; the characters '#' and '@' are not yet operative. The particular terminal operating at this time is determined by the hardware, but is conventionally named **/dev/console** in Unix.

The two booting programs should not be confused; the first executes from block 0 of the booting device, and is never called by name by the user; the second is called from the filestore and is specified by name by the user. The first may not exist in the filestore once it has been generated and moved to block 0.

(c) This program then prompts (usually the prompt is just a colon ':'), and calls for the name of the main Unix kernel. This is the program which will be main-store resident during the running of the system, and is usually stored in a file with a name such as **/unix**. Full systems allow this to be selected from any nominated (disc) device, and to have any name. The required file is specified by typing, for example,

```
rm(0,0)unix
```

There are four parts to this reply. The letters 'rm' indicate that the 'rm' disc controller is to be used; the first figure (zero in this case) indicates that the file is to be found on the first disc attached to that controller (drives are numbered from zero); the second figure (also zero in this case) indicates that a file-system 0 blocks offset from the beginning of the disc is to be searched (for other file-systems, the offset from the start of the disc in blocks must be known)†; and lastly, the letters **unix** give the name of the file within that file-system (the name may include '/' characters). This is very system dependent; you must consult your documentation for details. After the kernel has been loaded from the specified file, that file (or a copy of it) must be linked to the name **/unix** in the running filestore; this is the name by which the *ps* command finds out details of the position of the process tables in the kernel. For more information on the layout of file-systems, and the significance of block 0, see chapter 9 on file-systems.

The Unix kernel, when loaded, tests the size of the main memory by accessing addresses upwards until it finds an error, and then starts the first Unix process proper. This is the *init* process, stored as an ordinary binary program in **/etc/init**. This will run in super-user mode. This name is built into the Unix kernel, and cannot be changed; if a different *init* were wanted, the program in the file **/etc/init** could be changed by a 'super-user', but if the new program fails, it will be called after any reboot, so that it will be impossible to recover without booting from a different device – beware!

This is the first genuine Unix program to run following the booting sequence, and is responsible for all that follows. It is an ordinary program normally written in C, but could be written in any language supporting

† On some systems, the second number is the partition number; always check your documentation carefully.

facilities to enable it to make the system calls such as *fork*, *exec* and *wait* listed in section 2 of the on-line manual. The first and second stage boot programs do not run under Unix (they cannot make calls to the kernel, it is not yet running), but in a mode usually referred to as 'standalone'. They are written in C, but require special arrangements at the machine level for, for example, input and output to the console.

The *init* program is now running, and its first function normally is to fork a single 'super-user' shell onto the console (which is the device /**dev**/**console**, and must exist). This shell is to enable the system manager to perform various administrative functions before the system goes multi-user, while it is still quiet, such as setting the date, checking the consistency of the filestore, reconfiguring the list of on-line terminals to be active during the following session, and so on.

The filestore consistency check is performed by the command *fsck* (usually stored as /**etc**/**fsck**, but sometimes in /**bin**), which should be used to check all discs used as file-systems. It defaults to the list of filestore devices given in the file /**etc**/**checklist**. At this stage, most of the file-systems will not be *mount*ed, so will be inactive; only the *root* file-system will be active. The *fsck* command goes through each one in turn, reports any inconsistencies in them, and offers to correct them. The reply to each query is either 'y' for yes (correct the inconsistency), or 'n' for no (leave the file-system inconsistent). A parameter '−y' to the command assumes 'yes' replies to all questions, so that no further interaction is necessary; a parameter '−n' similarly assumes all 'no' answers, and therefore needs no write permission to the device. Any 'yes' reply may involve the loss of information, such as the complete removal of a suspect file. Suspect files on the file-system being checked are written to a directory **lost+found** on the device if such a directory exists; this directory must have been created, and be sufficiently large already to hold the names of all the files involved. This can be ensured by first creating the directory, then creating a number of files in the directory, and then removing them. The corrected systems will be consistent, and can later be mounted as and when required. It may be possible to recover information from deleted files by looking at the **lost+found** directory. There should be a **lost+found** directory at the head of each mountable file-system.

When checking the *root* file-system, there are complications, in that it will be active (even though, because it is *root*, it will not be formally *mount*ed as such, but is implicitly mounted as *root* during the booting process). If modifications are necessary, they should be completed, and the machine rebooted **without** first performing a *sync* (see section 4.5 below for the normal procedure for taking a system down). This is to ensure that the disc as modified by *fsck* is not overwritten by any in-core information, which may have been generated from information read from the original corrupt (inconsistent) version.

While this first 'single-user' shell is in operation, the program *init wait*s for the shell to terminate. To have such a super-user shell which appears on rebooting is obviously not sensible in certain situations, such as where a user could switch the machine off and on, since that user would then obtain 'super-user' privilege. Among the variants encountered by the author are:

- Some machines come straight up multi-user, with none of the above options of different boot programs and Unix kernels available. They must perform an *fsck* automatically before coming up multi-user.
- Others come up single user as 'root', but asking for a password.
- Other systems, for reasons of convenience rather than security, pause during the initialisation process; if, say, an escape character is typed during the pause, the machine comes up single user, otherwise it continues with the setting up of the multi-user system (including an automatic *fsck*).

The way in which the system comes up is determined by the *init* program, of which a simple example is given in the chapter of example programs. There are no file-systems mounted at this stage; the Unix kernel will at some point (either in the reconfiguring program *mkconf* or in the configuration details **c.c**) have specified which of the disc devices is to be the root system, and that will be the only system available on boot-up. Any file-systems that the manager wishes to modify must first be mounted (see *mount* and *umount* or /**etc**/**mount** and /**etc**/**umount** below).† If the manager is to reset the computer clock (by the command *date*) for example, the file-system containing the file /**usr**/**adm**/**wtmp** (which keeps the records of logins, logouts and time changes) must have been mounted.

As was mentioned earlier, a machine based on, for example, a single Winchester disc, needs the ability to come up off a different device for system recovery or re-initialisation of the Winchester. It is common and desirable practice to have, for example, a floppy disc or magnetic tape with a bootable system on it, which can be used in emergencies.

4.2 Going multi-user – the *rc* shell script

After the system manager has completed the operations that are needed in the single-user shell, the shell is terminated (by typing the end-of-file (EOF) character, typically 'control-d'). This releases the *waiting init* process, whose function is now to bring the system up multi-user. To do this, it is necessary to pass through two phases of activity as follows:

(a) Once-only operations such as:

mount file-systems as required;
initiate background processes such as *update* and *cron* of which exactly one instance must be running in the background;
save any precious files under /**tmp**, perhaps such as editor logging files.
delete temporary files such as those in /**tmp**.

These operations are performed once only, and must be followed by

---

† The *fsck* command checks and modifies the file-system by reading from and writing to the raw file-system device directly, and requires that the file-system should not be mounted during the check.

(b) Actions to be performed once for each line which is going to support a terminal which is part of the multi-user service, such as:

determine the number and type of on-line terminals;
set up the correct baud rates, parity settings, etc;
initiate the logging-in processes.

Once-only setting-up operations

The once-only setting-up commands needed prior to going multi-user are performed by executing the shell script contained in the file /etc/rc, a standard file name built into the source of the *init* program. This file will be edited by the system manager to the commands required for that particular installation and is, of course, executed from *init* in 'super-user' mode.

The contents of /etc/rc will be very configuration and installation dependent, but a typical example is given in figure 4.1 for information. It should be emphasised that this shell script is **very** system dependent, and subject to variations within a given installation. The operation of the /etc/rc illustrated in the figure follows the sequence:

(a) Set up the search path for this shell script
(b) Clear the files in which are kept lists of currently mounted file-systems (**mtab**, see the *mount* command), and currently logged-in users (**utmp**, see chapter 5 on 'logging-in' for more details), since currently no file-systems are mounted, and no users logged-in. If these files are read before they are cleared, they will give the state of mounted file-systems and logged-in users when the machine was previously closed down. If this information is required, execute commands such as

```
echo "Mounted at closedown:"; /etc/mount
echo "Logged-on at closedown:"; who
```

immediately before the files **mtab** and **utmp** are cleared.
(c) Mount any other file-systems which form part of the multi-user system under the required directories. If (as is usually the case) the /usr file-system is on a separate device from the root system, the extra commands under /usr/bin become available as soon as the separate disc containing /usr/bin has been mounted. Note that on the system for which this /etc/rc was written, the various disc devices are named by function (/dev/staff for staff files, /dev/spool for the spooler areas, and so on) rather than by the more usual /dev/disc1, /dev/disc2 notation. This makes reconfiguring more transparent. The devices also have their more traditional names with a second link. The /usr/bin entry set up in 'PATH' at the beginning of the *rc* shell script cannot be fully effective until /usr has been mounted. (To be pedantic, it would be possible to have special commands under /usr/bin on the root disc, which were available on booting, but became inaccessible when the /usr disc was mounted. This is highly unlikely.)

```
# a) set up path for finding commands - see later
PATH=/bin:/usr/bin
# It was a legal requirement on earlier systems
# to print a message such as the following
echo "Restricted rights: Use, duplication, or disclosure
is subject to restrictions stated in your contract with
Western Electric Company, Inc." >/dev/console
# b) Empty two files
        > /etc/mtab # the list of mounted file-systems
        > /etc/utmp # the list of logged-on users
# c) Now mount the major file-systems ; very system dependent
        /etc/mount /dev/usr /usr # /usr/bin is now available
        /etc/mount /dev/staff /staff
        /etc/mount /dev/stud /stud
        /etc/mount /dev/spool /usr/spool
# d) Mount and clear /tmp, see below for comment
        /etc/mount /dev/tmp /tmp
        rm −r /tmp/*
# some users prefer to "mkfs" /dev/tmp each time to clear it
# Clear other temporary areas
        rm −fr /usr/tmp/*
        rm −f /usr/spool/lpd/tmp/* # lpd's temporary files
# e) remake the directory for a modified learn command
        mkdir /tmp/playpen
        chown learn /tmp/playpen
        chmod ugo+w /tmp/playpen
# f) Unlock lpr spooler in case it was active
#        when the system went down
        rm −f /usr/spool/lpd/*lock
# g) Enable shell accounting
        /etc/accton /usr/adm/acct
# h) Initiate permanent processes
        /etc/update # regular main memory flushing
        /etc/cron   # the clock daemon
# Almost there, just for luck
        date > /dev/console
```

Fig. 4.1 A typical **/etc/rc** file

(d) Clear any files in **/tmp**; there are other temporary areas which also
require clearing. If **/tmp** is a separate device, some system managers
prefer to reconfigure the **/tmp** disc completely rather than simply clear it.
To do this, use the *letc/mkfs* command as in

```
/etc/mkfs /dev/rtmp 8192
```

to re-initialise the /**tmp** disc completely. The reason for preferring this approach is that there are likely to be open files on this device, which may therefore be corrupt, and completely re-initialising the disc effectively clears and empties the /**tmp** directory.

Some editors keep logging files to enable recovery of incomplete edits if a line or system goes down. If the latter is the case, care should be taken not to delete the logging files on rebooting (or to copy them to a safe directory), since this is the very time when they are likely to be needed. It is simpler if the editor keeps the logging files in the same directory as the file being edited.

The illustrated shell script also clears any directories under /**tmp**. If /**tmp** is on a separately mounted file-system, this will include the **lost+found** directory required by the *fsck* command; this will have to be replaced if required.

(e) Unfortunately, /**tmp** may contain a directory required by some command for its temporary files. In the above case the **learn** command has been modified to use a directory called /**tmp/playpen** for its temporary files. This directory must now be replaced, and correct ownership and access permissions established.

The correctness of having such a 'permanent' directory under /**tmp** (which is intended for temporary files) is open to question. If the temporary files and directories associated with the *learn* command, for example, are stored elsewhere (perhaps under /**usr/lib/learn/tmp**), it complicates the clearing out of temporary files, and may cause a normally settled file-system (such as /**usr/lib** which could be on a separate disc device) to overflow if the learning user creates a huge file. On the other hand, to use a directory under /**tmp** complicates rebooting in a different way; either the directory must be created whenever /**tmp** is cleared, or the clearing must remove files but not directories. There is no ideal solution.

(f) The printer spooler *lpr* normally uses a 'lock-file' in the directory /**usr/spool/lpd** to indicate when the printer is busy. If the file exists, no new spooler programs will start. If *lpd* was running when the machine was taken down, the lock-file may exist, so must be removed. (It would be more convenient if the lock-file were stored in, say, the directory /**tmp**, but this would enable unauthorised users to delete it; there is a detailed discussion in chapter 9 on the security of the *lpr* process.) Other spooling processes may require similar treatment. The exact names of any lock-files may vary from system to system.

(g) Switch on shell accounting if required; this is the accounting of individual commands, with results summarised and accumulated by the *sa* command. There is no shell accounting unless it is switched on at this stage. (Unlike shell accounting, the login accounting is operative if the file /**usr/adm/wtmp** exists; its needs no action within the *rc* script.)

(h) Start the two background processes *update* (which flushes the in-core buffers to disc at regular intervals) and *cron* (which runs timetabled processes, see later).

Some systems ask for the exact date and time at some point in the execution of the **/etc/rc** shell script, using a shell script such as that shown in figure 4.2.

```
echo "System time is" "date"
echo −n "Type actual time [dd[hhmm]]:"; read time
if test −n "$time"
then date $time
else echo "System time not changed"
fi
```

Fig. 4.2 A shell script for setting the date

Some *rc* scripts check to see whether a spooling directory such as **/usr/spool/lpd** contains files waiting to be printed and, if so, checks that the printer is ready and initiates the spooling daemon *lpd*. The files would otherwise wait until the first use of the *lpr* command before being printed. Similar considerations apply to *uucp* inter-machine spooling.

4.3 Starting up the multi-user system

4.3.1 The /etc/ttys file

The *init* process, after the once-only setting up specified in the **/etc/rc** shell script has been done, looks at the file **/etc/ttys** to determine which of the terminal lines are to be active (are going to be used as terminals to the multi-user service, for example) and in which way they are to be active (some may be lines to networks rather than to users, some may work at different baud rates from others, and so on). This information is stored in **/etc/ttys** in a form such as that shown in figure 4.3.

Each line in the file describes what is required of one terminal connection. The figure represents a machine with a total of 12 lines.

```
1−console
1ttty00
1ttty01
1ttty02
1ttty03
1Htty10
1Htty11
1Htty12
1Htty13
1+diablo
0&anadex
1Papple
```

Fig. 4.3 A typical **/etc/ttys** file

The first character of each line is either '0' (ignore) or '1' (put a process on this line). The second character is either the type of the process (one code letter for each type of line characteristics) or just a letter representing the baud rate of the device. The rest of the line is the name of the device in the **/dev** directory. If the first character is a '0', then *init* takes no action on that line; baud rate and parity will not be set, so that if such a line is for a serial printer, the program driving the printer must itself set the line characteristics and download fonts. During the initial super-user shell following booting-up, it may be necessary to edit this file to restrict the number of active lines. Alternatively, there may be several files representing different commonly required configurations, and the appropriate file is then linked to **/etc/ttys**.

If the first character is a '1', the program **/etc/getty** is invoked, with the second character of the line passed as parameter to it, with standard input, standard output, and error output redirected to the named device, and with the process forked off (to be independent of other activities). It is thus roughly equivalent to calling

getty t < /dev/tty00 > /dev/tty00 2> /dev/tty00 &

for the second line of the **ttys** above, where the 't' is passed over to indicate the type of the terminal expected on the line **/dev/tty00**. The *getty* also transfers the standard error channel (channel 2) to the terminal. After the whole file **/etc/ttys** has been scanned, there will be a *getty* process (still in 'super-user' mode, inherited from *init*) for each active line. A number of released *getty* programs have an error which causes them to loop if a line indicated as active in the **/etc/ttys** file does not exist.

The lines in the **/etc/ttys** of figure 4.3 which have a zero character in the first column might represent, for example, a line for transmitting but not receiving (a printer), or a terminal not currently available. Such lines are not strictly needed, but it is good practice to keep the **/etc/ttys** file in step with the complete set of lines on the machine.

4.3.2 The *getty* process
The job of *getty* (usually stored in **/etc/getty**) is to set the modes (features such as baud rate, parity, screen width and height details for VDUs, and delays at end-of-line for printing terminals) for that particular line, the type of the device being indicated either by the single letter passed as parameter, or being looked up in the **/etc/ttytype** file. In some earlier versions (V7) of Unix this is built into the source code of *getty* (in **getty.c** somewhere), so that for each new terminal type, that source code must be amended and recompiled. To avoid source licence problems, some vendors distribute the bulk of the *getty* command as an object (relocatable or semicompiled) file such as **getty.o**, so that the user writes a new module for the new terminal type, and combines it with the **getty.o** file using the loader *ld* to form the new *getty*. More modern versions of the program are table driven from the details in the **/etc/termcap** file.

The facilities specified and set by the *getty* command vary considerably between systems; for example, the EUUG version of Unix has additional paging facilities for video terminals and more sophisticated handling of 'tab' characters. This area of programming can become very system dependent.

4.3.3 The /etc/ttytype file

In System V and Berkeley versions, the second character in **/etc/ttys** is purely a baud rate; details of the types of terminals are stored in a separate file called **/etc/ttytype**. A typical common format for the **/etc/ttytype** is shown in figure 4.4.

```
la120 console
tvi912 tty00
tvi912 tty01
tvi912 tty02
tvi912 tty03
haz1500 tty10
haz1500 tty11
haz1500 tty12
haz1500 tty13
diablnet diablo
print anadex
applenet apple
```

Fig. 4.4 A typical /etc/ttytype file

The lines in **/etc/ttytype** give the type of each terminal on the system; the first entry on each line is the type of the device, the second entry is the name of the line in the directory **/dev**. The actual terminal protocols in this case then are picked up from details in the file **/etc/termcap**, where all details of each type of terminal are stored. For full details see the 'termcap' entry in the on-line manual.

The command *tset* can be used to set the complete modes necessary for a given type of terminal, and to set the TERM parameter, using a call such as

```
. tset vt100
```

in the Bourne shell, and

```
source tset vt100
```

in the C shell, to set the line and shell variable TERM appropriately for a 'vt100' terminal. (Note the need for the *tset* command to executed directly in the current shell by the use of '.' or 'source', so that its setting of the shell variable TERM is effective in the current shell.)

4.3.4 The invitation to login

After the modes have been set (*getty* uses the ordinary *ioctl* call within C) the *getty* process prints a heading message (earlier versions built this into the code; more recent versions list it from a file such as **/etc/logmessage** or **/etc/ident**), typically a message such as

> Addison-Wesley
> Unix System VI.3

and an invitation to login,

> login:

It then waits for a user to type a login name. When a name has been received (a newline character is encountered), the *getty* process *execs* to become a *login* process, the user's name being passed as a parameter.

If *getty* detects that all the characters typed in the login name are in upper-case, it assumes that the terminal is an 'upper-case only' device, and sets the line to upper-case mode by the system call *ioctl*, equivalent to the command

> stty lcase

before *exec*ing to *login*. This causes the system to interpret simple upper-case letters as lower-case, and to represent upper-case letters by escaped upper-case letters (i.e. the upper-case letter preceded by a back-slash).

The system normally interprets either line-feed (LF) or carriage-return (CR) as the same (end-of-line) character. Only one character is stored in text files at the end of each line, but on output it is printed as the two characters 'CR-LF', to obtain the correct effect. When either LF or CR is typed, both characters are echoed. This is the 'crmod' feature in the *ioctl* system call and the *stty* command. If the login name is terminated by an LF character, then *getty* does not activate this feature.

For lines on which the baud rate of the terminal may not be known (such as dial-up lines), there are *getty* entries which try different baud rates until a sensible answer is encountered.

4.3.5 Concluding state

Before users have started typing their login names, we have a machine with independent *getty* processes on each terminal line which was opened successfully, and a *waiting init* in the background. For lines which did not open successfully (for example, a telephone line waiting for a dial-up call) there will be an *init* process. The *init* is waiting on all its children, and will awake when any of its children dies. It will know from the process number returned when the *wait* terminated which of the children has died; it can then restart a new *getty* on that line, and the whole process restarts.

4.4 Variations on machine start-up procedure

The *getty* process on some machines is combined with either *init* (the *getty* code replacing the *exec* code after the *fork* in *init*) or with *login* (the *getty* code appearing at the beginning, see the next chapter for details of *login*). Thus inspection of all the processes running on the machine, by the command

```
ps lax
```

may show these as *init*s or *getty*s or *login*s. However, since *getty* has a distinct function to play, Unix philosophy decrees that it should really remain a separate process.

4.5 Taking the system down

4.5.1 Before switching off

It is essential to take a Unix system down with care. If this is not done (i.e. if the machine is simply switched off) the filestore may not be consistent when the machine is rebooted. This is because Unix has a sophisticated system to minimise disc traffic, by keeping as much current information as possible in buffers in the main memory. If a process is writing to a file, for example, the amended information may not be on the disc; the version on disc may still be the original, and the amended version may be only in buffers in memory. Any other program which accesses the file will, of course, be referred to the accurate memory version, not the out-of-date disc version, so there are no problems in general use. However, if the machine is switched off without any special precautions, the memory buffers are, of course, lost, and on rebooting, the files picked up from the disc may be a mixture of new and old contents. Corruption of this form with directories (which are written to whenever a file is created or removed) is equally likely to happen, and is much more serious. Special precautions must therefore be taken before switching a Unix machine off. It is necessary to

(a) kill all processes, including background ones such as *cron* which may fire programs off at any time, to ensure that no more background processes appear, and

(b) execute the command *sync*, to synchronise main memory and disc buffers.

The command to kill all other processes, and to return the system to a single super-user shell on the console requires that a certain signal be sent to the *init* process, so takes a form such as

```
kill −1 1
```

(send signal 1 to process number 1) since process number 1 is always *init*. Be absolutely sure to check the signal for your system before using this command. One signal is normally used for reconfiguring (after **/etc/ttys** has been altered), and another for bringing the system down to single user. To use the wrong signal can be catastrophic! There exist many variants of the particular signals to *init*; if the required signal is other than signal 1, the command should be changed appropriately. See the next section (4.5.2) for the effect of other signals on *init*. This command is then followed by

sync

to flush the main memory buffers, at which point it is safe to switch off the machine. On systems with slow discs, time should be allowed for all the transfers initiated by *sync* to complete before switching off.† Note that the *kill* command above kills all processes immediately, and it should be remembered that processes such as *lpd*, if active at the time the *kill* is executed, may then leave a lock-file somewhere, indicating that the printer is busy; this will have to be removed on rebooting the system.

For a user friendly shutdown, most systems provide (or if not, their system managers write) a shell script which

(a) stops new logins;
(b) gives countdown warnings using */etc/wall* (write to all logged-in users) at, perhaps, one-minute intervals for five minutes;
(c) executes the *kill* command;

The manager must then execute the *sync* command from the main console.

A typical shell script (called **/etc/shutdown** on some systems) might be as shown in figure 4.5.

```
for i in 4 3 2 1
do
            echo "Going down in $i minutes" | /etc/wall
            sleep 60
done
echo "Going down NOW" | /etc/wall
kill −1 1
```

Fig. 4.5 Outline *shutdown* shell script

It should be noted that the shutdown script should not be written in the C shell.

On many modern systems, the *shutdown* facility also includes a facility for rebooting directly, to bring the machine up again immediately.

It should be pointed out that the filestore problems associated with incorrect shutting-down of the machine are much less serious on the modern versions than on earlier releases of Unix, and that any problems which arise can usually be sorted out with the help of the *fsck* command.

† This is perhaps the origin of the myth that one should always type *sync* twice before switching off!

4.5.2 Reconfiguring

Different signals to the *init* process have different effects, and the signal numbers may be different on different systems. The different actions usually include the following:

(a) An essential action is to cause the machine to revert to single-user on the console similar to single shell after boot-up, except that various file-systems will still be mounted. The signal for this is often signal 1. At this stage the user may wish to perform a *sync* and switch off. Alternatively on some systems, logging-out on the console will then cause the system to come up multi-user again using */etc/rc*, which may attempt to re-mount mounted file-systems.

(b) Another standard requirement is to reconfigure according to a different (edited) copy of **/etc/ttys**, which defines the multi-access configuration. One signal therefore causes the current **/etc/ttys** to be checked, and lines whose first character has now become a '1' instead of a '0' will receive a *getty*; lines whose first character has changed from a '1' to a '0' may either be killed at this stage, or merely left until the user logs out, without a further invitation to login being generated at that point. These alternatives may be requested by two different signals.

(c) Particular sites use other signals to *init* to cause automatic reconfiguring of the system in different ways, typically at different times of the day, perhaps to open up networks during cheap tariff periods. System V has a number of different states of the *init* program.

Chapter 5   **Logging-in and logging-out**

5.1 Logging-in

The previous chapter described how the *init* and *getty* programs between them set up a process on each terminal line, waiting for the user to type a login name (followed by a carriage return character). As was described above, the 'login:' message on the terminal is typed by the *getty* command. When *getty* has successfully received characters followed by a newline, it *exec*s to a *login* process, with the string it has read given as parameter. It is thus more or less as if the command

    login jsmith

had been executed, for example, or, more strictly,

    exec login jsmith

since the *login* program overwrites the *getty*.

    The *login* program (again just an ordinary program, which could be rewritten by a user, and could be programmed in any language) now performs a number of operations in sequence. It must execute for most of its time in super-user mode, since it has to access special accounting files, and perform other privileged operations such as setting the UID of the current process. When forked from the *init* program, as above, via *getty*, it will automatically inherit *init*'s 'super-user' status. However, if it is required that the *login* command should work as an ordinary command executed by an ordinary user (if you want to), the file **/bin/login** must be root-owned, have public execute permission, and have its SUID bit set. However, many administrators prefer to operate with the *login* command being root-owned with mode 700 (access only by root). This then operates so that when a user tries to execute *login* as a command, the shell finds that it cannot *exec* to *login*, the shell therefore dies, and the *init* program starts up another *getty* and hence *login* anyway.

5.1.1 Looking up the user's name

The first action of the *login* process must be to look up the user's name (which has been passed to it as a parameter) in the password file **/etc/passwd**, which holds details of all users, one user's entry taking up one line of the file. A typical entry in **/etc/passwd** is

```
ef:ecqg6/1WZBoak:100:20:4000,,−2:/staff/ef:
```

It consists of seven colon-separated fields as follows:

```
<name>:<ecpasswd>:<uid>:<gid>:<special>:<homedir>:<shell>
```

The significance of the each of the fields is as follows:

<name> The user's login name, limited to a maximum of 8 characters.

<ecpasswd> The user's encrypted password.

<uid> The user's 'user identifier' or UID, an integer, normally limited to a maximum of 2 bytes, or about 31000.

<gid> The user's 'group identifier' or GID, an integer, with the same limit as the UID. (These two define access to files and processes, see chapter 9 on file-systems.)

<special> A spare field for installation dependent information. This field is ignored by the standard *login* command. In order not to confuse *login*, this entry must not contain any colons. If more than one item of information is to be stored here, the items must be separated by some other character, usually a comma. Typical information stored here is the user's full name, department, home telephone number, account codes on other machines, disc ration and priority. Such information should not be too long, since that would slow the *login* command down, and would make the file less readable. Obviously if the *login* command wishes to use this additional information, it must be specially written.

<homedir> The user's home directory. It does not need to have the same name as the login name.

<shell> The name of a program to act as the user's 'shell' (or 'command interpreter'). A blank entry here implies the Bourne shell **/bin/sh**. The program nominated here does not have to be a command interpreter in the ordinary sense of that word. If for example the named program is */bin/who*, logging in under this name will cause the *who* command to be executed, the termination of the command will act equivalently to a logout, and another request to login will appear; if the named program is, say, a chess playing program, the user will be asked to supply a chess-move!

If the *login* program is being written in C, the file **/usr/include/passwd.h** gives a mode definition for a structure suitable for holding this information and can be included in the program by the line

```
#include "pwd.h"
```

at an appropriate point. It contains the code specifying the types and names of the fields of a structure appropriate for holding the password entry information. Typical fields might include

```
char *pw_name;    /* (a pointer to) the login name */
char *pw_passwd;  /* the encrypted password */
int   pw_uid;     /* the user-id */
int   pw_gid;     /* the group-id */
char *pw_dir;     /* the home directory */
char *pw_shell;   /* the nominated shell program */
```

There are also available in the standard library a number of subroutines to read entries from the **passwd** file into such a structure. The subroutine *getpwent* reads a single entry from the file, the subroutine *getpwnam* searches the file for the entry with a given login name, and *getpwusr* or *getpwuid* (depending on the system) searches the file for the entry with a given numeric UID.

Having found an entry in the **passwd** file with the required user's login name (passed in as the parameter) in the 'name' field (if there are two entries with the same name, the second will never be accessed), the sequence of operations below continues. If no entry with this name can be found, the *login* program exits; at this point, the *init* process will re-awaken, since one of its child processes has died, and will restart the *getty* process for this terminal.

It is usual to ask for a password if the login name is not found, merely to make it less obvious to the user which names do not exist.

5.1.2 Checking the user's password

If the password field is empty, all actions concerned with checking the password are ignored. For security reasons, many systems insert a check at this point that all logins on dial-up lines must include a password. If the password field is non-empty, the program switches off the echo on the terminal (using the system call *ioctl* from C), asks for a password, reads the reply, and switches the echo back on again. The password just read is then encrypted, using the password as a key for additional security, and the result compared with the entry in the password field of the entry read from **passwd**. If the two differ, the program exits.

An improvement on some systems is for the entry '−' in the encrypted password field of the /**etc/passwd** entry to indicate that no password can be set; this particular login name must always be 'password-less'. This is useful for certain login names such as 'guest', which are designed to be freely available, but under which users (because they have a normal shell) can set passwords, thus inconveniencing any other users who wish to use that login name. This involves compatible modifications to the *login*, *passwd* and *su* programs. It is however fairly common practice for security reasons not to allow password-less logins over dial-up lines.

Users should be encouraged to use passwords, to change them regularly, and to invent passwords containing a mixture of letters, digits and other characters, not related in any simple way to their telephone number, age, address or date of birth!

5.1.3 Printing the message of the day
The program next prints out the 'message of the day', set by the system manager in the file **/etc/motd**, by simply reading the file and listing it onto the terminal. Some systems have separate messages of the day for users in different groups, so that the login command lists both the global message file, and the one for that particular group. The additional programming in the *login* code merely looks at the user's GID entry in the **passwd** record, and lists a file such as **/etc/motd23** for users with group number 23.

5.1.4 Checking the mail
Basic electronic mail facilities are available on Unix as it is usually supplied. On most systems, these facilities are extensively used. To indicate the presence of mail when a user logs in, the login program looks for any mail in the user's mail file, which is **/usr/spool/mail/$USER** on standard systems. Some systems then merely print the message

> You have mail.

if that file exists. Others are a little more helpful, and use the access dates on the file to perhaps

(a) print the date of the latest mail (which will be the date on which the file was last written to, available from the *stat* system call) or

(b) print the date of any unread mail (there is unread mail if the date of last writing of the file is later than the date of last reading).

More sophisticated mail systems exist whose 'mail agents' (the local program handling the user's access to the mail system) allow for mail to be searched by subject and/or keywords, and more helpful notifications (of subject, date and sender, for example) to be made during logging in. This part can be very system dependent; the more sophisticated versions are usually a great improvement, and may retain the basic mail mechanism, but employ different user interface programs (otherwise known as message agents or user agents). The simple *mail* command should always, however, be present, to function in a standard way when machines are connected.

In addition, the shell program may keep a check on mail, and can send information instead of, or in addition to, that sent by the logging in process, for example, to notify a logged-on user immediately of any new mail.

5.1.5 News and noticeboard
Some installations incorporate *news* and/or *noticeboard* facilities, which operate in a similar way to the mail system but which are intended, not for individual or group information, but for circulating system-wide news

information to all users (such as details of system changes) and notices (more temporary information such as details of meetings). In this case the login process will at this point announce new items of news or relevant notices in the same way as for the mail above. Such systems are often part of the mail system itself, and thus offer a uniform user interface for handling mail, news and notices.

5.1.6 Performing login accounting

The login process maintains two distinct files related to the logging on and off processes. One is a list of currently-logged-in users, and the other a history of all logins and logouts.

(a) It updates an entry for the current terminal in the file **/etc/utmp**. This is the file that maintains a list of the currently-logged-on users. Commands such as *who* and *wall* access it to find out who is currently logged on. Further commands such as *write* also access this file. Each entry in the file contains the user's name, the name within **/dev** of the line on which the login took place, and the time of the login. The format of the entries, in the form of a suitable structure mode for C programs, is in the file **/usr/include/utmp.h**, which can be included in a program by the line

```
#include "utmp.h"
```

This file contains a structure definition containing field types and names such as

```
char ut_line[8];/* tty name */
char ut_name[8];/* login name */
long ut_time;/* time logged on */
```

The length of the fields may vary from system to system; always check with the included file on your system.

Unlike the **passwd** file, this is a fixed-format file, so that individual entries can be overwritten when required; each entry can be read in a C program using the *sizeof* function on a structure of the above type to control the number of characters read.

(b) In addition to the **utmp** file of currently logged-in login names, a file is maintained of all *login*s and *logout*s on the machine. A record is appended to the end of the file **/usr/adm/wtmp** (if it exists), so that accounting of how many times and for how long each user has been logged-in can be performed. The record is in the same format as the **utmp** record. If the file **wtmp** does not exist, this action is ignored.

The **wtmp** file can be analysed to provide information by terminal, by hour of day or by user. The standard command for this is *ac*. The **wtmp** file will grow indefinitely, so must be processed and emptied from time to time.

5.1.7 Changing UID and GID

The *login* process then changes to lose its special super-user privilege, which it must have had for the above processes. It does this by executing the privileged calls *setuid* and *setgid* in C, using the values for UID and GID obtained from the /etc/passwd entry. Since *setgid* can be executed only in super-user mode, it must be done before the *setuid* call. The process now becomes owned by the user who is just logging in, and with their group identity.

5.1.8 Setting the user's directory

The user's home directory is known from the penultimate field in the /etc/passwd entry, and the login process next changes to that directory (by a call of *chdir* in C, equivalent to the command *cd*). Any failure, of course, causes the login to fail, and indicates an irregularity concerned with the user's directory, such as wrong access modes being set on the directory (or on one of the directories between it and the root of the file-system), or the complete absence of the directory.

5.1.9 Invoking the shell

Finally, the login process changes (*execs*) to the appropriate shell, using the shell field of the entry in the **passwd** file, with default as the file **/bin/sh**. Since the *chdir* to the user's home directory has already been done, the name may be given relative to the home directory.

Environmental parameters such as **$USER, $HOME** are set up before the *exec* call to the shell.

The shell will probably execute some initialisation code, depending on the particular shell, typically stored in a file such as **.profile** or **.login**; see chapter 6 for details. This is the responsibility of the shell itself, not of the *login* process.

5.2 Logging-out

The process of logging out is essentially the killing of the shell program, so cannot be executed by calling a program from **/bin** as happens with most commands. It must be executed within the shell, causing it to *exit*, and is usually invoked on receipt of (by the user typing) the standard EOF character.

If will be observed that the process number (the PID) of the shell is the same as that of the *getty* originally forked off by *init* (since PIDs are retained across the *execs* first from *init* to *getty*, then from *getty* to *login* and then from *login* to *shell*). The *init* process is waiting for any of its children to die; when it is woken up, it will be able to deduce from the process number returned by the *wait* call (the process number of the dying process) which terminal has logged out. It is therefore normally up to *init* to perform any accounting chores concerned with logging out. Having determined which terminal and user has logged out, the *init* program then

(a) updates the file **/etc/utmp** (marking the appropriate entry as no longer active), since that line is no longer logged in;

(b) updates **/usr/adm/wtmp** (by appending an entry with the date, terminal line, user login name and a character to indicate that it is a logout record, not a login record);

(c) forks a new *getty* as before, with its standard input and output and its error output redirected as before, and the whole logging in process on that terminal restarts.

Chapter 6 **The shell**

So far we have discussed the operation of the programs which form the skeleton of the multi-user time-sharing system. The end product of the logging in activity is that the user is presented with a command interpreter of some sort, whose standard input and output, and error output, are connected to the terminal. Most of a user's logged-on time in a development environment (the environment in which most early Unix systems were situated) is spent interacting with a general purpose command interpreter, known in Unix as a 'shell'. Until recently, most users have been happy to stay with the standard general purpose development shells which come with the system; as the exploitation of Unix develops in the commercial environment, and with a greater proportion of computer-naïve users, new shells should appear.

The function of a traditional shell (such as those provided with Unix and most other systems) is to read commands typed by a user at the console, and interpret them as required; the standard Unix shell as supplied is intended to offer the user a complete range of commands, not a set restricted to a particular application area. A good shell, such as the Unix shell, allows the user interface to be tailored to a given user's requirements to a certain extent. In more modern systems, the commands themselves may not have to be typed. A choice may be offered in the form of a menu from which one possibility is chosen by typing a single character or by pointing with a cursor or 'mouse'; on a number of very recent systems the interface may involve pointing to pictorial representations of commands or parameters, as in the use of icons. On other systems commands may be issued by implication rather than directly, but obviously some form of command mechanism must still exist behind the scenes.

6.1 Introduction

In most interactive computer systems, the command interpreter is an inextricable part of the operating system. In Unix it is a perfectly standard free-standing program, written and running using normal programming constructs available to any which can make standard system calls. The standard shells are written in C, but other languages producing **a.out** format loadable programs would be equally acceptable.

The program loaded as the user's shell (by an *exec* call from the *login* process) is the program specified in the last field of the **passwd** entry for that user. If the last entry in the **passwd** record is blank, the default program is **/bin/sh**, the Bourne shell. The program will be entered with its standard input, standard output and error output connected directly to the user's terminal. As was described in chapter 5 on logging in, the shell is entered by an *exec* call within *login*, so that it retains the same process number as the *login*, which itself retained the *getty* process number. The parent of the shell is thus still the *init* process. When the shell dies, its parent *init* wakes up and restarts the whole logging in process.

There are two distinct general-purpose shells in common use, one available on all Unix systems (the Bourne shell), the other only available on more modern systems (the C shell). They are geared to program development work, and are both fairly terse in command notations and error reporting. They are distinct developments of the original Unix Version 6 shell. The 'Bourne' shell was written by Steve Bourne at Bell Laboratories, and is the program in **/bin/sh** (hence is the default shell). Its more complicated constructs (particularly those for describing the flow of control in conditions and loops) were developed using Algol-like conventions, following Bourne's earlier involvement with Algol 68. The C shell (the command **/bin/csh**) was developed in parallel by Bill Joy at Berkeley with the idea of conforming, as far as possible, to the syntax of the C language, in order to unify the constructs of the programming and command languages. In addition to being C-oriented in its constructs, the C shell has very powerful process-control features. The C shell is not available on some Version 7 systems.

Users new to Unix often ask for advice on which is the better of the two main shells to adopt, and part of the research for this book consisted of asking for advice on this very point. It appears that those familiar with only one shell always think that it is the best one, so unbiassed advice is hard to come by; a similar situation holds with personal opinions of programming languages! Some advice on the choice of shell relates to efficiency, in the sense that, for example, the C shell is the slower of the two shells on start-up (since it creates a hashed index of the commands in all the directories in the $PATH list, and each new shell starts with the execution of the .cshrc file), but that it then runs faster (given the hashed index, it can locate command programs more quickly) than the Bourne shell. As far as features go, the general consensus of views from users familiar with both shells appears to be that the C shell is superior for interactive work, because of its process control features, while the Bourne shell has more powerful language constructs, and so is better for use in shell scripts. This implies that the use of both shells can be advantageous, but the author has seen the development of a number of extended Bourne shells, which now include a number of the C shell features such as the easy repetition of earlier commands, so that the decision on which shell to choose is becoming harder!

In this chapter the general features and principles common to both of these shells are discussed. The particular features of the Bourne and C shells are described separately in appendices.

6.2 General shell principles

There are several general aspects of shells which require discussion, and which apply to both the main shells and to most special-purpose shells. One is the general way in which a shell executes commands, and redirects their output and input; the technique used by a shell to perform these operations represents the general Unix techniques for controlling the execution of other processes from within a program.

A second area is the general one of the shell variables which form the user's environment. These include 'PATH' to define the search path for commands, and other user-definable parameters.

Another area from the user's point of view covers the functions of the general commands available. These are independent of the particular shell being used, and are described in section 1 on the Unix manual. Commands of particular interest to systems managers are discussed in appendix 3 to this book.

The final area concerns the constructs of the particular shell language being considered, such as the syntax for looping or branching, or for handling interrupts. This will vary between the Bourne and C shells, and is detailed in appendices 1 and 2 on the two shells.

6.3 Command execution

The first 'word' of the typed line (i.e. letters up to the first space, tab or newline character) is taken to be the command name. Once the command name has been determined, the shell searches for a file of that name, with execute permission, in each of the directories listed (colon separated) in the shell variable PATH: 'PATH' in the Bourne shell and 'path' in the C shell. A typical value of PATH is

    .:$HOME/bin:/bin:/usr/bin

in which the four directories '.' † then **/staff/ef/bin** (depending on the expansion of the $HOME shell variable), then **/bin**, and lastly **/usr/bin** are listed. These directories are searched in this order for a file whose name is the same as the given command. If an executable file of the required name is found, the shell executes *fork* and *exec* calls to start the execution of the file itself if it is an executable binary program, but if the command file turns out to be a shell script, a new shell will be started, with its input redirected to read from the file. The shell finds whether the file was a binary program by asking the kernel to execute it; the kernel recognises various different types of executable file, and on early Unix systems would reject anything that was not an executable binary. From this rejection, the shell would deduce that the file was a shell script. More modern systems (again with much variation) have a greater variety of files interpretable by the kernel, which looks at the first two

† You will often find the initial '.' omitted, but the effect is still to search the current directory first.

bytes of the loaded program, and deduces from the coded information just how the program needs to be run.

In the meantime, the main shell normally *wait*s for the command to complete before continuing, but will not wait if there was an ampersand ('&') character at the end of the command.

6.4 File name expansions – wildcards

It is assumed that the user is familiar with the use of the symbols '*' and '?' as 'wildcards' in filenames in command arguments, and the fact that they must be escaped if required as genuine characters.

Note that it is the shell itself which expands the parameter list; if the user types

```
prog chap*
```

the program *prog* will receive parameters as though the user had typed for example

```
prog chap1 chap2 chap5
```

with every possible filename in the current directory starting 'chap' included, and sorted into alphabetical order. This is very different from most other operating systems, in which any command which requires the possibility of interpreting various 'wildcards' has to include the code to interpret them.

If no files fitting the pattern are found, the C shell normally reports an error; in the Bourne shell the actual string given, still containing the 'wild-card' character(s) such as a '*' and/or '?', is passed to the program just as typed.

6.5 Commands executed in the shell

Certain commands cannot be executed as described above, by *fork*ing and *exec*ing from the shell. For example the *cd* command, if it were executed in a child process, would have no effect on the working directory of the parent process when it is re-entered at the termination of the command; the child process would change directory, but the parent (the shell) would be unaffected. Certain commands have, therefore, to be detected by the shell, and specially executed by system calls from within the shell itself. These may be thought of in general as any command which affects the environment (the values of shell variable, the working directory) for later running programs. Such commands include *cd*, *newgrp*, and setting values of shell variables.

There is a subtle distinction which must be understood between the command line

```
cd /etc; grep anon passwd
```

and the similar line in parentheses

```
(cd /etc; grep anon passwd)
```

In the first example, the (current) shell changes to the **/etc** directory, and there looks for the **passwd** file, to search for the string 'anon'. After the execution of the line, the shell remains in the **/etc** directory. The brackets in the latter cause a new shell to be initiated; this new shell will change directory, and execute the *grep* command in the new directory, and will then die; however, the original shell's working directory will not have been affected, since the original shell has not executed a *cd* command, but has been dormant while the new shell was in operation.

A similar consideration is involved in the execution of shell scripts. If the user has a file of commands which is to be executed, the normal command would be

```
sh filename
```

or simply

```
filename
```

if the file has execute permission, with parameters to the shell script following the filename if required. Either of these alternatives creates a new shell, and it is the new shell in which the commands are executed. Thus commands within the script such as *cd* and setting shell variable values will not affect the original shell. If the commands in the named file are required to have effect in the original shell (for example, if they set the values of shell variables), they must be executed without forking off a new shell. This requires another special command name which is recognised directly by the shell, and causes it to temporarily divert its input to read from the named file. The command to do this is

```
source filename
```

in the C shell, and

```
. filename
```

(a full stop, a space and the filename) in the Bourne shell. This is typically the way to execute an amended **.login** or **.profile** file, or using the *tset* command. For example, if a **.profile** file in the Bourne shell includes the lines

```
PS1="next: "
export PS1
```

the reset the command prompt string, to simply execute

```
.profile
```

would create a new shell, whose prompt string would be reset, but which would then die. However, executing

```
. .profile
```

in the Bourne shell would reset the prompt string in the current shell, giving the user a new prompt from now on.

6.6 Special files

Most command interpreter systems have means by which a user can tailor a system to their own particular needs and foibles, and can arrange for these facilities to be set up whenever they log in.

In the Bourne shell, a file named **.profile** in the user's home directory will be executed on logging in if such a file exists. It will be executed within the shell (see the previous section) before any commands are read from the terminal, so that any values assigned to shell variables will be available to the user. The file is not executed at the start of other shells started by the user.

In the C shell, the file **$HOME/.login** is executed whenever a user logs in, and the file **$HOME/.cshrc** is executed every time a C shell starts, even within shell scripts. This can slow down the execution of forked-off shells.

The C shell executes the file **.logout** on logout, when the user logs out; this can be used to perform any tidying-up operations the user requires. To obtain an equivalent effect in the Bourne shell, the user's **.profile** executed on logging in may include a *trap* command to pick up the logout signal, as in

```
trap $HOME/.logout 0
```

which causes the **.logout** file to be executed on receipt of signal 0.

A typical **.profile** or .login file might set a user prompt, set an initial directory other than the default one (perhaps to the directory the user was in when the last logout occurred), check for noticeboard items if the *login* command does not do so, switch off access to the terminal from others using the command *mesg*, and so on.

6.7 User-provided shells

Any ordinary program can act as a shell, and users with particular applications in mind are encouraged to write a special shell to suit the application and the likely users. A typical application area might be more suitably served by a shell which offers at each stage a choice of legitimate commands, possibly as a menu of options, with more helpful error messages, and not allowing the user to do anything except a limited range of commands. For example, in a documentation environment, a shell might allow the user access only to commands for editing files, removing them, viewing them on the screen through *nroff*, and obtaining hard copy through *troff*.

In addition, system managers may like to think of setting up a shell which would run under super-user privilege (entries 0 for the UID and GID fields in the **/etc/passwd** record for this login name), and would allow an assistant to perform certain specific administrative tasks which require super-user status, without allowing him or her full access to all commands as root. Such commands could include just, say, dumping and performing accounting runs.

Chapter 7 Control of users on a Unix system

This chapter is devoted to describing a number of aspects of Unix related to the control of users, including topics such as the creation of new login names, the deletion of all traces of departed users, and the creation and control of their shell environment.

7.1 Creating a new user

The sequence of operations necessary for creating an additional login name on the system is described below. We show here just the shell commands for installing a new login name; other administrative considerations such as whether there is enough filestore space to accommodate the new user's requirements, are obviously required before the new name is implemented. Most of this can, of course, be written as a shell script; such a script is outlined.

(a) Determine the required login name, user identifier (UID) and group identifier (GID). The latter are numeric values used internally by Unix to identify ownership of files and processes, and to protect them. In general the UID will be unique to a particular user, and so a value which will be chosen is not already assigned to any other user. However, in general the GID will already exist, and will reflect the category/classification of the user in some way. The usual practice is to divide users into a number of categories, each of which will become a Unix group. Members of a particular group will share certain privileges intermediate between those of the general public and those of an individual user. Typical groups may be different sections of a company such as sales, production and purchasing; in an academic environment, the groups might be system staff, other staff, postgraduates and undergraduates. (See section 5.3.3 below for some further system and management implications of group numbers.)

The user identifiers will normally be unique to each user, but are often blocked into certain ranges of number for each group. If however two different login names are assigned the same numeric UID, the two users have complete interchangeability of access to files and processes,

78

but can login to different directories. Processes which convert from numeric UID to login names will, of course, always come up with the first one to occur in the file **/etc/passwd**, which may cause problems with mail systems.

Having decided on the login name for the new user, its uniqueness must be checked. This can be done by a *grep* command, as in

```
grep "^name:" /etc/passwd
```

to search for a line containing the proposed name between the start-of-line and the first colon.

To find the first free number within a given range which does not already occur in the file **/etc/passwd**, some kind of program is necessary. The simplest technique in Unix is to use an *awk* script; *awk* is a C-like language intended for the easy analysis of files whose format is essentially 'one record per line'.

(b) Edit **/etc/passwd**; care must be taken to ensure that two processes are not editing this file in parallel, or the result may not be what you expect. The source code of some early versions of Unix included outline code for Dijkstra-style semaphores† to enable parallel processes whose execution might interfere with each other to synchronise their actions, but this was never fully implemented. More recent versions of Unix include file-locking as a primitive, and it is included as a modification in Xenix, but the bulk of the system source has not yet been modified to make use of them.

The usual way to overcome this problem in Unix is to use what is commonly referred to as a 'lock-file'. All processes with a common interest which might interfere (such as the amendment of the file **/etc/passwd**) agree on the name of a file. That file will be present when such a process is active, and absent otherwise. Each process when it needs to access that particular resource then checks for the existence of this lock-file, and if it exists, knows that another process with which it might interfere is active. It can then be programmed either to wait for a given length of time and try again, or to print a message and abandon ship. If, on the other hand, the lock-file does not exist, the process creates it, does whatever processing is required, and at the conclusion of the process, erases the file. The file must be erased under all possible process terminations, including break-ins, or the resource will appear to be permanently locked. During the processing, if any other process requiring this resource starts, it will find that the file exists, and will not interfere.

The critical time interval ('window of vulnerability') is that between checking for the existence of the lock-file, and creating it if it is absent. It is possible that one program could check, find the file absent, but that

† see E. W. Dijkstra, 'Co-operating Sequential Processes' in *Programming Languages*, editor F Genuys, published by Academic Press 1968, pages 43–112.

a second process could check before the first has created the file; both programs would think that the resource was free. In C programs, for example, the system call

```
creat( filename, 0 );
```

will create the file if it does not exist, with no read or write permissions (given by the second parameter). If the file does exist (because a similar call in another program has created it), it has no access permissions, so the *creat* call will fail, and will deliver a negative value. The program code becomes something like

```
if ( ( f = creat( "thislock", 0 ) ) < 0 ) {
        ... print error message, and/or wait or exit ...
}
```

The critical time for possible interference between two processes is now reduced to the time for the *creat* system call. Note that this cannot work for root-owned processes, which have permission to access any files.

A better solution is to use a *link* system call or command rather than to create a file; *link* always fails if the new name being created already exists without write access, and is equally effective under root-owned processes.

In System V, there is an 'exclusive open' mode for files, which can be used as the basis for process locking.

Some Unix-like systems (such as Xenix, but not System V) have added record-locking facilities, allowing individual records within a file to be locked. These are however non-standard, and should be used bearing non-portability in mind.

The *passwd* command itself has to be careful of such problems, since any change to a record will in general alter the length of that record, so that the file must be completely rewritten. It uses a lock-file **/etc/ptmp** as inter-process protection for this purpose. Some users alter their editors to create locks, to ensure that two users cannot edit a file simultaneously.

(c) If necessary, edit the file **/etc/group**, if the new user is expected to require the ability to change groups. (See below for further discussion on the significance of groups.)

(d) Create the home directory, and *chown* and *chgrp* it to the user. (If you wish to provide the user with a default **.profile**, **.login** or **.cshrc** file, this is the point at which it can be inserted.)

(e) If necessary, create other items such as the user's mail directory. The requirements here will differ from system to system; the basic default mail system requires no further actions, and most sophisticated mail systems create the new files necessary for a mail user when the mail system is used by that user for the first time. However, it may still be necessary to add the user's name to appropriate interest groups, and to certain inter-machine mail directories.

(f) If appropriate, store the user's full name, address, internal telephone extension number and other administrative details in files kept for this purpose. It is undesirable to clutter up the **/etc/passwd** file with too much information, but most installations require further details about each registered user beyond that appearing in the **passwd** entry.

A simplified version of a possible interactive shell script (it assumes that the name of the directory is the same as the login name of the user) using the Bourne shell is given below.

```
PASS=/etc/passwd
PASST=/etc/passwdtmpnewu
LOCK=/etc/ptmp
#
#    Check authorisation
#
if test ! -w $PASS
then echo "Sorry -- you do not have authority to add new users"; exit 1
fi
#
#    Check lock file
#
if test -r $LOCK
then echo "Passwd file locked"; exit 1
fi
#
#    Create lock file
#
if cp /dev/null $LOCK
then chmod 000 $LOCK; trap "rm -f $LOCK;exit 2" 1 2 3 15
else echo "Cannot lock passwd file"; exit 1
fi
echo -n "Proposed identifier? "
read iden junk
if grep -s "^$iden:" $PASS
then echo "Identifier $iden exists"; rm -f $LOCK; exit 1
fi
echo -n "Parent directory? "; read home junk
home=$home/$iden
if test -d $home
then echo -n "Directory $home already exists - continue?"
    case `read ans` in
      y*) if mv $home ${home}.old
        then echo "$home renamed ${home}.old"
        else echo "Cannot rename $home"; rm -f $LOCK; exit 1
        fi;;
      *) rm -f $LOCK; exit 1 ;;
    esac
fi
```

```
while echo −n "uid? "; read uid junk
do
    case $uid in
        # if this check isn't made, the user could
        # end up as root with uid 'a' or something
        [0−9]*) break;;
        *)   echo "UID must be numeric";;
    esac
done
if grep −s ":.*:.*:$uid:.*.*:" $PASS
then echo "UID $uid exists"; rm −f $LOCK; exit 1
fi
while echo −n "gid? "; read gid junk
do
    case $gid in
        [0−9]*) break;;
        *)   echo "GID must be numeric";;
    esac
done
echo −n "shell if non-standard? "; read shell junk
if mkdir $home
then :
else echo "Cannot create home directory"; rm −f $LOCK; exit 1
fi
if chown $uid $home && chgrp $gid $home  # uid not iden
then :
else echo "Problem setting uid/gid on $home"; rm −f $LOCK; exit 1
fi
(cat $PASS; echo $iden::$uid:$gid::$home:$shell ) | \
    sort −t: +2n +3n  > $PASST
if cp $PASST $PASS
then :
else echo "Failed to copy passwd - saved in $PASST"; rm −f $LOCK; exit 1
fi
rm −f $LOCK; exit 0
```

A non-interactive version, in which the information is passed as parameters, follows.

```
PASS=/etc/passwd
PASST=/etc/passwdtmpnewu
LOCK=/etc/ptmp
case $# in
    5|4) ;;
    *) echo "newuser : usage : newuser name homedir uid gid shell" 1>&2
        exit 2;;
esac
```

```
if test ! -w $PASS
then echo "Sorry -- you do not have authority to add new users"; exit 1
fi
if test -r $LOCK
then echo "Passwd file locked"; exit 1
fi
if cp /dev/null $LOCK
then chmod 000 $LOCK; trap "rm -f $LOCK;exit 2" 1 2 3 15
else echo "cannot lock passwd file"
fi
iden=$1
if grep -s "^$iden:" $PASS
then echo "Identifier $iden exists"; rm -f $LOCK; exit 1
fi
home=$2 uid=$3 gid=$4 shell=$5
home=$home/$iden
if test -d $home
then echo "Directory $home already exists "; rm -f $LOCK; exit
fi
if mkdir $home
then :
else echo "cannot make $home"; rm -f $LOCK;exit 2
fi
if chown $uid $home && chgrp $gid $home
then :
else echo "Problem setting uid/gid"; rm -f $LOCK; exit 1
fi
case ` grep :.*:.*:$uid:.*.*:    $PASS ` in
   *:$uid:*) echo "UID $uid exists already"; rm -f $LOCK; exit 1;;
esac
(cat $PASS; echo $iden::$uid:$gid::$home:$shell) | \
   sort -t: +2n +3n > $PASST
if cp $PASST $PASS
then :
else echo "Cannot copy passwd - saved in $PASST"; rm -f $LOCK; exit 1
fi
rm -f $LOCK; exit 0
```

The shell scripts operate as follows:

(a) Check that the user running the shell script has permission to write to **/etc/passwd**; access should also be restricted by permissions on the file containing the shell script.

(b) Perform a locking check, to ensure that no other process is accessing the **passwd** file.

(c) Set the identifier for the new user.

(d) Check whether this identifier already exists. The *grep* command delivers the value 'true' if it finds at least one occurrence of the requested string, and 'false' otherwise. The option flag '−s' causes *grep* to deliver the command status (true if it found an occurrence, false otherwise) without generating any output.

(e) Read the name of the parent directory for the new user, the proposed UID and GID, and the shell if non-standard. On the author's full version of the shell script, we merely request a category of user; the shell script then looks up the category in a table, deduces the parent directory, GID and shell from that, and computes a convenient free UID from **/etc/passwd** using an *awk* script.

(f) Report an error if the directory or an entry with the chosen UID already exists. The UID should perhaps be checked after evaluation using the *expr* command to avoid problems with representation.

(g) Edit a temporary copy of **/etc/passwd** to append the new entry, and sort it by UID (the third colon-separated field). It is usually convenient to keep **/etc/passwd** in a known sorted order.

(h) Create the user's directory (with *mkdir*), and set its UID and GID correctly (using *chown* and *chgrp*). Note that the *chown* command cannot be performed using the login name to specify the user

```
chown name files
```

until the new user's entry exists in **/etc/passwd**. Until that time, a number UID must be given.

At every exit, the lock-file must be removed. Strictly, it is necessary to lock the **passwd** file only during the last few instructions, where a record is appended, the file is sorted, and is copied back to the original. However, it would be frustrating using the interactive version for the user to have typed the earlier information only to have to wait for the file to be free.

7.2 Deleting a user

The steps here are more dangerous than the above steps creating a new user, since it is always easier to delete information than to create it. The steps can again be written as a shell script.

(a) Delete that user's line from **/etc/passwd**.

(b) Delete any references to that user in **/etc/group**.

(c) Remove the user's home directory and subsidiary files by a command such as

```
rm −r directory
```

It is possible that other users may own files in this user's tree; such files will be deleted by this command.

(d) Remove the user's mail directory, secret mail directory, and spooled files.

(e) If you really want to purge the user completely, and remove all the user's files, wherever they may be, use a command such as

```
find / −user 234 −type f −exec rm −f {} ";"
```

which removes every normal file in the system which is owned by that user, but not directories! This operation will take a considerable time, so is usually forked off. If the user's login name were specified as a name rather than as a numeric UID, the command would have to be executed before the login name is removed from **/etc/passwd**, since the *find* command looks up that file to determine the numeric UID. The extent to which the user's files should be expunged completely is debatable. The step (c) above would leave in existence any files to which other users have created links (who presumably in general would wish to continue using those files even after the deleted user has left). This would be convenient for those other users, but the files would be left belonging to a non-existent user, and if the UID were re-used at a later time, a new user would own the files. Perhaps a more comprehensive scheme would involve sending mail to all users who have links to the deleted user's files, instructing them to take copies if they wish to continue using the files, and the files could then be deleted after a given length of time. For safety's sake, UIDs should not be re-used straight away, so that problems such as the above have time to settle before the UID becomes that of another user.

A possible simple shell script is shown below as an interactive Bourne shell script, followed by one in a non-interactive form. Access to the shell script must of course be safeguarded.

```
PASS=/etc/passwd
PASST=/etc/passwdtmpdel
LOCK=/etc/ptmp
if test ! −w $PASS
then echo "No permissions"; exit 1
fi
if test −r $LOCK
then echo "Passwd file locked"; exit 1
fi
cp /dev/null $LOCK
echo −n "Identifier? "; read iden junk
home=`grep \`$iden: $PASS ^ sed "s/.*:\/\//" ^ sed "s/:$//" `
if test ! $home
then echo "Can't find in passwd"; rm −f $LOCK; exit 1
fi
if test −d $home
then ls −ld $home; ls −l $home; echo "du $home" `du $home`
else echo "$home doesn't exist"
fi
```

```
echo −n "OK to continue? "; read ok
case $ok in
    y*) echo "OK...continuing";;
    *) echo "Abandoned"; rm −f $LOCK; exit 1;;
esac
if test −d $home
then echo "Clearing $home"; rm −r $home
fi
rm /usr/spool/mail/$iden
nice find / −user $iden −print  −exec rm −f {} ";" & sleep 10
sed "/^$iden:/d" < $PASS > $PASST
cp $PASST $PASS
rm −f $LOCK; exit 0


PASS=/etc/passwd
PASST=/etc/passwdtmpdel
LOCK=/etc/ptmp
if test ! −w $PASS
then echo "No permissions"; exit 1
fi
if test −r $LOCK
then echo "Passwd file locked"; exit 1
fi
cp /dev/null $LOCK
iden=$1
home=`grep \^$iden: $PASS ^ sed "s/.*:\/\//" ^ sed "s/:$//" `
if test ! $home
then echo "Can't find in passwd"; rm −f $LOCK; exit 1
fi
if test −d $home
then ls −ld $home; ls −l  $home; echo "du $home" `du $home`
else echo "$home doesn't exist"
fi
if test −d $home
then echo "Clearing $home"; rm −r $home
fi
rm /usr/spool/mail/$iden
nice find / −user $uid −print  −exec rm −f {} ";"
sed "/^$iden:/d" < $PASS > $PASST
cp $PASST $PASS
rm −f $LOCK; exit 0
```

The author uses the script described in the previous section for creating a new user in an interactive form, since it can take several attempts to find a new and unique (and short) login name; but the non-interactive user deletion script is preferred, since deletions usually occur a number at a time (such as at the termination of a course), and the list of login names of those users can be generated automatically from a course list. The scripts operate as follows:

(a) Check whether the user running the script has permission to write to the **/etc/passwd** file.
(b) Perform the usual locking check.
(c) Read the identifier and find the corresponding home directory from **/etc/passwd**.
(d) List details of some of the files as a check before proceeding with this dangerous exercise.
(e) Clear all the user's files throughout the filestore; this is very time-consuming, so may be forked off.
(f) Clear the home directory and its contents.
(g) Clear the mail file (or its equivalent on your system).
(h) Delete the entry from **/etc/passwd** (but no sorting is required this time).

7.3 Use of groups

There is often confusion among Unix users about the significance of user and group ownership of files, and the effective use of groups, so a brief discussion of such points is given here.

Associated with each user is both a user identifier and a group identifier; these are set up on logging in from the data in **/etc/passwd**. Each process and file has an associated user identifier and group identifier; those for a process are inherited from the process that spawned it (with the exception of the *setuid* and *setgid* system calls which are available to super-user), while those for a file are set at the time when the file is created to those of the creating process. The access permissions on the file relating to user and group access (the ones set by 'chmod o+x' and 'chmod g+x', or 'chmod 770', for example) refer to permissions relative to the file's user and group. Thus, during a normal logged-in session, the user and group identifiers of the shell are those set in the **/etc/passwd** file, so that files created have that user identifier and group identifier, and files accesses are checked relative to the user and group identifiers in the **/etc/passwd** file.

7.3.1 The /etc/group file

If you execute an *su* command (don't forget that *su* can have a login name as parameter; most people just think of it as being for going into 'root' or 'super-user') a 'login name' is specified, and results in a new shell with both a new user identifier and a new group identifier, picked from that login name's entry in **/etc/passwd**. There is no command to change only the user identifier, but to leave the group identifier unchanged. However, the command *newgrp* changes the group identifier, but leaves the user identifier intact. It uses the file **/etc/group**, which should be of the form shown in figure 7.1. The colon-separated fields on each line represent the name of the group, a password (function unknown, but it may be wise to insert a dummy entry here), the GID of the group (cf the GID entry in **/etc/passwd**), and a comma-separated list of login names of users permitted to change into that

```
root::0:anw,ef,wja
bin::1:anw,ef,wja
uucp::4:
system:ayej8fQoKeEmQ:9:al,jrw,wja,anw,ef
csstaff::20:anw,ef,wja,annet
statstaff::21:ams
otherstaff::22:drw,gfp
roget::23:ef,anw,wja,al,daa
postgrad::30:al,jrw,wja,jch,daa,aah
unixcs::71:annet
project::100:ef,aah
unixbook::101:ef,wja,jpo
```

Fig. 7.1 Typical **/etc/group** file

group using the *newgrp* command. In the example **group** file shown, the users 'anw', 'ef' and 'wja' are permitted to change to group 0, and the users 'al', 'jrw', 'wja', 'anw' and 'ef' are permitted to change to group 9, called 'system', and so on.

The name of each group and its numeric identifier enable groups to be named as in the command

```
newgrp staff
```

which changes the current group of the shell process to that named as 'staff' in the **/etc/group** file. The *newgrp* operation is permitted only if the logged-in login name occurs in the last entry in the appropriate line of **/etc/group**. The **/etc/group** file is not involved in the logging in process, so login names do not need to appear unless the user is expected to need the *newgrp* command (i.e. is expected to need to change to a group other than the one specified in the **/etc/passwd** entry). Notice that *newgrp* changes the group identifier of the current shell, whereas *su* creates a new shell. To perform this function, *newgrp* must be a special command detected actually inside the shell, but executed via a root-owned SUID command to obtain the privilege to be able to change GID. In the process, the user's environment is usually lost, but this can be corrected.

The use of group names instead of numeric identifiers in commands such as *chgrp* also requires access to this file, using only the first and third entries of each record.

For work which is shared across users in different groups (such as project work involving staff from both senior and junior groups), the project can be assigned a new group identifier, and all those involved in it allowed to *newgrp* to that group. An example is the group 'project' in the example file above, with users 'ef' and 'aah' from different login groups both being able to *newgrp* to the 'project' group.

A parallel facility to the **group** file and the *newgrp* command which permitted a user to change the current logged-in UID rather than GID (which would involve a file **/etc/user** and a *newusr* command to enable users named in the file to change to a new login name) would be useful, and can easily be implemented by those with source licences in a similar way to the group facility.

7.3.2 The *chown* and *chgrp* commands

The above discussion clarifies problems which sometimes occur when, as often happens, a file is created for a user by the system manager running as 'super-user'. When created, the file will belong to user 0 ('root') and group 0. If you wish to pass ownership in full to the user, you should execute both of the commands

    chown usersname file

and

    chgrp usersgroup file

Often the person who created the file remembers only the *chown* command, and the user later finds that group permissions appear not to be acting correctly. The source of an appropriate command to change both the UID and the GID of a file (which might be called *chuser*) is shown in the chapter of example programs.

7.3.3 Effective use of groups

Note the use of special groups called 'project' and 'unixbook' above. Normally staff at different levels of seniority are in different groups, but project work will involve staff at different seniorities in common software. To enable the sharing of files for a research project which involves some people from each level, a special group can be created, to which all those involved can change using the *newgrp* command.

Similarly, if the basic distribution of groups in the logging in details in the **/etc/passwd** file is performed in a vertical sense (i.e. the company staff are divided into groups by section rather than by seniority), the same technique can be applied to enable inter-sectional work to take place.

7.3.4 The *umask* facility

The *umask* facility sets the default permissions given to newly created files, and is available both as a shell command and as a C system call. The parameter is an octal number of three digits, where the bits set to one in the first digit define the owner's permissions (read, write, execute/search) which **cannot** be set, and the second and third digits define the group and public permission limitations similarly. The command

    umask 077

will cause any files created later in that session to have access only to the user, while

```
umask 022
```

prohibits group and public write access. Some users set the default mode to 222, to provide additional default protection from accidental overwriting by themselves. However, since deletion of files usually involves a check on the permissions of the owner (the command *rm* will prompt before removing for any file of which the remover does not have ownership, or does not have write permission) temporary files will often not get deleted. In addition, and even more catastrophic, editors cannot write to their own temporary files, so cannot function correctly.

7.4 The user environment

Both the Bourne and C shells allow users to set up their own environments (shell variable values, prompts, command and directory search paths, etc). Some details are given here; more details can be found in Appendices 1 and 2.

7.4.1 The Bourne shell

For the Bourne shell, the file **.profile** in the user's home directory is executed on logging in, so that the user enters any personalised commands here. The system manager can set a global **.profile** script (to apply to all users) in **/etc/profile**, to set global *umask* and search path values, for example.

Note that this type of file normally sets up shell variables within the user's shell, and so must be executed within the shell, rather than by a forked shell; in the Bourne shell, this is equivalent to executing

```
. .profile
```

7.4.2 The C shell

For the C shell, the files **$HOME/.login**, **$HOME/.cshrc** and **$HOME/.logout** are executed on logging in, starting any new C shell, and logging out, respectively.

7.4.3 Additional commands

As part of tailoring your Unix system to the requirements of the local user community, you will wish to add new commands to the system. These will be added as described the chapter 3, under the section on **/bin**, and you will maintain source code and manual entry with the command. The user interface of any new commands (the way they handle flag parameters, for example) will, unless you are developing a completely new environment, conform to the 'Unix standard', whatever that may mean. In appendix 5 is a summary of discussions at a recent Unix meeting at which these standards were discussed. It is not a definitive document, but gives a good feel for what experienced users considered important in this area.

7.5 User directories

By tradition, user directories were always *mount*ed under the directory /**usr** (hence the name). They do not need to be, and it may be more sensible to use a structure more closely related to the structure of the organisation of the personnel using the machine. In such an arrangement the directories at the 'root' level rather than below the /**usr** directory could represent the different sections of the company, with names such as /**sales**, /**purchasing**, /**support** and so on. Similarly in an academic environment, there might be directories at the top level named /**staff**, /**graduate**, and /**undergrad** representing the major divisions.

7.6 User monitoring

The basic principle of Unix is to be as helpful as possible to the users. It is thus easy for any user to create new files and directories, which can cause problems when discs are accidentally over-filled. An additional problem is that, when a disc is full, the messages appear on the console, not at the terminal of the user trying to create a new file. It would be a simple matter to add to the *login* command or the global login profile the use of the *quot* command or some equivalent to check on total disc usage. However, since on a large file-system the *quot* command takes a long time, such a check is usually done overnight, and the overnight results checked on logging in. The dummy field in the /**etc/passwd** entries (or a separate file) can then be used to keep a user disc usage upper-limit. In general however this field should not be extended more than is essential, and a separate file is probably necessary for information such as each user's maximum disc space allocation, name, address and telephone number. The use of a separate file for this information avoids modifications to the *login* command.

The *ac* command should be used to check users' total logged-on time, if appropriate. This is not generally a problem in commercial environments, but in an academic environment it may be necessary to detect and report on over- or under-use by an individual. A shell script run nightly (see the command *cron* in chapter 12) could check for new large files using the *find* command and report on them, and output from the *du* command (total disc use under a given directory, see chapter 10) used to detect users whose usage is increasing too rapidly.

There will be an occasional need to move individual users to new file-systems, to balance the total disc load on the system. Users should be encouraged to use a shell variable such as HOME to refer to their home directory whenever possible, to reduce problems after reconfiguration.

7.7 guest

Many Unix systems in general environments maintain a login name 'guest' to which any user is welcome to login. This is mainly for use by visitors, or by users who are checking whether the system offers the facilities they require; in the latter case, if the facilities are as required, they are then expected to apply for their own login names. A login name such as 'guest' (with no password) would normally not be allowed to login on dial-up lines.

7.8 Special users

It is often convenient to have a number of usernames with non-standard shells for particular purposes. Typical examples include a login name 'who' with shell **/bin/who**, a login name 'learn' with shell **/usr/bin/learn**, and even (for those sites with spare machine capacity) a login name 'chess' with shell **/usr/games/chess** (the chess program). If the default logout and login message clears the terminal screen, the 'who' username needs a command which leaves a delay for the information to be read before terminating and clearing the screen. To have a 'learn' or 'chess' login name, with the command available only under that UID, may simplify monitoring of its use.

Chapter 8   Devices in general

Unix devices fall into two categories, character serial devices (those from which characters can be read from or written to only in a serial fashion, such as terminals, printers and magnetic tapes), and block-structured devices (those used in the file-system, usually shared, normally usable only after actions to position the read/write head, and readable by ordinary users only through file input/output requests). The Unix kernel attempts as far as it is able to make serial devices look like ordinary files to the user; however, different devices obviously involve very different actions at the system hardware level when reading and writing, and such differences must be handled by the kernel. Block structured devices are hidden from the users by the kernel, and are accessed only through filestore requests.

The directory entry for a device gives, as usual, a name, and an inode number. In the corresponding inode area is a flag to indicate that this is a device rather than a file, and to indicate whether it is a character serial or block-structured device. The inode also contains details of which particular device it is. This is in the form of two numbers (see below), the first or major device number representing the type of device, and the second or minor device number representing a particular device among perhaps several of identical type. This information is then passed over to a part of the kernel which performs the actual input/output, and takes into account the physical characteristics of the device.

The normal convention is that devices reside in the directory /**dev**, but this is not essential.

8.1 Making a Unix device

The code to support any device which you wish to interface to the Unix system must already be in the kernel; the methods for adding new device drivers to the kernel varies very much from system to system, and are very licence dependent. Further, the problems of driving different types of device (discs, networks, memory-mapped displays) are so diverse that details could not be given here. In early versions, all modifications need access to the system source, which would be changed and recompiled. Later versions allow the reconfiguration of existing devices by the amendment of configuration tables without any recompilation, but the addition of new devices still needs access to the system source. Some non-Bell releases gave rules by which the user could add new modules written by himself according to a given interface. These methods are so variable and system dependent that they are not discussed further here.

Each device is defined by two numbers, known as its 'major' and 'minor' device numbers. Typically the major device number for a block device would refer to a disc controller, and the minor number to the particular disc drive number on that controller; for a serial device, the major number may refer to the multiplexer, and the minor number to the particular line number on that multiplexer. More precisely, the major number refers to the software section within the kernel which handles that type of device, and the minor number to the particular device of that type. Thus it is normal for all multiplexers of the same type to be treated as one major device, while the minor device number specifies both the multiplexer and the line within it. Thus if each multiplexer handles eight lines, minor numbers 0 to 7 might be on the first multiplexer, numbers 8 to 15 on the second, and so on. On some systems, the same physical device may be available with different minor numbers to allow different modes of access (such as a magnetic tape working in different formats).

Major and minor numbers can be displayed by using the long form of *ls* output on the **/dev** directory, as in

```
ls −l /dev
```

This command gives output such as is shown in figure 8.1. The lines beginning with a 'c' indicate a character serial device, those beginning with a 'b' indicate block-structured devices.

Device entries in a directory are created by a command such as

```
/etc/mknod /dev/newdev c 5 7
```

which creates a device to be named **/dev/newdev**, of type character serial (the 'c'; use 'b' for a block device) and to be major device 5, minor device 7. The code to handle major device 5 must already be in the kernel, and it must handle device number 7 of that type correctly. Major numbers for character and block devices are independent, so that there may be two devices with the same major number, one a block device, and one a character device.

Devices can be linked to give two names to the same device, if convenient. Whichever name is used, data transfer goes to the one real device. This technique can be useful in giving use-oriented names to devices, and can enable the console (often the only hard-copy device on a small system) to double as a printer by linking **/dev/console** to **/dev/lp**. In addition to the typical names of discs such as **/dev/disc1** and **/dev/disc2**, reconfiguration is made less troublesome if alternate names are given which relate more closely to the use of the disc. It is often sensible, for example, to link a name such as **/dev/root** to whichever device the root file-system is on, or to have the name **/dev/spool** for the spooling device which will be mounted on **/usr/spool**.

```
total 41
crw--w--w-  1 mt     0,   0 May  2 10:12 console
crw-rw-rw-  1 tdl    6,  31 May  1 23:32 diablo
crw--w--w-  1 mt     0,   1 May  2 10:32 dl11
crw-rw-rw-  1 root   6,  16 Apr 10 14:43 dz20
crw-rw-rw-  1 root   6,  17 Apr 10 14:43 dz21
crw-rw-rw-  1 root   6,  18 Apr 10 14:43 dz22
crw-rw-rw-  1 root   6,  19 Apr 10 14:44 dz23
crw-rw-rw-  1 root   6,  20 Apr 10 14:44 dz24
crw-rw-rw-  1 root   6,  21 Apr 10 14:44 dz25
crw-rw-rw-  1 root   6,  22 Apr 10 14:45 dz26
crw-rw-rw-  1 root   6,  23 Apr 10 14:45 dz27
crw-r-----  1 root   8,   1 Jan 10 1979  kmem
crw-r-----  1 root   8,   0 Jan 10 1979  mem
crw-rw-rw-  1 root   8,   2 May  2 10:00 null
crwxrwxrwx  1 root  17,   0 May  1 13:37 tty
brw-r-----  2 root   9,   0 Oct  2 1983  rm00
brw-r-----  3 root   9,   1 Oct  4 1983  rm01
brw-r-----  2 root   9,   2 Oct  2 1983  rm02
brw-r-----  2 root   9,   3 Oct  2 1983  rm03
brw-r-----  2 root   9,   4 Oct  2 1983  rm04
brw-r-----  2 root   9,   5 Apr 11 22:08 rm05
crw-r-----  2 root  19,   0 Oct  2 1983  rrm00
crw-r-----  3 root  19,   1 Apr 27 12:13 rrm01
crw-r-----  2 root  19,   2 Apr 26 15:06 rrm02
crw-r-----  2 root  19,   3 Oct  2 1983  rrm03
crw-r-----  2 root  19,   4 Apr 26 15:07 rrm04
crw-r-----  2 root  19,   5 Apr 13 11:33 rrm05
brw-r-----  2 root   9,   3 Oct  2 1983  swap
brw-r-----  2 root  10,   2 Oct  2 1983  usr
```

Fig. 8.1 Typical list of **/dev/**

In this way a regular arrangement for dumping information, in which the name of the device to be dumped must be given, can be performed using the functional name; any reconfigurations can keep the same names for each physical device, but move the functional names round as convenient.

8.2 Block structured (file-system) devices

In this section we look at ideas of making a Unix block-structured device, making a file-system on it, and mounting it in the system. It must be emphasised that the actual code to drive the device must already be in the kernel before any of the following actions will be effective. The device must first be created using

```
/etc/mknod /dev/name b maj min
```

in the way described above. A typical new disc may then well need formatting, using a special program provided by the suppliers, which will also enter
any bad block information in the appropriate place. It must then be initialised with certain information before it can become part of a Unix file-system;
this is performed using the *mkfs* command as in

    /etc/mkfs /dev/name 4871

(*mkfs* stands for 'make file-system'). This simple version of the command
initialises the disc to contain the basic initial information, such as a super
block and a head directory, and to reserve space for the inodes, and so on
(see chapter 9 on file-systems). The amount of space reserved for inodes is
set to a default proportion of the total space available, assuming 'average-
sized' files.

A more complex use of the command allows various extra features to be
defined. It may be necessary to allow the number of inodes to be controlled
(if the disc is to hold a file-system of very many small files, for example, as
happens with a disc dedicated to a mail system). The command also allows
a known pattern of files and directories to be established on the initialised
disc; the default version of the command leaves the disc with only the head
directory. Other parameters to the command allow the manager to specify
the 'skew' of the device, i.e. the rotational distance which the system will
then attempt to keep between consecutive blocks of a file. This affects the
efficiency of access to files on the device, and for optimal performance may
be best set to different values for different file-systems; experimental benchmarks on an otherwise quiet machine will show the changes in performance.

Each file-system should have on it a directory named **lost + found**, which
is used by the *fsck* command for checking the consistency of a file-system,
and for removing corruption. The command is described more fully in
chapter 4 on booting-up a machine.

The device is then ready to be mounted as part of the file-system using
the command

    /etc/mount /dev/name /directory

8.3 Raw and block-structured devices

For all file-system devices, it is normal to have a character serial device
(known as a 'raw' device) corresponding to each block-structured one. This
device represents the same disc, but when it is read serially through the raw
device, the read starts at the first sector of the first track, and works through
the whole disc serially. This facility is provided so that certain operations
which involve reading serially can be performed more efficiently. Typically
such operations include device-to-device copying (see the command *dd*) in
which one disc may be copied identically to another pack or to a magnetic
tape. A number of commands start by reading in the inode area of the disc;

dump does this, to check the modification date of the files, *ncheck* does it to determine the ownership and sizes of files. Reading through the inode area is always fastest when done serially, using a straight *read* instruction on the raw device, and using the structure which represents the format of an inode, contained in the file **/usr/include/inode.h**. Thus disc devices usually occur in pairs, one block-structured, and the other character serial. The latter by convention has the same name as the former, preceded by the letter 'r', as in **/dev/disc** for the block device and **/dev/rdisc** for the character serial one. The 'r' stands for 'raw'. Examples of such pairs can be seen in the 'ls −l' output shown above. If a *read* is performed from a raw device, the user must be careful to read whole blocks at a time, and to allocate the correct number of bytes for first the super-block, then the inodes, and then the data blocks. A serial read on the corresponding block-structured disc device is buffered by the kernel, and so runs slower, but allows any number of characters to be read.

8.4 Character serial devices

The character serial devices on a typical Unix system include terminals, the main console, printers and magnetic tape devices. Such devices are created by a command such as

```
/etc/mknod /dev/name c maj min
```

The major device number for a terminal will usually correspond to a multiplexer or block of multiplexers, and the minor device to the number (starting at zero) within that block of lines. Typically a number of multiplexers with consecutive memory-mapped addresses will all be treated as one major device. The names traditionally used for terminal lines always begin with the letters 'tty', followed by two digits; in Version 6 Unix this form of nomenclature was compulsory. The only exception usually is the console, which on some machines is a special line, but on small machines is more usually the first line of the first multiplexer. This must be named **/dev/console**. It is suggested that names other than the traditional **tty01** can often bring more clarity to a system. For example, the first letters could be used to represent the room number or building in which that particular terminal is located, with names such as **c30a**, **c30b** and **c30c** for terminals in room C30, and so on. The part of the output from the *who* command which gives the line on which the user is logged-in can then be used to find the location of a given logged-in user, and commands such as the *mail* command will be able to indicate the location from which the mail was sent. However, those using Berkeley systems should bear in mind that they run more efficiently if the last two characters of the terminal line names are distinct.

To rename a terminal line, just use the *mv* command. Devices do not need to be removed and re-created.

8.4.1 Some special devices

There are a number of special files/devices on Unix which live in /**dev** and look like devices, but which do not represent an actual physical device. The more common ones are listed below.

/dev/tty

This device always refers to the currently connected terminal. It can be used, for example, in the shell in conjunction with the *tee* command to bring one copy of output to the screen, while sending another copy down a pipe, as in

```
... | tee /dev/tty | ...
```

The information from the first part of the command will appear at the terminal, and will also be sent on down the later pipe.

/dev/null

When this device is written to, it acts as a 'sink' for arbitrary amounts of output, and can be used to, for example, absorb output if the output is not required, as in

```
... > /dev/null
```

In this case, only error messages (on stream 2) will appear at the screen. When the device is read from, it delivers end-of-file, and can therefore be used to create empty files, as in

```
cp /dev/null newfile
```

or

```
cat /dev/null > newfile
```

/dev/mem

This device refers to the current program's memory, and is a character serial device. If the run-time layout of the program is known, information can be read from it, and interpreted using *adb* techniques.

/dev/kmem

This device refers to the kernel memory, and is again a character serial device. It is opened and read by programs such as *ps*, which look up the relocation tables for the kernel (attached to the file /**unix**) to find the position of the information such as the process tables, and read them to obtain information on the state of currently active processes.

8.5 Terminal lines

The properties of serial lines are set using the *stty* command from the shell, or the *ioctl* call from a program. These offer facilities for setting baud rate, parity, the number of start and stop bits, and other features related to the user, such as the end-of-file character. They also allow setting features such as screen height and width for video terminals, and tab settings; these latter features can be very system dependent, and may cause problems with portability. See your own documentation for details.

8.6 The Makefile in /dev

Just as with all other system directories, it is useful to keep a **Makefile** in the directory /**dev** so that all devices can be easily reconstructed. Separate sections of the file should make terminal lines, file-system devices, and so on. The *mkfs* parameters can also be indicated, so that file-system devices requiring non-standard parameters can be easily regenerated when required.

Chapter 9   **File-systems and their maintenance**

We discuss here various aspects of Unix file-systems as a whole. Some of the discussion is of routine system manager tasks such as maintaining backup copies of the filestore for security purposes, other parts are explanations of the way in which the file-system operates. A thorough understanding of how file-systems are laid out is of great help in appreciating many of the characteristics of the Unix system.

9.1 Dumping and restoring discs

On any disc-based system, care should be taken to keep backup copies of the disc-based filestore on another medium, the generic term for this activity being 'dumping'. This form of security is necessary as a precaution against two distinct occurrences. The first reason for dumping is in case a disc crash occurs (an event still possible even in these days of Winchesters) when the complete file-system must be restored. Even if only part of the disc surface is destroyed, it is very unlikely that the other information can be retrieved, since pointers to file information are also stored on the disc itself. Users of disc systems expect all their files to be retained carefully by the system, and would not tolerate even a politely worded message telling them that a file had been lost. The second (and much more likely) reason for dumping is to cope with the user who accidentally erases a file, and comes to the system manager hopeful of being able to retrieve a not-too-out-of-date version.

There are several distinct ways of dumping and restoring discs in Unix. Each has different benefits and drawbacks, and a wise decision may be to use different methods at different times and for different discs. In addition to the different ways of dumping under Unix, the frequency with which the dumping is performed must be carefully chosen between the extremes of infrequency (most of the files have been changed since the last dump, so that the dump is not very helpful), and incessant dumping (most of the machine time goes into dumping activities). Users of typical small modern Winchester-and-floppy systems should be aware also that the Winchester disc will be many times larger than the floppy disc. Dumping can then be a significant headache for the system manager. Systems with cartridge or streamer tape backup, or with good network connections, are much more convenient in this respect.

Programs for dumping file-systems to exchangeable media can, of course, be used also for the transfer of information between machines, by dumping the required files to any exchangeable medium, and restoring them on a different machine. Problems may then arise due not only to the obvious features such as the physical differences between media, and the non-compatibility of binary programs between different processors, but also due to processor differences such as the sequence in which the low and high order bytes are stored within a word, which is different on different machines; such problems should be borne in mind whenever transfer of information between non-identical machines is considered. Formats in which all information is stored in ASCII characters (all-ASCII archive formats) such as one developed at Berkeley, overcome this problem, but are not generally distributed.

9.1.1 The *dump* and *restor* commands

The standard Unix utility *dump* is intended for dumping complete block-structured file-system disc devices to a serial device such as magnetic tape, or to dump just those files on a given disc which have changed since a certain date. The command *restor* can then be used to restore from the dumped information. The serial device will usually be an (exchangeable) magnetic tape or cartridge, but can equally well be a raw disc device such as a floppy disc.

Dumping

The *dump* command does not dump from a given directory, but from a given device. It obtains its basic information by reading the inodes on that device (using the 'raw' device). From these it can find the names and positions of the files, which of the files are directories, and when they were last modified; all this information is stored in the inodes. The program can then dump the complete file-system on that device, or, from the modification dates and a record of when the last dump was performed, can find which files have changed since the last dump, and therefore require dumping selectively. By inspecting the data areas for the directory files (the directories themselves) the file hierarchy and the files themselves can be reconstructed.

Dump privileges

Because it reads from the raw device, the *dump* command can be run only by a privileged user (see chapter 11 on security for details of why the public cannot be allowed access to the raw disc devices). Because the *dump* program is reading the inodes directly, it can then over-ride user access permissions on files, reading all data directly from the raw device. The dump program, using the information it reads from the inodes, can determine the last modification date of each file, and can then easily choose to dump certain files dependent on the modification date; a typical requirement is to dump any file modified since the last dump. However, from the inode information directly it cannot determine the hierarchic relationship of files (i.e. which files are in a given directory), so cannot conveniently dump files defined by their position in the filestore hierarchy.

In the author's installation, the raw disc devices are owned by group 'bin', and have read access to that group. All users who share the dumping chores are permitted to change to group 'bin' through entries in the file **/etc/group** and the *newgrp* command, and can perform the dump within that group.

Dumping levels

Most mainframe computer systems (it was on mainframe computers that large filestores first developed) have arrangements for dumping to magnetic tape which allow the whole filestore to be dumped (a 'total dump'), or only those parts which have changed since the previous dump to be dumped (a 'partial dump'). On a large machine, the time taken to perform a total dump is considerable, so combinations of total and partial dumps are used in sequence. A typical possible sequence would be to dump the complete filestore once per week, and on each other day, dump what has changed since the previous day. To restore a complete filestore, it is necessary to restore firstly the most recent 'total' dump, and then all of the following 'partial' dumps. In addition, if a user wishes to recover the most recently dumped version of a given file, it is not obvious from which tape it must be restored; it must be searched for on each of the partial dumps, starting with the most recent, searching back eventually to the total dump.

The partial dumps contain information other than just the changed files. They will obviously contain some completely new files, created since the total dump. In addition, they will for example contain information about files deleted between the time of the total dump and that of the partial dump, since the deletion of a file will alter the directory which contains that entry. The dumped information enables the file-system to be reconstructed from the dumps exactly to its state at the time of the partial dump.

In Unix, the concept of 'dump-levels' was introduced. Instead of having only the two types of dump, 'total' and 'partial', dumping at different 'levels' can be performed. At a given level (levels run from 0 to 9) all files which have changed since the most recent dump at that level or a higher numeric level are dumped. The level 0 (zero) is a total dump; every file is copied, and is available for restoration from the single† dump output. If a dump at level 4 is performed at a later time, all files changed since the level 0 dump will be dumped. A complete restoration of the file-system would now require first the level 0 dump to be restored, and then the level 4 dump to be restored; the latter would overwrite some of the files with new versions, and restore some completely new files. Files for restoration would be found on the level 4 tape in their most recent form if they had been modified, but on the level 0 tape otherwise. The next dump can be done in three distinct ways.

† Although referred to as a 'single' dump output, the information may spread across several magnetic tapes or cartridges; as one is filled, the system will request another.

(a) If it is done at level 4 or higher, only files changed since the level 4 dump will be dumped. Files for restoration could now be on any of the three dump tapes, depending upon when they were last modified.

(b) If the dump is done at level 3 or 2 or 1, all files changed since the level 0 dump will be dumped. The level 0 dump and this one now form a complete set for restoration, since all files on the previous level 4 tape will have been dumped again. The level 4 tape is now redundant, except as a back-up facility.

(c) If the new dump is done at level 0, all files will again be dumped. A complete restoration can be done from only one tape. The previous level 0 dump tape is redundant, except as a back-up. This option will generally take much longer than the previous ones.

On a typical system, the complete disc will not be dumped very often, since it involves a large amount of information, only a small percentage of which will be changed on a daily basis. The 'total' dump will perhaps be performed once per week. Typical dumping sequences for the rest of the week could follow any of the three patterns outlined here.

(a) All dumps at the same level; each day, only the one day's changed files will be dumped. Each dump will be small, so that dumping time is small, but if an individual file has to be restored, finding the most recent version may be a problem by the end of the week, when there may be six possible tapes on which it could exist. Restoring the whole file-system late in the week would again involve a large number of tapes being loaded.

(b) Dump on successive days at levels 5, 4, 3, 2 and 1, for example. Each day, the complete set of files changed since the total dump will be dumped; at any time, only the total dump and the most recent partial dump are current; earlier partial dump tapes become redundant except as back-up. The dumps will get steadily bigger each day, the last one containing a complete week's changes. After the first day, dumps will be slower than with the above method. However, to restore an individual file, or a complete file-system, only two tapes would need to be involved, which is much more convenient.

(c) Dump on successive days at levels such as 3, 2, 3, 1, 3, 2, 3. This is known as the 'ruler sequence', and forms a compromise between the two extremes mentioned above.

The choice between these (and other) dump sequences must depend very much on experience; if the time taken dumping turns out to be a major problem, the first method should be used. If there are found to be frequent requirements to restore files, the second method is best. It may well be appropriate to use different tactics when dumping different file-systems; a file-system consisting mainly of the files of users involved in developing programs may change very rapidly, and need frequent dumping, while a file-system consisting mainly of, say, system documentation may well not be subject to such rapid change, and weekly dumping may be adequate.

Another management decision relates to the length of time for which dump tapes (or other dumping medium) are kept before being re-used. The more valuable the information is, the more security is required, and the more backup tapes should be kept; typically a cycle of about four tapes (or sets of tapes) might be kept for each file-system. Some installations perform a master total dump once a year, and keep the resulting tapes 'for ever'; this practice is becoming less feasible as larger and larger filestores become used. Another aspect to be considered is whether a set of dump tapes should be kept in a different building, in case of total destruction by fire. Such a system is easy to manage, and could reduce the significance of a catastrophe considerably.

The file /etc/ddate is maintained by the *dump* program, and is used to keep the date of the most recent dump at each level; this is the file used by the *dump* command itself to determine which modification date to base any partial dump on. A flag 'u' to the *dump* command causes the file /etc/ddate to be updated; if the flag is absent, the file is not updated, so that future dumps will not be aware of that particular dump.

Typical dumping commands
Typical commands to dump a file-system are as follows.

        dump 4u /dev/rdisc3

where the '4' is the level, the 'u' requests that the level and date be recorded in /etc/ddate, and the last parameter gives the name of the raw device containing the file-system which is to be dumped. The device onto which the dumped information is copied is built into the dump program; an additional key 'f' and parameter is necessary if the device being dumped to is not the default built into the *dump* command. The command is then typically

        dump 4uf /dev/cartridge /dev/rdisc3

A competent supplier will ensure that the default is the sensible one for your machine. If the default device built into the command is a magnetic tape name such as /dev/mt0, which does not exist on your machine, you can easily execute the command

        ln /dev/cartridge /dev/mt0

to make your cartridge the dumping device.

However automated the dumping process becomes, it is still wise to keep a handwritten log of all important system activities such as dumping and error reporting in a notebook next to the console; a notebook is always readable even when the machine is down! The book also serves as a record for shutdowns and reboots.

Checking the names of the dumped files
The command *dumpdir* lists the names of the files actually dumped on a particular dump tape; again, a default device is built into the program, and

can be over-ridden if necessary. A shell script could obviously be written to perform a *dumpdir* on each tape after it has been dumped, and to store the results. These results could then be used with another script to find automatically the most recent version of any file among a number of dump tapes.

A drawback of the Unix dumping system is that no record exists on the tape of the date, time, level and filestore device of the file-system being dumped. This is a general criticism of the lack of tape labelling in Unix handling of magnetic tapes generally. At one stage, the author's system was modified so that the shell script for dumping, before calling the *dump* command, created a file at the head of the disc, to which was written the current time, the dump level, and the name of the disc being dumped. This file was always included on the dump tape, and could be listed directly from the tape to check on the origin of the tape.

The way in which a large disc is partitioned into a number of file-systems may be significantly affected by dumping considerations. There may be cases when it is wise to choose an upper limit to the size of file-systems in order to ensure that a completely full file-system can be dumped onto a single tape or cartridge, if this does not affect other considerations too severely. It may similarly be wise not to break the disc into too many small file-systems, since these would all have to be dumped separately.

Restoring

To restore a complete file-system (perhaps after corruption has occurred, or after the disc has been reformatted in some way) requires the most recent complete dump to be restored, followed by any relevant partial dumps. A typical command to restore a whole device is

    restor r /dev/rdisc3

Again, the device from which the dumped information is to be read should be set to an appropriate default in the program, but can be specified in combination with an 'f' flag. To restore from partial dumps, use the command

    restor r /dev/rdisc3

first with the full dump tape, and then with each of the partial dumps in the order in which they were created. Each tape restored will overwrite earlier versions of amended files.

A complete dump can be used to move a file-system from one disc device to another, or to replace a file-system after reformatting its own device in some way. Such an activity might be necessary to balance the requirements of groups of users between the available file-system space from time to time, or to move selected groups of users to a new disc when it is installed. The sequence for a reconfiguration might be

```
dump 0 .... { a total dump of the system }
/etc/mkfs .... { reconfigure the disc }
restor r .... { restore the information }
```

This allows a file-system to be moved to a disc of different size from its earlier base; it cannot, of course, be restored to a disc which is too small for the amount of information in the file-system, since the *restor* will fail before the complete system has been restored.

The above operations involved restoring a complete file-system from dumped information. One of the other uses of dumping is to recover individual files for users who have accidentally erased or corrupted a file. To restore a single file, the command is

```
restor x filename
```

('x' for extract) which will look for the file of the given name on the tape. The name must agree exactly with the name on the tape (this can be checked using the **dumpdir** command, see above), and will be the name relative to the directory at the 'head' of the device which was dumped (the directory under which it was mounted). Thus if one disc is mounted under /**usr** (very common practice), say on device /**dev/rdisc3**, it will be dumped by a command such as

```
dump 4u /dev/rdisc3
```

The file /**usr/bin/xxxx** will now be referred to on the dump tape as /**bin/xxxx**, and must be restored using that name. The names on the tape reflect the system's view of that tape as representing a complete file-system, starting with / at its head.

The *restor* command will restore the named file from the dump tape to a file in the current directory of the restoring program; the restored file will be owned by the user who has done the restore, and will appear with a name which is a simple number (actually the inode number of the file). After restoring, this file must then be located, moved to its correct position, and its name, owner, group and permissions set as required. Restoring complete sub-trees correctly is an obvious candidate for an *awk* script. The *restor* command has been replaced on later Berkeley systems by a *restore* command (with a terminating letter 'e' in its name) which overcomes the above problems; this command will probably be adopted more widely as time goes on.

Beware of using a dump tape from one machine to restore files to another. Any command which retrieves files from an external medium which may have come from another machine will have the problem that file ownership is specified by numeric UIDs, and the imported files may be owned by a user or group which does not exist on this machine, or by one who exists, but is irrelevant to the new files.

9.1.2 The *tar* command

The *tar* command in Unix is intended mainly for copying a sub-tree of a file-system (that area below a given directory) to a serial device (normally a magnetic tape of sorts). Its name is an abbreviation for *t*ape *ar*chive, and its function bears some similarities to that of the *ar* (archive) command. Because this command dumps by directory, reading the filestore as an ordinary user, it requires user permissions to access the files, and will be unable to read those files for which read permission (to a file) or execute permission (to a directory) is not available. Thus files to which the user performing the operation does not have read permission will not get copied. The *tar* command can also optionally append to the end of a tar tape only those files which have changed since the original files were written to the tape. Since *tar* reads its information through the normal filestore mechanisms, files which have been dumped will be marked in the file-system as having been read (in information from the *stat* system call, or the *find* command, for example), whereas the *dump* command (reading information through the raw disc device) leaves them unmarked.

The *tar* command is frequently used for the transfer of applications software between installations. This is because all control information is in ASCII characters, and not in any direct dump of binary information such as that contained in directories, which may be machine dependent. Even machines with a floppy disc as their exchangeable medium normally use the floppy disc in serial mode as the output device for *tar* to perform program transfer between machines. In serial mode, the floppy disc runs fast, since it is transferring with a minimum of head movement.

Typical *tar* commands for functions comparable with some of those described for *dump* and *restor* above are as follows:

(a) To copy a sub-tree of the file-system to a tar tape, use

```
cd /usr/dir; tar c .
```

where the flag to the *tar* command is simply a 'c' to indicate the creation of a new *tar* tape. A further flag parameter 'f' is available in a similar way to that for the *dump* command to indicate that the next parameter represents the device to which the output is to be sent (there will normally be a default, which your supplier should arrange to compile into your version of the command). The final parameter is the name of the directory whose sub-tree is to be dumped, or the name of a single file to be dumped. The simplest approach generally is to change to the directory which is to be copied, and to specify '.' as the directory to be *tar*red.

(b) To check the names of the files on a *tar* tape, use the command

```
tar t
```

This compares with the command *dumpdir* above; note that all aspects of *tar* are covered by the same command, but with different flags.

(c) To restore a directory and its sub-tree complete, use the command

```
cd /usr/dir; tar x .
```

where the 'x' stands for 'extract', and the second argument to *tar* is the name of the directory to be restored, given just as it occurs on the *tar* tape (which can be checked with the command 'tar t'). The directory and sub-tree to be restored need not be the whole directory dumped by the *tar* command. The files will be placed as named, relative to the current directory when restoring, and will be owned by the current user. It is generally dangerous to use absolute pathnames when dumping with *tar*, since this leaves no flexibility for positioning the data when it is being restored.

There is an optional flag to prevent the overwriting of existing files, if required.

To restore a single file, use

```
tar x filename
```

where again the filename must be exactly as on the tape. All file names when the *tar* tape is produced or restored are relative to the named directory. When restoring, the exact name as on the tape must be given, and files will be restored to the same position relative to the current directory at the time of restoring.

9.1.3 The *dd* command

The *dd* command does a direct device-to-device copy between named character serial devices, or files, with specified block size for the transfer. An example was given earlier when discussing the booting process. A typical command for dumping using the *dd* command could be

```
dd if=/dev/rdisc3 of=/dev/cartridge
```

where **/dev/rdisc3** is, for example, a Winchester disc on which a file-system exists, and **/dev/cartridge** is assumed to be a cartridge tape of capacity greater than the disc; the letters 'if' stand for 'input file', and 'of' for 'output file'. The transfer will run faster if done in larger blocks, as in

```
dd if=/dev/rdisc3 of=/dev/cartridge bs=16k
```

to transfer with a blocksize of 16 kbytes. On magnetic tape devices (such as cassettes and cartridges) the use of a larger block size also increases the amount of information which can be dumped, since the 'inter-block-gaps' on the tape occur less often. However, for rough-environment or long-term storage, a smaller block size is recommended.

When using *dd*, we generally wish to copy the disc identically, track-by-track, to the magnetic tape. The disc will therefore be specified as a raw device. These commands can be executed only by a user who has the privilege required to access the raw devices.

The machine must be quiescent during the *dd* process, since otherwise the disc produced may not be consistent; the safest way is to unmount the file-system during the dump.

There are further problems (very system dependent) concerned with bad blocks on the disc supporting the file-system. All systems can handle bad blocks on file-structured devices. However, when using the raw serial disc device with the *dd* command the presence of bad blocks may cause some systems to fail in the *dd*; other systems may skip over them, but if the information is restored to another disc with different bad block positions, the file pointers may now refer to the wrong blocks. For these reasons, *dd* should only be used as a last resort, for perhaps dumping and restoring the root disc before and after maintenance.

To restore a cartridge created using a *dd* command, the input and output parameters are reversed, as in

    dd if=/dev/cartridge of=/dev/rdisc3 bs=16k

where the cartridge is now the input device. There are further parameters to the *dd* command which are irrelevant here, but offer facilities for, for example, ASCII to/from EBCDIC conversion. This is particularly useful in exchanging tapes with mainframes.

9.1.4 Transfer of files to other systems

If information is to be transferred from one system to another, such as an update or new package being distributed by a supplier, or local data files being exchanged between machines, there are a number of possible solutions. For transfer using an exchangeable medium, it is normal to use the *tar* command. This is simple to use, and runs fast even from floppy discs, since they are used serially.

If there is any form of direct connection between the systems, then direct transfer is usually preferable, the only exceptions being for security reasons, or because there is an excessive amount of data to move. Since there are many proprietary communications systems available, all working to different user interfaces, we will mention only the two simplest here. These both relate to systems connected by a simple serial line.

cu

The command *cu* allows a user on one machine to login through that machine onto another connected by serial line to the first. The user's local machine must not have an active *login* process on the port connected to the remote machine, since it would interfere with the data traffic. The remote machine on which the user is logging in must, of course, have a *login* on the connecting line to allow the login. Files can then be transferred between the machines, but there is little error checking, and this is usually only a very temporary method, perhaps used to bootstrap communication software to the remote machine.

uucp and uux

The *uucp* command allows a serial connection to be used for the spooling of files and mail automatically between linked systems. There are unfortunately many variants of *uucp*. The more recent ones are very comprehensive, and form the basis of a number of major networks. The *uucp* command saves a copy of the file to be transferred, and its spooler logs in to the remote machine under the login name 'uucp'. Permission names for any file accesses on the remote machine must therefore be permitted relative to the 'uucp' login name.

The related command *uux* provides for the execution of commands on a remote machine, again spooled, and logged in as 'uucp' rather than as the original user issuing the command.

9.1.5 Quiescent systems

Whenever a file-system is being dumped by any of the above methods, it is important that it should be quiescent, since Unix does not lock the information in any way, and the information in a file can change while it is being dumped. As far as possible therefore, file-systems should be quiescent while they are being dumped. Ideally this would mean unmounting them, making them unusable for the period of the dumping activity, but in practice, it is usually good enough to dump them during a slack period. Systems with sufficient disc capacity may find it useful to dump to a disc overnight, and to transfer the disc to tape during the day. This practice also overcomes the serious degradation on performance which dumping can cause.

9.1.6 Other devices for dumping

The serial device assumed above has been, as is most usual, a magnetic tape type of device, such as a full magnetic tape, streamer tape, or cartridge. It can, of course, equally well be any serial device, such as the raw device corresponding to a floppy disc, which can to dumped to and read from just like a magnetic tape. However, if the machine has no tape device, but has a floppy disc, it may sometimes be more convenient to use the floppy disc as a block-structured copying device, not a serial device; see below for details.

9.1.7 Dumping and restoring the root file-system

There will, of course, always be problems in restoring the root file-system, since it cannot be unmounted, and will have some activity going on such as the access to the dump program's inode. Further if it is restored, the information in main memory may be out-of-line with that on the disc. In general if any significant activity has to take place with a given root file-system (such as reformatting or restoring the disc), the best solution is to run the machine temporarily from another disc. Typically a small machine would have a floppy disc for various purposes, and the suppliers would offer a small maintenance system which runs on the floppy disc; on a larger machine, there would be multiple hard discs, and multiple boots and kernels so that alternative discs could be run as root at different times. The boot programs and Unix kernel on the backup system would be different from the standard one, but would have to be compatible in their interpretation of all the file-system devices. The need for this type of emergency activity should be borne in mind when the filestore layout is being decided, perhaps leaving space on a second disc for a duplicate root system with the necessary different kernel.

9.2 Copying to block-structured exchangeable devices

If the main exchangeable medium is a block-structured device such as a floppy disc, it may be easier to exchange information between machines using a proper file-system on the disc rather than by using it as a serial *tar* or *dump* device. To do this, it must be *mount*ed (usually under the directory /**mnt**), and the required directory and sub-tree copied to it. It may be necessary before mounting the device to reformat it and use the *mkfs* command to set up a Unix file-system on it. To restore the information which has been copied out, the process can be reversed.

To copy complete sub-trees of the file-system, the *tar* command can be made to act completely internally. To copy the tree below the directory **fromdir** to the directory **todir**, use a command such as

```
( cd fromdir; tar cf − . ) | ( cd todir; tar xf − . )
```

The 'c' parameter to the first *tar* command specifies that a complete new *tar* output is to be generated. The 'f' flag states that the output/input file will be as specified by the next parameter, and with the next parameter given as '−', this indicates that the standard output is to be the device for dumping. For the second *tar* command, the '−' parameter indicates on this occasion that the data (this time the input to the *tar*) comes from the standard input.

The verbose version of *tar* can be used to give a commentary on the files being copied; to do this, replace the 'xf' flag in the second command by 'xfv'.

This technique of dumping and restoring information is obviously sub-ject to problems when transferring between different types of processor. The problems of, for example, bytes being ordered differently within a word has already been mentioned, and files such as directories may well contain integer values for inode numbers, stored in two bytes.

9.3 Filestore usage/occupancy

There are several commands for checking on filestore usage, some of which work at the directory/sub-tree level, and the others at a user level. All give their output as a number of blocks rather than bytes, since filestore is claimed a block at a time, even if that block is only partially filled.

9.3.1 The *du* command

This command summarises the *d*isc *u*sage in blocks below the current direc-tory if no parameter is given, or below the named directory if one is given as parameter, irrespective of the ownership of the files. Totals are normally given for sub-directories, unless a '−s' flag is present, in which case only the total is given. Files linked within the sub-tree are counted only once in the total, but files with links from outside the sub-tree are counted as if they were full size. Thus if files totalling 100 blocks in one sub-directory are linked to another sub-directory, then they will be counted as 100 blocks in each sub-directory calculation, but only as 100 blocks in the total calculation. Thus totals may not appear to add up! Typical output from a command such as

    du /staff/ef/notes

might be as shown in figure 9.1.

24	/staff/ef/notes/arts
57	/staff/ef/notes/papers
34	/staff/ef/notes/pascal/intro
80	/staff/ef/notes/pascal/if.case
157	/staff/ef/notes/pascal/loops
122	/staff/ef/notes/pascal/functions
75	/staff/ef/notes/pascal/procs
1471	/staff/ef/notes/pascal/arrays
236	/staff/ef/notes/pascal/recursion
11	/staff/ef/notes/pascal/ex6
2339	/staff/ef/notes/pascal
38	/staff/ef/notes/informatics
1116	/staff/ef/notes/unix/book
1183	/staff/ef/notes/unix
68	/staff/ef/notes/languages
3713	/staff/ef/notes

Fig. 9.1 Typical *du* output

9.3.2 The *quot* command

The *quot* command in the form

    quot ef

scans the complete set of file-systems (or a specified subset of the file devices) looking at the ownership of each file, and adding together the sizes of the files belonging to the named user. It is thus inevitably slow on a large system, but includes all files owned by that user wherever they are, including spooling and mail files, as well as owned temporary files under **/tmp**. The output in this case from a command such as

    quot ef

is a single number such as

    6169

indicating that there is a total of 6169 blocks somewhere in the system owned by the user 'ef'. The use of *quot* with no parameters gives totals for all users in the system.

If the result for a particular user is larger than expected, you may want to find out why by searching the complete filestore for files owned by a named user. This may be done by the *find* command as in, for example

    find / −user ef −print

or

    find / −user ef −exec ls −l {} ";"

to show more details of that user's files. This is again a command which will execute very slowly, since it searches the complete filestore.

An alternative is to use a combination of the *ncheck* command (to give the name, owner and size of each file) and the *awk* command (to add up the totals for each login name), a method which was used before the *quot* command was available, and is still convenient if only one file-system is being checked.

Because the execution of *quot* is inevitably slow, it is often run overnight, and its output used to inform the manager of exceptionally high usage by any user, and perhaps used also to control the logging-in process.

9.3.3 The *df* command

The *df* command (*disc freespace*) gives the amount of disc space free on that device (if a device-name is given), or by default, all devices involved in the file-systems. Some versions also give the amount of disc space used on each device. The default file-system list may be in a special file (see your documentation for the name, it varies between systems), so that it can be accessed automatically by commands such as *quot* and *df*. Alternatively, it may be obtained from the output of the /etc/mount command on a running system (which will indicate the names of all mounted devices, but will not indicate the name of the root device on normal systems). Typical output of the *df* command is shown in figure 9.2.

```
/dev/rrk6 1522
/dev/rrm02 3709
/dev/rrm04 1364
/dev/rrm11 17005
/dev/rrm12 10046
/dev/rrm13 15751
/dev/rrm14 4089
```

Fig. 9.2 Typical *df* output

Some more modern variants of *df* give the size of the device, the blocks used, and the blocks free; and even the name of the directory under which it is mounted.

The system manager should obviously keep a regular watch on the amount of free space on the discs; areas directly under the manager's control (such as the documentation for the manual, under **/usr/man**) may not change much, so may not need much free space, but user areas generally need quite a large free space to allow for temporary extra use. Some managers recommend that 25% of the disc should be kept free on average, but this is obviously a very subjective figure. A warning should certainly be sent to users on a particular file-system if the free space falls below some agreed figure, the critical figure being when the first 'disc overflow' messages begin to appear on the console. Whether the manager should run an overnight shell script to remove files which may be assumed to be of a temporary nature (files with names such as **core**, **a.out**, ***junk*** for example) is again open to debate, and depends on the institution.

9.4 Special access bits to files

In addition to the nine commonly used access bits for a file (read, write and execute permission for each of owner, group and public) there are three other bits with special significance.

9.4.1 The SUID bit

Commands such as *passwd* (change a user's password) can only do that by altering the file **/etc/passwd**. This file cannot, of course, have public write permission, for obvious reasons of security. To enable the *passwd* command to amend it, it must run with some sort of privilege. In most computer operating systems, such commands are part of the 'system' itself, and so can obtain their privilege that way. In Unix, commands are nearly all ordinary programs or shell scripts, or are special functions executed by the shell (such as the command *cd*), and therefore normally have only the same privilege as that of the shell, i.e. that of the user running the shell. To overcome this, Unix has a way in which executed commands are able to change their 'effective user identifier', and become privileged in some way.

This is done by having one extra bit associated with each file, the SUID or 'set-*user*-*id*' bit. This is stored with the access permission bits in the inode area. If this bit is set in the inode of a file containing an executable program, then when that program executes, its process temporarily (for the duration of that process only) takes on the user identity of the owner of the file. Thus if the file is owned by 'root', the program will have 'super-user' facilities as it executes. This is the means by which the *passwd* command can be made so that, when it is executing, it can, in fact, write to files such as **/etc/passwd**, even though the user who called the command does not have that permission.

The SUID bit is set by the command

```
chmod u+s files
```

using mnemonic modes, or

```
chmod 4??? files
```

for modes specified numerically.

The most well known examples of SUID files are concerned with root-owned files, since there are a number of situations where special privileges are required in commands executed by an ordinary user. There are, however, great dangers associated with root-owned SUID files. Firstly, if public write permission is accidentally left on, any user can write any program to that file, and execute it with 'super-user' privilege; the user could, for example, easily create root-owned SUID files in their own directory. Secondly, if the program has an escape to the shell (as with the '!' facility in *ed* or *write*), the shell generated will be a 'super-user' shell unless special precautions have been taken.

On Version 7 Unix systems the use of SUID bits applies only to programs, not to shell scripts, so that a minimal program of the form

```
main()
{
    system( "command" );
}
```

needs to be written to cause the shell script to execute under the effective UID.

It is a common requirement that a process should be able to append information to a file, but should be prohibited from reading that file. A typical example is where different sales staff append information to a common sales file, but must not be permitted to read the file, which would enable them to see the results of other staff. Similar considerations apply where students are appending coursework results to a common file. The program in cases such as these needs SUID facilities to enable it to access a file which the user running the program would not normally have permission to access. The file and the program would be owned by a special user, the program would have SUID facilities, and the file would not have public access. The program can then be run by any user, and can append information to the file (or access it in any other predetermined way), but the user cannot access the file directly. It should be noted that the command cannot however by written in the shell as, for example

```
program >> file
```

since at the stage when the shell is redirecting the output, access to the file is not permitted. The file must be opened from within the program, since by that time, the program has assumed a new effective user-id.

Another use of SUID files, this time for ordinary users, concerns the scheduling program *cron*. This runs in the background, and forks off programs according to a given timetable. The *cron* program itself usually runs under the 'daemon' login name. Thus any children which it forks will also be owned by 'daemon', and may not therefore be able to write to the user's own files. If an ordinary user requires a program to be run regularly, it should be made SUID with the user as owner; it will then be as though the user had started the program.

The use of SUID bits in the *lpr* spooler enables confidentiality of output to be improved. The command *lpr* is called by a user, and stores output in a file under the directory **/usr/spool/lpd**. That directory must therefore have public write permission, for new files to be created. The implication of this is that other users can delete files from the directory, since create and delete permission are effectively just write permission to the parent directory. To overcome this, the following scheme is normally operated.

> The directory **/usr/spool/lpd** is owned by the user 'daemon', and has no public access, but full owner read and write access. The command *lpr* is also owned by 'daemon', and has its SUID bit set. It then has permission to create files in the spooling directory, since when it is executing, its effective user identity is that of 'daemon', not of the user who called it. In addition, the spooler *lpd* must also be owned by 'daemon' and with SUID, and the printer can be owned by 'daemon' with no public access, so that it can be opened only by the *lpd* spooler. The lock-file in the spool directory is then protected from accidental erasure by an ordinary user, and the files can be daemon-owned with no public read access, for confidentiality.

Similar considerations apply to the other spooling activities such as the *mail* and *at* commands, and to *uucp*, all of which are really a form of spooling.

Standard commands which require root ownership and SUID facilities include *ncheck* (to enable it to read the raw disc device), *mkdir, mv, newgrp* (to enable it to set a new group-id it must run as super-user), *passwd* (to enable it to amend the file **/etc/passwd**), *ps* (to enable it to read the process tables in memory; ordinary users must not be allowed access to memory), *quot* (to enable it to read the raw disc devices directly), *rmdir, su* (rather like *login*), *mail* (owned by mail), *uucp* (owned by uucp), *lpr* and *lpd* (both owned by daemon), and perhaps *login* (if you wish to enable the *login* process to be called from an ordinary shell).

9.4.2 The SGID bit

The SGID (*set-group-id*) bit is similar to the SUID bit, but causes the permissions of the program while running to take on the group identity of the group owner of the file. The same considerations apply as to SUID facilities, except that in general, the facility is not so dangerous, since many privileged operations require the super-user identity, irrespective of the current group identity. The SGID bit on a file is set by the command

    chown g+s files

Commands such as *df* which read their information from raw disc devices are usually SGID and owned by group *bin*, with the devices also owned by that group. This allows the command to read the raw discs, and is less dangerous than using root-ownership and SUID facilities.

9.4.3 The 'sticky' bit
This is the last of the twelve access bits of the file, which are stored in the inode area for the file. If this bit is set, the system will try not to lose the core image of the program when it terminates. It is therefore good to set this bit on frequently-used commands, since it reduces swapping activity, and speeds access to the program (when called, it is more likely to be already in memory, instead of having to be called in from disc). Care should be taken not to set this mode on too many programs, since the system will then tend to be too reluctant to swap anything out at all, and any benefits will have been negated. Typical frequently accessed programs for which this facility might be sensible include *ed*, and, in a program development environment, *ld*, *as*, and *cc*. In addition, it may be good policy to make *login* sticky; although it is not often accessed compared with the above commands, users like a quick response to their initial login.

9.5 File-systems
In this section the layout of file-system information is discussed. Some understanding of this helps considerably in the appreciation of a number of Unix features.

9.5.1 Disc layout
Each disc device is divided into blocks, which were uniformly 512 bytes long on Version 7. A size of 1024 is selectable as an option on System V, and later BSD releases allow a wider variation in units of disc allocation, although the block size of the device is still 512. The first block is the boot-block and is followed by one or more file-systems. The layout is thus roughly

    boot-block; file-system; file-system; file-system

The division of the body of the disc between a number of file-systems is determined by the Unix kernel, and can make a single physical disc look like several virtual discs to the user. To alter the way in which the physical disc is subdivided needed a drastic reconfiguring of the kernel in early versions of Unix. The disc driver is a system source file such as **/usr/src/sys/dev/disc.c** for example, and within the source are the details of the number of blocks allocated to each subsystem, and their offsets from the start of the disc. To reconfigure the disc, this source had to be amended, recompiled, relinked with the rest of the kernel, and the new kernel loaded. On more modern versions, the divisions are table driven, with the details of the subdivisions picked up at the boot-up stage from tables in a file.

Each file-system on a disc consists of a super-block (containing details of the file-system's size, the most recent modification date, the maximum number of files, etc), an area for inodes, and an area for data blocks. Thus each file-system consists of three areas

> super-block; inodes; data

These are set up using the *mkfs* command. The inode area contains space for a number of fixed size inodes, each containing the details of one file. The maximum number of files on a file-system is thus fixed by the size of the area allocated for inodes. Each inode contains details of the positions of that file's data blocks (or the address of a block containing further pointers, see below), the times of the most recent accesses for reading and writing, the access permissions on the file, the type of the file, the owner's UID and GID, and various other items, but **not** the file's name. Files are accessed by looking up the name in a directory, which contains entries for each file, with a name and inode number for each file. To access a file, its name is looked up in the directory, and from the corresponding inode number, the inode (and hence all details of the file's ownership and access permissions) can be found by a single further disc access.

9.5.2 Directories

Directories contain a list of file-names and the corresponding inode number (but no device number; the file must therefore be on the same disc as the directory in general, the exception being *mount*ed devices). The exact format of a directory entry can be found by listing the file **/usr/include/sys/dir.h** on your machine. It contains basically a C structure suitable for storing one directory entry, with one field for the inode number (perhaps two bytes long) and one for the file name (perhaps fourteen bytes long; this determines the maximum length of file names). Some newer Berkeley systems have more complex directory structures to allow variable length file names.

It should be remembered that the 'read' permission on a directory allows a user to *read* it (for example, using a *read* in C into a structure of the mode declared in the **dir.h** file) or to perform, for example, an *ls* command on it. Any user with read permission on the directory can then find the names and and inode numbers of the files named there; however, without appropriate privilege the user will be unable to access the inode (since that requires access to the raw disc device).

Furthermore, 'write' permission may be set, but only the system itself is permitted to write to directories. The 'write' permission on a directory allows the system (and hence the user) to create, rename and delete entries. Confusion occasionally arises when the system call *access* is used; it indicates whether the user has permission to access a file in a specified way. If the file is a directory, the user may find that there is write permission, but that writing to the file fails.

The 'execute' bit allows directories to be searched by the system as part of a filename, but not to be read directly by the user. Thus to execute an *ls* command on a directory with read permission but without execute permission would succeed, but a *cd* to it or an access to a file in it would fail.

If a file is removed, its entry is marked as unused in the directory, but still occupies a record; it will be re-used when another filename is created, but the directory will never decrease in size. If it is required to tidy up a directory, the directory mus be renamed, then re-created under its original name, and then the files moved back to it, as in

```
mv directory tempdir
mkdir directory
mv tempdir/* directory
rmdir tempdir
```

Files are sometimes created accidentally whose names contain strange or unprintable characters. It can be difficult to remove such files, since the exact character sequence in the name is not known. If the *od* command (octal debug) is used to search the byte pattern of the directory, the exact characters in the name can be found.

9.5.3 Inodes

The format of an inode can be found by listing the file **/usr/include/sys/inode.h** on your machine. This file contains a C structure declaration which matches an inode on your machine. The fields include areas for

the collection of one-bit flags for features such as access permissions;
the number of links to the file;
the owner's numeric UID and GID;
the size (number of characters) of the file;
thirteen addresses of blocks on disc.

The one-bit flags in the flag field represent information such as

the type of the file (directory, character device, block device, regular);
the SUID, SGID and sticky bits;
the read, write and execute permissions for each of owner, group and public.

It should be noted again that files have an owner, group and size, but no name; the name comes from the directory entry in which an inode number is given for each name. One file can thus be referred to from a number of different directories on the disc, giving the Unix concepts of 'links' to a file. The file to which the links point is a single file, and access permission for the file relate to the inode information (access permissions and owner's UID and GID), not in any way to the directory (or directories) in which the filenames reside.

There is an entry in the inode giving the number of links to the file. Each time a new link is made, this is incremented. When a link is broken (the command *rm* in the shell, the system call *unlink* in C), the number is decremented. When the number decrements to zero, the file is no longer referenced, and its data blocks can be added to the free space list. As long as the number of links is greater than zero, the file will remain (even though the user who originally created it has removed it from the directory, or in an extreme case, may no longer exist on the system).

Note also that there is no 'end-of-file' character stored in the file data area; the inode knows the size of a file, and will know how many characters can be read from it, for example. Having read that number of characters, a *read* will report that no further characters are available. The 'file size' entry in the inode is updated whenever a *write* occurs at the end of the file.

The inode contains pointers to 13 data blocks on disc. The first 10 of these are direct pointers to the first 10 data blocks of the file; any of these can thus be accessed directly once the inode has been fetched, so that file up to 10 blocks in size (or the first 10 blocks of a larger file) can be accessed very quickly. The pointers are set to the null value if the block does not exist.

If the file is larger than 10 blocks, the inode uses the eleventh pointer to contain a pointer to a disc block (stored in the data area of the disc) containing a number of pointers to further data blocks, the exact number being a system parameter. Assuming a value of 128 (the Version 7 value), this block gives the addresses of the next 128 data blocks of the file, enabling the system to address files of up to 138 blocks (69k bytes with blocks of 512 bytes) with at most one extra disc access.

If the file is still larger, the twelfth pointer in the inode is then a pointer to a block containing the addresses of a further 128 blocks, each of which contains the addresses of 128 more of the file's data blocks; at this level, the file can grow to $10+128+128*128$ blocks in size.

There is one further level of indirection for files over this size, using the thirteenth pointer in the inode, giving a total possible size for the largest file of $10+128+128*128+128*128*128$ blocks.

The value 128 in all these calculations is a system parameter, and may be different on different implementations.

If an *lseek* system call is used to move the current position beyond the end of a file, and then a *write* is performed, intervening complete blocks which have not been accessed are represented by null pointers in the inode or associated blocks of pointers. There are no actual data blocks allocated. Reading from such blocks will deliver blocks of null characters.

9.5.4 Raw and block disc devices

To read inodes from a device, the device is read as a 'raw' or 'serial' device. For every block-structured device on a Unix system, there is both a block special file (device) associated with it, and a serial special file for the same physical device. The serial version of the device traditionally has the same name as the block device, preceded by the letter 'r'. Thus a typical 'ls −l' on /**dev** might include details such as is shown in figure 9.3. The lines starting 'b' indicate block devices, those starting 'c' indicate character serial devices.

```
brw-r----- 1 root     9,  0 Oct  2 11:24 /dev/rm00
brw-r----- 2 root     9,  1 Oct  4 17:37 /dev/rm01
brw-r----- 1 root     9,  2 Oct  2 11:24 /dev/rm02
brw-r----- 2 root     9,  3 Oct  2 11:24 /dev/rm03
brw-r----- 2 root     9,  4 Oct  2 11:24 /dev/rm04
brw-r----- 2 root     9,  5 Oct  2 11:24 /dev/rm05
crw-r----- 1 root    19,  0 Oct  2 11:24 /dev/rrm00
crw-r----- 2 root    19,  1 Oct  4 17:03 /dev/rrm01
crw-r----- 1 root    19,  2 Oct  2 11:51 /dev/rrm02
crw-r----- 1 root    19,  3 Oct  2 11:24 /dev/rrm03
crw-r----- 2 root    19,  4 Oct  2 11:24 /dev/rrm04
crw-r----- 2 root    19,  5 Oct  2 11:24 /dev/rrm05
```

Fig. 9.3 Long listing of /**dev**

The raw device can now be read with a simple serial *read* in a language such as C, providing that read access is permitted. Reads must be in whole blocks, and must take account of the disc layout of superblock, inodes and so on.

9.5.5 Buffer pool

All file input/output takes place via a general buffer pool operated by the Unix kernel. This is very sophisticated to minimise disc traffic, and allows buffers to be shared between different processes where possible. If a second process opens a file which is already opened by a running process, as it requests blocks of the file for input or output the system will check to see whether these are already in buffers before fetching them from disc; if that particular block is already in a buffer, the processes will share the buffer. The problems that this causes when the buffers and the disc files become out-of-step were discussed earlier, in chapter 4.

9.6 Other filestore maintenance commands

Other commands of which the manager should be aware include *fsck* (see the chapter on booting-up); *ncheck* (gives the inode number, name and owner of files on a given device); *clri* (to overwrite the contents of an inode; the file-system should be unmounted, the inode number of the file must be determined, the inode cleared, and an *fsck* command executed to clean up the file-system; this is a dangerous command and should be used only by experts); *fsdb* (filestore debug, again for experts only, this is for for patching discs, and the user must be very familiar with the raw structure of discs); and finally here *sync* (see chapter 4).

9.7 *mount* and *umount*

To mount an exchangeable device such as a floppy disc (which must have been formatted, and initialised using the command *mkfs*) use the command

/etc/mount /dev/floppy /mnt

where **/dev/floppy** is the name of the device, and **/mnt** is the directory under which it is to be mounted. The disc now looks to the user like part of the ordinary filestore; creating a file such as **/mnt/file** will create the file on the disc. The disc must be unmounted before removal using the command

/etc/umount /dev/floppy

The command

/etc/mount

with no parameters lists the currently mounted file-systems.

Access to the contents of the disc when mounted is controlled by the permissions and ownership of the directory at the head of the disc which has been mounted; these are set by using commands such as *chown* and *chmod* on the directory while the disc is mounted. There is an error on some implementations of Unix in which an 'ls -ld' command on the mounted directory still shows the permissions on the original directory, not those of the mounted directory.

The *mount* and *umount* commands live under the directory **/etc** in Version 7 Unix; many distributors move them to **/bin** so that they may be called without the '*/etc/*' prefix.

Files which are under the directory used for mounting before the *mount* command is executed become inaccessible while the directory is used for mounting, but reappear when it has been unmounted.

Discs created at other sites and then mounted may have UIDs and GIDs of file owners which do not exist on the current machine, and may possess files owned by 'root'. The inodes contain only the numeric values of the UID and GID, and a particular UID or GID will normally represent completely different users on different machines. The use of the *mount* and *umount* commands should therefore be restricted for security reasons; details are given in the chapter on security.

Chapter 10 Performance considerations

Unix is a complex multi-processing system, with sophisticated techniques for optimising the sharing of the main memory and the disc channels between processes. There is, however, much scope for a system manager to tune the system to the particular characteristics of the local workload. Effort spent in careful monitoring of performance by the system manager, and adjustment of various parameters, can lead to considerable improvements in response time for users. Performance monitoring is also essential in the planning of hardware and software enhancements, so that the relative cost-effectiveness of different upgrade paths can be compared.

Careful consideration should be given to the generation of sharable code for common commands, and of the sticky bit (see elsewhere) to minimise swapping. Unix provides commands for monitoring both hardware and software performance; these commands are described below, together with suggestions for adjustments to the system to respond to the performance which has been observed.

10.1 Standard commands for monitoring performance

A number of standard commands exist; we deal first with hardware performance then software performance. The two are inextricably related when the corrective measures are considered later.

10.1.1 The *iostat* command
This command should give details of traffic to filestore and magnetic-tape-like devices. Typical output from the command

```
iostat 30
```

is shown in figure 10.1. The first three columns in this particular configuration represent the performance of an 'RM' disc, and give the average transfers per minute, the number of milliseconds per seek, and the number of milliseconds per transfer. The first line of figures gives the average values since boot-up; each succeeding line gives the values over a 30

RM			RK			HT			PERCENT			
tpm	msps	mspt	tpm	msps	mspt	tpm	msps	mspt	user	nice	system	idle
208	16.2	0.5	13	52.6	3.2	0	0.0	0.0	5.09	10.53	12.01	72.37
2104	21.3	0.5	36	50.5	2.8	0	0.0	0.0	0.00	17.73	38.84	43.43
2399	19.6	0.5	36	60.5	2.8	0	0.0	0.0	0.20	21.64	38.28	39.88
2099	19.6	0.5	89	55.8	2.8	0	0.0	0.0	1.79	15.31	50.70	32.21
2064	20.7	0.5	0	0.0	0.0	0	0.0	0.0	0.40	11.67	35.01	52.92

Fig. 10.1 Output from *iostat*

second interval, the time interval being given as the parameter to the command. If no parameter is given to *iostat*, only the first line of figures is given. The first line, being the average since boot-up, appears low in the above example, since the data comes from a system which runs 24 hours per day and 7 days per week. The later lines represent more accurately the performance of the disc in real time. The 'millisecond-per-transfer' will be roughly constant in Version 7 Unix for an ordinary filestore device, since all transfers are of length one block. (Later Unix releases can vary the block size on different devices.) For the disc on which the swapping device resides, the times will be longer, since swaps are performed in large units. The 'milliseconds-per-seek' figure should be compared with the average expected of the device. If it is greater than the expected value, then the information is not well laid out on the disc. There are suggestions below for action to be taken in this event.

The next three columns on the configuration being illustrated represent an 'RK' disc, a much slower disc. The next three represent an inactive magnetic tape type of device.

The last four columns give the percentage of processor time being spent in the four categories 'user' (ordinary on-line and forked off user activity), 'nice' (low-priority processes, started with the *nice* command to reduce their priority), 'system' (time spent in the system on behalf of processes, handling systems calls such as *read*s and *write*s) and 'idle' (the processor has no waiting processes).

The alternative call of *iostat* is

    iostat −i 10

which gives output of the form shown in figure 10.2. The first four columns have the same significance as the last four columns of the previous output. The next two columns give the percentage of time for which the processor has been held up waiting for an input/output request to be satisfied (a request on a filestore device, for example, but not a request for input from the terminal), and the percentage of time during which input/output has been active. The last three columns give the percentage activity of the three devices already mentioned.

idle	user	nice	sys	IO wait	IO act	RM act	RK act	HT act
70.07	5.08	10.52	12.01	2.33	6.73	9.94	0.18	0.00
0.00	0.22	16.48	33.63	49.67	76.26	23.22	0.00	0.00
0.20	0.00	14.60	34.00	51.20	75.40	45.00	0.00	0.00
0.00	2.40	11.00	50.40	36.20	65.00	33.40	0.00	0.00
0.00	0.20	8.40	39.00	52.40	73.00	32.20	0.00	0.00
0.00	0.20	13.97	38.72	47.11	73.85	17.20	0.00	0.00

Fig. 10.2 Alternative *iostat* output

The additional parameter '−t' gives terminal activity (in average characters/second) as well as the above information, and an example is shown in figure 10.3.

TTY		RM			RK			PERCENT			
tin	tout	tpm	msps	mspt	tpm	msps	mspt	user	nice	system	idle
2.7	87.1	205	14.2	0.5	22	52.0	3.1	6.86	2.79	15.62	74.72
25.5	485.6	82	16.5	0.4	0	0.0	0.0	5.44	52.30	42.26	0.00
25.5	516.2	299	14.0	0.4	0	0.0	0.0	6.59	42.71	50.70	0.00
23.9	545.2	358	13.6	0.4	0	0.0	0.0	18.49	17.30	64.21	0.00

Fig. 10.3 Terminal activity *iostat* output

The *iostat* command uses kernel information, and so must be changed to reflect different hardware configurations; some companies supplying Unix systems have been known not to match the *iostat* command with the configuration provided, or not to supply the command at all. This performance information is sufficiently important that you should check that it has been supplied correctly. This is a very system and machine specific area, and you should check your manuals for details of the particular implementation on your machine.

The traffic shown by *iostat* is for a complete disc, and is not normally split between the different 'virtual' discs and file-systems which may reside on a single device in Unix. For those with source licences, it is a simple matter to generate much more useful information by altering the driver firstly to monitor traffic by separate virtual disc, and secondly to monitor separately the inode and data areas of each disc. This gives additional useful information on the relative amount on traffic to different parts of the disc.

10.1.2 The *sa* command

The *sa* command is for shell command accounting. The accounting process is initiated by the use of the

/etc/accton

command within the **/etc/rc** file, executed on going multi-user. This makes a system call such as

    acct ("/usr/adm/safile");

which defines the name of the file to be used (if any) for process accounting. (The call returns the value '−1' if it fails for any reason.) If this call has been made successfully, the system will log all processes (their name, the name of the user executing them, the processor time used, and the elapsed time) in the named file. This file grows very quickly on a large system (one entry for every command executed), so must be watched carefully.

The file can then be analysed in various ways by the *sa* command. Typical output from the command

    sa

is shown in figure 10.4.

1	386.13	374.04	gaussint
31	3561.02	208.14	comp
2	92.98	14.98	ch
631	2501.23	14.16	tar
57	849.33	12.95	h7
27	30.60	12.60	h3b
100	371.00	11.92	restor
43469	406243.50	11.09	ed
72	67.23	10.50	ttable
25	56.37	9.73	clust
13	17.93	9.52	lex.ft
973	3684.45	9.41	cdm
340	804.25	7.83	ljf
237	3180.98	7.68	dump
62	58.78	6.27	preproc
62	54.02	6.18	io
7820	17819.14	5.57	apd
478	198926.89	5.32	display
184	730.72	4.81	alged
266	120.82	4.70	uucp
182	231.37	4.32	rules
8937	2520.30	4.13	lint1
47	15.72	4.08	timetable
47076	4995946.50	3.65	sh
12755	266661.42	3.50	nnroff
84	73.72	3.43	realoc

Fig. 10.4 Output from the *sa* command

The figures give the total number of calls of the command, the total elapsed time involved in those calls (in minutes), and the total processor time (also in minutes). For this call of the *sa* command, entries are ordered by the third figure.

The command

```
sa −n
```

gives the same information ordered by the number of times the command was called, and typical output appears in figure 10.5.

59587	35713.85	0.00	sleep
47076	4995946.50	3.65	sh
43469	406243.50	11.09	ed
31478	22659.27	2.70	cat
31472	701.13	0.31	cp
31042	618.58	0.07	tr
30522	3368.75	0.10	ls
29839	3842.10	0.50	cpp
27270	941.38	0.51	atrun
25120	1032.43	0.11	rm
23316	6998.70	0.13	echo
22717	17613.21	0.14	cc
20321	2647.58	0.93	c0
18213	3996.88	1.09	as2
17662	2458.60	1.23	c1
17495	1101.93	0.23	f
15646	30721.23	0.36	link
15578	3887.55	0.56	who
14645	−74215.18	0.30	fs
13745	3125.20	0.65	notify
12987	5280.35	0.80	ld
12755	266661.42	3.50	nnroff
12361	2129.33	2.33	grep
11663	13472.57	0.16	a.out
11147	616.77	0.11	termtype
11084	25643.01	0.09	nroff

Fig. 10.5 Output from *sa* −*n* command

Other parameters to the *sa* command give other summaries; see the manual for full details. The *sa* command has an option to enable it to keep a summary file of commands used and their resource requirements, so the actual accounting file (which can grow very quickly on a large system) can be truncated at regular intervals. The format of the entries in the accounting file is in the include file

#include <sys/acct.h>

The structure has fields so that for each command executed, the following information can be kept, for later analysis by the user as required: command name, user time, system time, elapsed time, beginning time (the time the command execution started), user ID, group ID, memory usage, and the name of the typewriter from which the command was issued. The author's version has been modified to log the disc traffic from each command, since this is a common Unix bottleneck.

10.1.3 The *ac* command

The *ac* command is for the accounting of logged-on time on the system. As described in chapter 5 on logging-in, if the file **/usr/adm/wtmp** exists, then every login and logout will be recorded, with the time, the name of the user, the terminal line being used, and so on. The format of each entry is according to the structure given in the standard 'include' file **/usr/include/utmp.h**. The **wtmp** file should be processed regularly to produce a summary, and all obsolete entries removed. When **wtmp** is processed, the 'login' entries for any session not yet ended must be left in the new **wtmp** file, ready for the next accounting run.

In addition to the login and logout entries, the **wtmp** file contains other entries arising from system reboots and system time changes. A special entry is inserted after rebooting, at the time the system goes multi-user, and any accounting program using the **wtmp** file should assume when such a record is encountered that all current users have been logged off, even though there are no logout entries. A further complication when clearing out the **wtmp** file arises from the fact that the *date* command, when used by super-user to alter the system's idea of the current time and date, puts two entries (the old and the new time) into the **wtmp** file. These differences must be taken into account when accumulating logged-on times for any user who was logged on when the time change occurred, since the difference between their login and logout times will not be the actual time spent logged on. The time-change entries must be retained in the new **wtmp** file if they occurred after the 'login' entry for someone who has not yet logged out. It should be noted that the **/usr** disc is not normally mounted during the initial super-user shell after rebooting, so that any changes to the system clock at this stage will not be recorded. It should be changed after the **/usr** has been mounted.

The *ac* command analyses the **wtmp** file simply, ignoring the above complications. Typical output from the command

ac −p −d

(where the flag '−p' causes separate user totals to be given, and the flag '−d' causes different days to be accounted separately) might be

```
ef      0.22
jaa     0.10
```

	zoo	0.31
	jpo	0.03
	raw	0.28
	mp	0.40
	daa	0.19
	jch	0.04
Sep 29	total	1.56

where the units are hours and minutes of logged time.

The *ac* command, unlike *sa*, does not keep a separate summary file, or empty the **wtmp** file. The matter is a little more complex than with *sa*, because when the **wtmp** file is cleared, any 'login' entries for current users (who have not yet logged out) must be replaced, together with any 'time-change' entries which have occurred since they logged in. It is, however, a fairly simple matter to write a more sophisticated program which performs these functions and, for example, gives details summarised by terminal line and/or time of day. The format of each record in the **wtmp** file is the same as the **utmp** records (for details check your **/usr/include/utmp.h** file) and includes fields for storing the line name, the user's name, and the time.

This type of accounting is one area where vendors have often greatly extended the standard distributed facilities; see your manual for details. Statistics of the login activity analysed by location of terminal and time-of-day can be particularly useful in assessing demand from users.

10.2 General disc performance considerations

10.2.1 Introduction

The discs on a Unix system are one of the major keys to machine performance; any effort spent improving their efficiency will have considerable benefits to the installation.

In Unix, a single physical disc device can appear to the system either as one device, or as a number of devices. In the latter case, each device is specified by an offset from the beginning of the disc, and a size. Within each 'virtual' disc, the first part of the area is reserved for the super-block and inodes (see chapter 8), and the second part for data blocks.

10.2.2 Disc head movement

The most important objective of disc performance improvement is to minimise the average head movement between transfers. On typical discs (as can be seen from the *iostat* output shown above), the seek time is generally far greater than the transfer time. Considering a single Unix disc, the data blocks of a given file will be scattered about the disc, the blocks being obtained on request from the free space list. In addition, there will typically be alternating access to the inode area (to find the address of a data block), then access to the data block, then back to the inode area for the next address. Since the inode area is at the start of the disc (typically the outermost extremity), head movements can be considerable. To reduce this cause of head movement, a large disc can be divided into a number of 'virtual' discs, each with its own file-system, consisting of a super-block, and inode and data areas. When a given file (or file-system) is being accessed, the distance between the inode accesses and the data blocks will be smaller than when the whole disc is treated as a single unit. In addition, the data blocks themselves will be closer together.

Thus a system will normally perform better if a large disc is subdivided. Having divided the disc, the areas with most traffic should be placed on file-systems situated approximately half-way out from the centre of the disc, and the least used areas at the outer and inner extremities. The traffic to individual 'virtual' discs is not monitored by normal system programs such as *iostat*, but it is usually possible to estimate the busiest areas. A possible way to measure the traffic on a particular file-system is to move it temporarily to a separate device. The ordering on one carefully monitored installation in decreasing order of traffic was:

> Highest traffic: root disc
> /tmp
> user areas
> Least traffic: /usr : manuals, documentation etc

The traffic to the **swap** device must also be considered, but unlike ordinary filestore accesses, the effect of swapping can be reduced by either reducing the traffic, or by speeding up the disc. The amount of traffic can be reduced by adding more main memory, and by carefully selecting the programs which have the sticky bit set. Since swapping on a non-virtual memory machine occurs in larger-than-standard units (the whole program is swapped on a non-virtual machine), the considerations concerning the speed of the disc become slightly modified; it may be feasible to use with advantage a disc with a slower seek time, but a faster transfer rate. For separate file-systems on distinct discs, the division of users and system areas between the file-systems should be adjusted to balance the total demand on each disc relative to its maximum throughput capacity.

There are, unfortunately, other considerations militating against the division of a disc into a number of small file-systems, and the decision may not be an obvious one. With a number of small file-systems, the overflow of the available disc space in a file-system is more likely; each user or group of users sharing a file-system will have less flexibility for the creation of temporary files in their area than if they all share one large file-system. The file-systems have to be dumped separately, and this again puts an upper limit on the number of file-systems which it is reasonable to operate. A lower limit on the number of file-systems may be set by the consideration that a file-system small enough to dump onto a single magnetic tape simplifies dumping.

10.2.3 Making a new file-system

The command /*etc*/*mkfs* for creating file-systems has two performance-related parameters available which can be set only at the time the file-system is created. The first is effectively a 'skew' factor, requesting the algorithm which claims data blocks from the free list in such a way that consecutive blocks in a file have an agreed skew (rotational distance) between them where possible. An appropriate factor can be found only by experiment, by setting up a shell script of commands representing a typical workload for the installation, and running it repeatedly on an otherwise empty machine.

10.2.4 Reordering directories

A last (but still worthwhile) performance improvement can be obtained on non-Berkeley systems by ordering the entries in directories to minimise searching time; Berkeley systems perform the search in a more efficient way using a hash table, making this point unnecessary.

To reorder the directory, first create a new temporary directory, then move the items to it in the required order, then delete the original directory and move the temporary one to that name. Beware that if the machine goes down during this process, vital commands may not be available when it comes up.

The output from the *sa* command can be used to order the entries for the commands in the **/bin** and **/usr/bin** directories, and to determine which commands should be in **/bin** (any commands required during the initial single-user shell, and the most frequently used ones), and which in **/usr/bin**.

Beware that if you are reordering **/bin** while the commands are in another temporary directory they will have to be accessed by a full path-name, and that if the machine goes down, there may be problems!

10.3 Varying system parameters

Certain key system parameters, such as the maximum number of processes, of opened files, and of in-core buffers, can be changed on Version 7 Unix only by recompilation of the source code. Details are not therefore given here. Those who can adjust such parameters should try careful tests with fixed benchmarks to determine the effects of such variations. Benchmarks in the form of looping shell scripts are easily generated and executed in Unix, and should be designed to reflect the typical workload which is expected.

10.4 Holding some files open

To ensure rapid access, it may be desirable to hold a certain file open, so that its inode is held in main memory. This requires that it be opened by a program which remains running the whole time. It is normally done by the *update* process (the *open*ing of the file is done at the entry to the *update* program) but will militate against the best overall performance. It could perhaps be done in the *init* process, but one would generally not want any such special arrangement to take effect before the system has gone multi-user.

10.5 General performance figures

Selecting machine configurations to support a given user community is a hazardous exercise. Some machine vendors advise that a configuration should be based on a main memory size of 256 kbytes for the system plus 256k for each active terminal, and a disc throughput capacity of 4 blocks per active terminal per second. This is however very much a ballpark figure, and particular heavily used applications will give a wide variation of demand.

The total filestore size is also difficult to estimate; newcomers to multi-user systems often underestimate the file space which users will require. The system area required will depend on decisions to support or otherwise the on-line manual, documentation and *learn* systems.

A point raised by several existing managers was the use of *cron* to switch certain facilities off or on at different times of day. It is obviously feasible to reconfigure the system (perhaps by editing **/etc/ttys**) at different times of the day or week to allow a greater or lesser number of terminals on, or simply to forbid access (perhaps by *chmod* on the directory) to, for example, the games programs at certain times if it is felt that to remove them completely would cause a user revolt.

Chapter 11   The security of Unix systems

The term 'security' in this chapter refers to security against deliberate or accidental damage to the system, or access to private information by users of the system, rather than to security against, for example, disc failures. The latter is covered in the section on dumping in the chapter on file systems. The confidentiality aspects of security in Unix systems have been mentioned in various places above where the relevant topics were being considered. In this chapter all aspects of this type of security are gathered together.

One sometimes hears criticisms of Unix from uninformed users, in which it is described as poor in its security aspects. The fact of life is that Unix is very secure when managed correctly. Any lack of security in a given installation can be traced to some feature which has not been implemented, or has been implemented incorrectly, or where user-friendliness has been deliberately chosen in preference to security.

The following points are all worthy of consideration.

11.1 Permissions on files

11.1.1 Command permissions

With a few exceptions listed below and elsewhere, all system commands (all files in the directories **/bin** and **/usr/bin**) should have an access mode such as 771 (for binary programs) or 775 (for shell scripts), to ensure no public write permission, and no public read permission except where necessary (shell scripts). The group permissions should be set so that users with permission to change to the system administration group can perform system changes without need for super-user status; if this arrangement is not used, the modes should be set to 711 and 755 respectively. If the execution of shell scripts does not require read permission, then they also should be with mode 771; read permission should in general be avoided, to prevent people from taking copies of programs or shell scripts to, for example, a floppy disc attached to a terminal. The exceptions are those commands needing SUID facilities, listed in section 9.4.1 describing SUID facilities earlier in the book. For such commands, it is particularly important that there should not be public write permission.

11.1.2 Root-owned writable files
There should be no root-owned public-writable files.

11.1.3 Directory permissions
Directories such as **/bin** should not have public write permission. It is surprising how many managers carefully check the access permissions on the files in their main directories, but do not check the directories themselves. If there exists public write permission on the directory, users can then save a copy of a command in their own directory, delete the original, and insert a replacement of the same name. The command to check the permissions on a directory is, for example,

```
ls −ld /bin /usr/bin
```

A suitable mode would be 775, to allow them to be searchable and readable by the public.

In general each user's home directory, **.profile** and **.login** files should be owned by that user, and should have write permission only to that user, for similar reasons to those above.

11.1.4 Escapes to the shell and SUID permission
There are potential dangers associated with any command which has an escape to the shell (such as the '!' facility in the editors *ed* and *vi*, and in the *write* command). In general, none of these should be a root-owned SUID command, since the shell forked off would then be a 'super-user' shell. If for any reason this is unavoidable, the source code must be amended to reset the effective UID before the escape is activated. It should be noted that the system call 'setuid' for resetting the user-id of a process is permitted to 'super-user', and to processes resetting to their original UID. (It is a poor feature of the system that such information cannot be nested.)

11.1.5 General file permission default
The default file permission for ordinary users' files can be set by the *umask* command before a user's shell is entered. In a research environment, general public read on most files is acceptable, and is to be encouraged, since it improves co-operation between users. However, in a more restrictive environment, it may be advisable to default to no public access to general users' files with a *umask* setting of 007.

11.2 Access to devices

11.2.1 Access to raw devices
There should be no public access to the 'raw' disc devices used for the public filestore. If so, users could read from the inodes, and find the position of any information on the disc, and read it. Any command which is to be accessed by ordinary users, but which to perform its function requires access to a raw device (for example, *df*), must then be an SUID or SGID file of some sort, with its owner having access to the device.

There may be devices outside the general filestore, perhaps used for image processing where large amounts of data and high access rates are required, for which public read access is legitimate.

11.2.2 Access to memory
There should be no access to /**dev/mem** and /**dev/kmem**, again because it would give users access to information not belonging to them. The command *ps* looks up the process tables in kernel memory, and so thus needs SUID privilege and to be owned by whoever owns those devices.

11.2.3 Access to terminals
Public access to any terminal device on a serial line is dangerous, particularly if the line is connected to an 'intelligent' terminal. For example, some terminals can be instructed by a particular escape sequence to re-transmit information just received and displayed on the screen. If there is public write permission on such a terminal, a message sent to it can be made (as part of the message) to be retransmitted to the system, and then it will appear as though it came from that terminal, although it was not originated by the person sitting at that terminal. For maximum security, use the command *mesg* to inhibit public access at such terminals. Any user who is prepared to take the risk can then use the same command to reset public access.

11.3 The *mount* command

If there is public access to the *mount* command and to a demountable device, a user with, for example, a root-owned SUID shell from another machine stored on a floppy disc, can bring it to the local system, load it, and execute it there. Access to the mount command also allows a user to mount an appropriately prepared disc as /**bin** or /**etc**, with system-blowing results from new commands or **passwd** files. Access to the *mount* command and the mountable devices should therefore be restricted.

11.4 Other general points

11.4.1 Passwords
Important passwords should be changed regularly, and should be known to only a minimum of staff; the minimum number should, of course, allow for individuals to be away ill, or to be run over by a bus! Logins on usernames without a password should be prohibited on dial-up and network lines. The passwords chosen should, of course, not be obvious ones, and should contain a mixture of upper and lower case letters, digits and punctuation. The *passwd* command could be modified to include some such checks, but cannot be expected to know people's telephone numbers.

11.4.2 A suggestion for .*secure*
A very standard danger to security is the problem of a user leaving a program running at a terminal (overlaying the shell by an *exec*) which leaves a prompt looking like a standard 'login' prompt. When a user approaches the

terminal, the program reads the typed login name, requests a password, and stores both, then exits with a message such as 'Invalid password'. A normal 'login' then appears, and the new user just assumes that the password had been mistyped. For those concerned at the security of logging-in, some installations have implemented a system in which, before the password is checked (or even instead of the password system), the *login* process activates a program called .**secure** in the user's home directory, if it exists. This program is written by the user, and can ask for responses in any way that is thought appropriate. This gives a much more flexible approach, and avoids the collection of passwords by a program which is left on a terminal, which prints the usual 'login' message, and stores the name and password typed before exiting.

As an additional precaution, the *login* command itself should be executable only by root, with no access at all to the public. It can then be entered only from the *init* and *getty* processes, but not by an ordinary user.

11.4.3 Search path for super-user

For users permitted to use the *su* command, the search path should include the current directory at the end rather than at the beginning. This avoids users being able to leave non-standard commands with standard command names lying in the current directory, and having them executed in super-user mode.

11.4.4 Encryption

Sensitive information is best stored in an encrypted† form. The command *crypt* can by used as in

    crypt < clearfile > codedfile

which will ask for an encryption key at the terminal, and will store the encrypted version of the information in **clearfile** in **codedfile**.

Echo is suppressed while the encryption key is being typed. However, the key is asked for only once, which can be dangerous, and should be checked immediately by recovering the information with

    crypt < codedfile

The key can be given as a parameter, but is then visible on the terminal (since echo is not switched off), and may in addition be visible in the output from the command

    ps −al

for a short while.

† Arrangements for encryption in System V Unix are different in the USA and non-USA versions.

To overcome the problem that encryption asks for the key only once, it is possible to write a shell script which asks for it twice, as in the Bourne shell example

```
stty −echo; echo −n "Key: "; read key1
echo −n "Again: "; read key2
stty echo
if test $key1 = $key2
then ... ok ... crypt $key1 < $1 > $2
else echo "Keys differ"
fi
```

but again there can be problems with the key passed to the *crypt* command appearing on *ps* listings for a short while.

The '−x' flag in the standard Bell editor *ed*

```
ed −x file
```

asks for an encryption key, and writes the file back in an encrypted form. However, the drawbacks are twofold. Firstly, like *crypt*, it asks for the key only once (which is satisfactory for an existing file being decrypted, since the recovered version will immediately be seen to be incorrect, but is unsatisfactory when creating a new file). Secondly, some versions do not hold the temporary files in **/tmp** in encrypted form. The files produced by 'ed −x' are compatible with *crypt* output.

11.4.5 Use of 'super-user' status

It is a good policy to minimise the use of super-user privilege as far as is possible. Never login as root, but as an ordinary user, and then use *su* just when necessary. In addition, make as many tasks as possible performable by the group 'bin' or your system group; thus if the commands on your system are owned by group 'bin' and have group write permission, anyone with permission to *newgrp* to 'bin' (hopefully all systems staff) can install amended commands without having to become super-user or login as root. Similarly, if files such as **/etc/passwd** are owned by group 'bin' and have group write permission, the need for 'super-user' status is reduced. The status of super-user gives so much power that it should be avoided whenever possible. The careful use of different groups for different system functions reduces the possibility of security breaks.

One of the standard requirements for super-user facilities is when a *chown* has to be performed, since files restored from magnetic tape often appear under the login name of the user who restored them, rather than the original user. Amended versions of *chown* are available which run with SUID facilities, but check passwords for the previous and new owners of the file before allowing the ownership to be changed, and thus remove the need for going into 'super-user' mode to *chown* the file. Systems III and V and later Berkeley systems allow anyone to use *chown*, but the command unsets any SUID and SGID bits, thus avoiding breaches in security.

11.4.6 Storage of system backup tapes

A general point on security which relates to all systems, not just to Unix, involves the security of backup tapes. Obviously, all the information on the system is stored somewhere (perhaps in more than one place) on backup tapes. These tapes can be restored to another machine if stolen or copied, so must be kept in a physically secure place.

11.5 Conclusion

The above is by no means a complete list of possible security problems; there may be some of which the author is not aware, and there are others of which he is aware, but which are best not revealed here. One aspect not even mentioned above is the possibility of human error, such as the leaving of a terminal logged in, or problems related to the security of communication lines. It is worth making a shell script to run nightly or weekly to check some of the more straightforward problems mentioned above, but the manager who has users determined to break the security must be always on guard.

Chapter 12   Some major commands for managers

In this chapter we describe some of the more complex commands which are of interest particularly to system managers. The first two (*make* and SCCS) are general-purpose commands for the maintenance of any non-trivial programming package involving a number of source code and/or data files. The third (*awk*) is a simple pattern recognition and processing language, which many managers have reported as being of great use on a range of occasions. The last section of this chapter covers commands for the initiation of other commands and processes on a pre-scheduled basis, very useful for, for example, regular accounting runs.

12.1 The *make* command

The *make* command is designed to assist in automating the maintenance of programs and/or files whose integrity depends on suites of files which must be combined together in some way to create that program or file. The maintenance aspect is automated to a high degree and actions invoked by the *make* command can be made to depend on the files involved in a number of ways. A typical problem with a large program (or suite of programs) written as a number of modules arises when an alteration is necessary, and one source code module is changed. The user then has two options: the first is to recompile the whole system, which can take a considerable time, the second is to recompile just those parts of the system which depend on the amended module, to save time. The first option is usually very slow. However, with the second option, if one of the dependencies is forgotten, the resulting system will have inconsistencies which will cause it to fail. The *make* command is intended to automate this type of situation, recompiling only those modules requiring it, and guaranteeing a consistent new system without performing unnecessary compilations. Some dependencies of files on other files can be deduced by the *make* command itself (for example, the fact that a '.o' file depends on a corresponding '.c' file) where other dependencies must be specified by the user (for example, the fact that since one file '#includes' another, the first depends on the second).

The use of *make* avoids the need to recompile a system completely when one module has been changed, in case that one change has repercussions on other modules, and avoids at the other extreme the problem of finding the new version corrupt, because one module which should have been recompiled was forgotten. The use of *make* ensures the minimum of recompilation consistent with the amendments to the various files involved.

The actions invoked by *make* take the following points into account.

- The action may depend on the date that a file was last written to; this is available from the ordinary Unix file-system, and the system may need to compare the dates of modification of two files to see which has been modified more recently.
- In addition, it is necessary that the programmer be able to stipulate the dependencies of the target program on its various constituent files. Although it might be possible for a sophisticated system to look for '#include' lines and deduce the corresponding dependencies, other cases would be harder to find, and it is left to the programmer to specify all such relationships.
- The *make* software itself understands certain important implicit dependencies. For example, it knows that an object '.o' file can be generated from a corresponding text '.c' or '.f' file by performing a compilation of some sort (a *cc* command for a '.c' file, or an *f77* command for a '.f' file).

By default the *make* program expects to find, in the current directory, a file called **makefile** (or **Makefile**) which contains details of the program or programs that can be constructed from explicitly named component files together with an indication of the way in which the programs depend on these constituents and on various other files. The usual difficulty encountered in the writing of **makefile**s is the combination of the explicit relationships given by the programmer with the implicit rules understood by the *make* command itself.

As a simple example consider a **makefile** which contains the following lines.

```
fred : fred.o
    ld −o fred fred.o
```

This is interpreted to mean that the file **fred** (a binary program) is the result of this particular maintenance activity. The *make* command is now called with argument 'fred' as in

```
make fred
```

The first line of the **makefile** specifies that the program **fred** depends on the file **fred.o**, and the second line specifies that **fred** is to be re-made by executing the command

```
ld −o fred fred.o
```

This command (or it could be a sequence of commands) is to be carried out only if the file **fred.o** has been modified since the file **fred** was last modified; that is the interpretation of the statement '**fred** depends upon **fred.o**'. When the *make* command is invoked, it looks for a **makefile**, and this particular one will cause it to examine the directory first for a file **fred.o**, to see if it is up-to-date. To do this, it will then look for a file **fred.c**, since it knows by its internal rules that a '.o' file is always made from a '.c' file. It will then compare the dates of most recent modification of the files **fred.o** and **fred.c** and see whether it should remake **fred.o** using built-in rules. If **fred.o** did not exist then *make* would issue its built-in rules anyway to construct **fred.o** from **fred.c**. If the file **fred.c** does not exist, *make* will give an error message. The *make* command now returns to the rules above, and compares the modification date of **fred.o** with that of **fred** to see if it should carry out the rules in the above example.

The above example is trivial by the usual standards of *make*, but the *make* command still does a significant amount of work. The more usual **makefile** script is one in which a program depends on several '.o' files and some '#include' files as in the next example.

```
fred : fred.o jim.o chuck.o
     cc −o fred fred.o chuck.o jim.o −lm

jim.o chuck.o : defs.h
```

In this example, **fred** is loaded from three modules, two of which (**jim.c** and **chuck.c**) have a '#include' line including the file **defs.h** in the source. The first line is interpreted as 'fred depends on fred.o, jim.o and chuck.o', and the last line as 'jim.o and chuck.o depend on defs.h'. Thus if **defs.h** is changed, both of these two modules will need to be recompiled. However, if the **defs.h** file is unchanged, and one of the '.c' files is changed, only that one module will need recompilation. This script has two visible levels which *make* has to consult. First it has to check whether the file **defs.h** has been modified since **jim.o** or **chuck.o** were last modified. If it has, then *make* will have to remake one or both of the '.o' files.

In order to remake the **fred** file, it is now necessary only to type

```
make fred
```

The minimal form of the command, just

```
make
```

will default to the first rule in the **makefile**. In addition, the command has enough built-in understanding to interpret

```
make jim.o
```

as an instruction simply to remake **jim.o** from **jim.c** if **defs.h** or **jim.c** have a later modification date than **jim.o**.

The *make* command also allows a form of macro definitions. These are defined and used in the **makefile** by instructions such as†

```
LIBRARY = −lm
OBJECTS = jim.o fred.o chuck.o

fred : $(OBJECTS)
        cc −o fred $(OBJECTS) $(LIBRARY)
```

The last two lines now have the interpretation

```
fred : jim.o fred.o chuck.o
        cc −o fred jim.o fred.o chuck.o −lm
```

This script is equivalent to the one described in detail above, but is much easier to modify if an extra module is to be included in the program. The *make* command also allows macros to be defined as parameters in the command line, and any such override any ones of the same name specified in the file. Thus to change the library called in the above example on a one-off basis, without editing the **makefile**, it is possible to type

```
make "LIBRARY=−ldbm" fred
```

and so use the 'dbm' library instead. Macros of this type are used internally by the *make* command to create its own rules, and the built-in rules can be overwritten by either specifying new definitions in the **makefile** or as parameters. The default compiler name is defined by default for example as

```
CC = cc
```

When *make* uses a built-in rule involving the C compiler it uses the macro-value of *CC* rather than actually using the compiler *cc* directly. By redefining the macro *CC*, it is now possible to invoke a different C compiler (such as a cross-compiler for generating microprocessor code, for example), or even a different program entirely. In a similar way, the default flags for the *cc* compiler are defined by the macro-value *CFLAGS*, which can be redefined as required by the user.

All of the built-in rules used by the *make* command can also be redefined; the built-in rules appear in the source of *make* in Version 7, requiring a recompilation, but appear in a separate file in System V. The System V version of *make* has itself a '#include' facility for use in **makefile**s, whereby other files of *make* instructions can be included in a given **makefile**.

† Note that this notation is inconsistent with both the C preprocessor '#defines' and the setting of variables in the Bourne shell.

The source code of the *make* command then includes only a single built-in instruction, typically

```
#include /usr/lib/template.mk
```

and the file **/usr/lib/template.mk** contains the default *make* rules. Such modifications would enable one to overwrite the existing automatic relationship between for example '.c' files, '.o' files and the C compiler, or to add a new compiler with its own set of suffices, or perhaps to *unpack* files automatically before use in System V.

Rules involving built-in relationships between suffices involve the use of some other predefined macros, mainly the following

```
$?    is the string of names younger than the target file.
$*    is the prefix common to both dependent and current file.
$<    is the name of the file that caused the action.
$@    is the name of the file to be made.
```

In order to build in an automatic rule for generating an object '.o' file from a source '.c' file, the related suffices must be given, in the order that later suffices depend on earlier ones. A typical rule† is

```
.SUFFIXES : .c .o
```

There must then be provided the rule for conversion

```
# is the make comment, rather like the Bourne shell
.c.o :       # .c to .o depends on no other files.
    $(CC) $(CFLAGS) −c $<
# compile the .c file with the −c flag
# using compiler $(CC)
# and with other flags if any defined in $(CFLAGS)
```

As *make* operates, it reports the commands being executed, the output appearing on the standard output. To inhibit this output, include the line

```
.SILENT :
```

The *make* command itself has a **makefile** for its own maintenance. The source involves both C and 'yacc' program modules. Any 'yacc' file (the suffix '.y' is understood by *make*) has to be passed first through the 'yacc' compiler, then the result (which is always in a file named **y.tab.c**) compiled under C. The built-in rule for 'yacc' files consists of

† English users should note that the spelling in this rule is SUFFIXES, not SUFFICES!

```
.y.o:
        $(YACC) $(YFLAGS) $<
        $(CC) $(CFLAGS) −c y.tab.c
        rm y.tab.c
        mv y.tab.o $@
```

Note that the intermediate **y.tab.c** file needs to be removed, and the output file needs to be moved to an appropriately named file. It is now possible using these built-in rules to keep *make* itself completely up-to-date with the **makefile** shown in figure 12.1.

```
OBJECTS = ident.o main.o doname.o misc.o files.o dosys.o gram.o
SOURCES = ident.c main.c doname.c misc.c files.c dosys.c gram.c
FILES = makefile ident.c defs main.c doname.c misc.c files.c dosys.c \
        gram.y gcos.c
LIBES=
LINT = lint −ps
CFLAGS = −O
LDFLAGS = −s −n
LPR = lpr

make: $(OBJECTS)
        $(CC) $(LDFLAGS) $(CFLAGS) $(OBJECTS) $(LIBES) −o make

$(OBJECTS): defs

cleanup:
        −rm $(OBJECTS)
        −du

install: /bin/make
/bin/make: make # copy only if bin version is older than local version
        cp make /bin/make

print: $(FILES)   # print recently changed files
        −pr $? | $(LPR)
        touch print

lint : $(SOURCES)
        $(LINT) $(SOURCES)
```

Fig. 12.1 A typical **makefile** for the *make* command

To remake the **make** program, one now calls either

```
make make
```

to create a new version of the command in a local file named **make**, created
by calling the *cc* command with appropriate parameters, or

```
make cleanup
```

to tidy the filestore by removing all '.o' files, or

```
make lint
```

to generate a *lint*-type output, or

```
make install
```

to install the new version (see below for more explanation), or

```
make print
```

to print out any changed files.

The 'install' version of the command is perhaps worth some further
explanation. The entry beginning 'install' indicates that 'install' (which is not
actually a file) depends on **/bin/make**, and this is interpreted by the *make*
command as meaning that it needs to carry out the given command to construct a new version of 'install' regardless. It then finds an entry specifying
how it is to construct the file **/bin/make**, and so checks whether to construct
/bin/make from the given rules by checking the respective modification dates.
Thus when (and only when!) it is known to be safe to release the new version
of *make* to the world, the command

```
make install
```

will complete the process.

The 'print' parameter command is also useful. This is interpreted as a
request to print out all files that have changed since a 'print' parameter was
last given. It does this by keeping a marker file called **print**, which is empty
(and hence occupies no data blocks), to show the date on which the files were
last printed. This is then compared against the list of source files in FILES
and the list of newer files contained in '$?' is printed out.

On System V, features of SCCS (see below) have been built into the
make command, so that it can automatically extract source files from the
SCCS area for compilations.

12.2 Source Code Control System (SCCS)

The Source Code Control System is one of those programming tools, like
make, which perhaps appears to be a non-essential luxury until you have used
it, but once it is in regular use, survival without it cannot be contemplated.
Basically, the SCCS system allows the manager to keep all the backup files

relating to a suite of important programs that has been created, and is being maintained. It allows the manager to experiment with different versions of commands and to always have the certainty that if serious problems arise, it will be possible to return to an earlier version which worked correctly.

12.2.1 How it works

The SCCS system may be thought of as a base file of one particular version of the code, with a *diff* listing to represent each variant.† Thus, if the current file is kept complete, in order to obtain a copy of the previous version of the file, a sequence of editing commands is executed on that file to reduce it to the previous version. Generally all this information is kept in one file, together with certain administrative data in what is termed an 's-file.' The administrative information generally contains such things as:

> the dates of the various versions;
> the name of the user who made each of the versions;
> comments accompanying the versions;
> a list of people eligible to edit the file;
> various checks such as checksums.

The SCCS system really shows its worth in large projects worked on by several people. In this case, it prevents the editing of files that are already being edited, keeps backups of all previous versions and allows people to branch out on different paths when experimenting with their own ideas.

12.2.2 The SCCS commands

There are several variants of the SCCS system in existence, differing in the syntax of the commands, but generally with all of the features discussed below.

Creating SCCS files

This is generally done with the command *admin*. It is normal practice to keep all the 's-files' in a separate sub-directory, usually called **SCCS**; in this way only the files that are being worked on at the present time are visible in the current directory. So typically a directory **SCCS** will be created, and then the *admin* command is used to install the file. Here again, the actual command varies, but it is generally of the form

> admin −ifile SCCS

or

> sccs admin −ifile SCCS/s.file

with the parameters representing the name of the file to be included, and the

† If two similar files are required, it is always more economical of disc space to store one of the files as it stands, and instead of storing the other file directly, store a file of the edit commands necessary to generate it from the first file. These edit commands can be obtained from the *diff* command.

name of the directory to be used. In some systems this command removes the original copy of the *file*, while in others it leaves it, but assuming that all went well, the *file* is now stored in SCCS format in the directory **SCCS**. The *admin* command has other uses as described later.

How to use the SCCS file

To reclaim a file (for example, to use it in a compilation), the command is generally of the form

>   get file

or

>   sccs get file

This then extracts the latest version of the file from the SCCS directory for use in compilation or printing. The file is extracted with modes 444 (read only) as a reminder that you are not supposed to edit it. To extract a file for editing, the command is

>   get −e file

or

>   sccs get −e file

or even

>   sccs edit file

This extracts the file for editing, makes a note in the SCCS file of who is editing the file, and locks the SCCS file against further parallel attempts to edit this file. (Remember that the standard Bell editor allows any number of users to edit a file simultaneously; the last person to write it back overwrites any amendments by others.)

Putting back amended files

This action is called 'making a delta', and is usually done with some form of the delta command.

>   delta file

or

>   sccs delta file

This has the effect of making the current version of the named file the latest version of the file; it also unlocks the SCCS file to allow others to edit the file, and prompts for comments about the latest version. These comments would normally include information such as the reason for the changes made, the parts of the program that were affected, and the effect the changes will have on other files. Previous versions are retained as deltas or *diff* listings.

SCCS metacharacter expansion

When *get*ting a file without the '−e' or *edit* switch, certain strings in the file are expanded by the *get* command. These strings take the form of

    %x%

and are expanded into useful parameters.

The most commonly used string is the %W% form, which is expanded into the sequence

    @(#)filename version-number

The string @(#) is sufficiently rare that it can be searched for by a *grep* type of command, even in binary programs (but, of course, the standard *grep* cannot be used for binaries). Thus if a line of the form

    static char sccsid[] = `@(#)cat.c 1.2';

is inserted at the top of each module of C program when compiled, it is possible to determine exactly which versions of the various modules have been used to compile the program. Other strings expand into the date of the version, the file name, the release number, and the @(#) field.

12.2.3 More advanced features

Both the forms of the *get* command can also take a version number such as

    get −r1.2 file

or

    sccs edit −r2.6 file

This may have one of two effects; if the version number is lower than the latest one, it will extract that particular version. If however the file is being extracted for editing and the version is greater than the latest version, the latest version of the file is extracted, and when that file is *delta*d (replaced in the SCCS directory) the version number will be the number with which it was extracted. This feature is generally used when a major revision of a program is done. Thus a typical numbering system will be that versions 1.1, 1.2, 1.3 are all the first release; when a major revision is to be made to the program, it is extracted with the '−r2' flag. The new version number will be 2.1, and later versions of the file will now be numbered 2.2 and 2.3.

Other features of *get* are the ability to exclude certain versions when extracting a file

```
get −x1.2 −r1.6 file
# get file version 1.6 but excluding the changes made
# in version 1.2
```

Other features of the *admin* command include the ability to add users to the SCCS file, thus allowing them to edit and delta files. It also allows various operations on the SCCS file, such as the ability to make branches, to stop further editing on a file, to set the maximum release number, and to add a description text to the SCCS file.

Another useful command is *info* or *prt*, which prints out useful data about the SCCS files, such as those things set by *admin*, or the user's comments about *delta*s.

The SCCS system can be made to work with the original Version V7 Unix *make*, but generally various extra lines have to be added to extract files if they are not already present. With the augmented *make* which is supplied as standard with various newer releases of Unix, there are rules built-in to extract files automatically if they do not already exist. In this way most **makefile**s in SCCS systems look very similar to those in non-SCCS systems.

12.3 Awk

Although not a system management command *per se*, discussions with many managers during the planning of this book produced comments on the usefulness of *awk*† as a general tool. The *awk* command is intended for performing operations on files which consist essentially of 'one line = one record' entries, with the fields in the records separated by some character. A typical such file is **/etc/passwd**, with a colon as the field separator. Output from the *ls* commands is again in a suitable format for *awk* analysis, this time with the space character (the default) as field separator.

The essential features of *awk* are an editor- or grep-type syntax for selecting particular records, and an interpretive form of C for operating upon them. The selection expressions can use arithmetic operations as well as character expressions. A common form of simple *awk* program thus takes the form

```
selection expression { instructions }
```

with the possibility of further different selection expressions and corresponding instructions. In addition to the main program, which defines which records are to be acted upon in what way, there is an optional initialisation section at the start, and a summary section at the end. An *awk* program is thus typically of the form

† The name of the command originates from the initials of the three original authors, A V Aho, P J Weinberger and B W Kernighan.

```
BEGIN { initialisation instructions }
selection expression { instructions }
END { summary instructions }
```

The full details of *awk* are to be found in a document under **/usr/doc**, but a few typical simple applications of *awk* will serve to illustrate some of the principles.

12.3.1 Summarising *ls* output

The fields in the output from

```
ls −l
```

are the permissions (field 1), the number of links (field 2), the owner (field 3), the size in bytes (field 4), and various other items. The fields in an *awk* record are referred to in the program as '$1','$2', and so on. An *awk* program to add together the sizes of those files with two or more links can be written

```
$2 >= 2 { total += $4 }
END { print total }
```

where the selection criterion is now that 'field 2 has the value 2 or more', and the action to be taken on these records is 'increment *total* by the value of the fourth field'. All variables are automatically declared and initialised to zero. The summary instruction just prints out the accumulated value of *total*. This program would be called by the command

```
ls −l | awk −f file
```

where the named file contains the above program. The variable '$0' refers to the complete record, and to print the above records as well as summing the sizes of the files, the first line would be replaced by

```
$2 >= 2 { total += $4; print $0 }
```

To print the number of records involved, use

```
$2 >= 2 { total += $4; number ++ }
END { print total, number }
```

Note that the semicolon symbol here is a separator, not the terminator as in C. The last statement does not need a following semicolon.

12.3.2 Analysing /etc/passwd

This example illustrates the definition of a new field separator (by assignment to the variable *FS* in the initialisation section), and the use of arrays. Arrays are not declared, and new elements are created (and initialised to zero) whenever a new suffix is encountered. To find, for example, the number of users in each numeric group (the GID is the fourth field of each line of **/etc/passwd**), an appropriate program would be

```
BEGIN { FS = ":" }
{ num[ $4 ] ++ }
END { for ( i in num ) print i, num[ i ] }
```

The elements are, with this simple program, printed out in the order of first occurrence. The *for* construct shown runs through all suffices of the array, in the order of creation of the elements. The subscripts do not have to be numeric, and can be strings if required; to analyse output from the command

```
ls −l
```

to calculate the total bytes of file (the size of the file is the fourth field) per user (the username is the third field), the program could be

```
{ num[ $3 ] += $4 }
END { for ( i in num ) print i, num[ i ] }
```

where the array subscripts are now the usernames.

12.3.3 Producing the index for this book

The production of this book uses a modified form of the system suggested in Steve Bourne's book. The original index information is in the form of entries

```
<string>:<pageno>
```

for each item, generated by *nroff/troff* macros. These are then sorted using the command

```
sort −u −t: +0f −1 +1n −2
```

to the form where the index strings are alphabetically sorted (with upper- and lower-case folded together) and page numbers for the same string are in numeric order. The data is now ready for adjacent entries with the same first field to be compressed into a single entry with two page numbers, so that the entries

```
passwd:111
passwd:123
```

become the single entry

```
passwd:111,123
```

For formatting reasons, this is produced in the *nroff* form

```
.tl 'passwd''111,123'
```

This can easily by performed by the *awk* script shown in figure 12.2.

```
BEGIN { FS = ":" }
/:/ {
    if( $1 == old ) x = sprintf( "%s, %s", x, $2 );
    else {
        print  old " : " x ;
        x = $2;
    }
    old = $1;
}
END { print old " : " x }
```

Fig. 12.2 A simple *awk* program

Such a solution is much cleaner and quicker than the writing of a complete C program or shell script.

12.4 Process scheduling programs

System managers have a greater need than ordinary users for the ability to run regularly scheduled programs. Typically, certain accounting programs will be run each night during the early hours (or whenever the particular installation is at its quietest), and different accounting may need to be run at weekends. In addition, it may be desirable to set a given program, which needs to be run only once, but is best on a quiet machine, to execute at a given future date and time. The two relevant commands in Unix are *cron*, for regularly scheduled programs, and *at*, for one-off runs.

12.4.1 cron

This command performs regular process scheduling according to a timetable specified in the file **/usr/lib/crontab**. Each line in the file represents one regular event; the space separated fields on each line represent the minutes past the hour (0 to 59), the hour of day (0 to 23), the day of month (1 to 31), the month (1 to 12), and the day of week (Monday = 1, Sunday = 7), and the name of the command to be executed. Fields may be an asterisk (any value), an integer (that particular value), or a series of values or ranges separated by commas, contained within square brackets. Thus an entry

```
30   3    *    *    *    prog
```

will cause the named shell script to be activated at 30 minutes past 3 each day. An entry

```
[0,30]  *  1   *    *    shscr
```

will cause execution on the hour and half hour throughout the first day of each month. An entry

```
30  3   25  12  *    xmas
```

will cause the named file to be executed each Christmas day at 0330 hours. The entries

```
30  3   *   *   1–5  nightly
30  3   *   *   6    weekly
```

cause the command *nightly* to be run each weekday at 0330 hours, and the command *weekly* to be run at each weekend.

The named programs are forked off by the *cron* program, and so are initialised under the username under which *cron* is running; this is usually 'daemon'. Its forked off processes may therefore well need to be SUID for each user, and will need to set up the environment of shell variables and current directory. The *cron* program runs all the time, and after each activity is forked off, computes the time until it next needs to wake, and sets a sleep for that length of time. Thus if the table is altered, and a new event introduced which will occur before the next event scheduled previously, it will be overlooked; *cron* must be woken up (or killed and restarted) to make it note the new entry. To overcome this, some versions of *cron* wake themselves up regularly, and look at the modification time of **crontab** to see whether it should be re-read.

A very standard use of *cron* is to initiate each night, shortly after midnight, the *calendar* command. This searches a central file such as **/etc/calendar**, and individual user files such as **$HOME/calendar** for lines containing today's or tomorrow's date, and sends the user a mail message consisting of that complete line. Thus a file containing the line

```
Jan 23 Get final copy to publisher
```

will cause a message consisting of that line to be received on January 22nd and 23rd. The *calendar* command is a shell script, which can be easily tailored to an individual installation's requirements. It invokes a program **/usr/lib/calendar** to perform the main date calculations, which is clever enough to ignore weekends, and to send messages early if a weekend intervenes.

12.4.2 at

The *at* command is for executing a given command at a given future time, the command being executed just once. A typical call is

```
at 2200 file
```

or

>   at 2200 June 4th file

requesting that the named file be executed as a shell script at 2200 hours (for a.m. and p.m. specification see the manual) either in the first example, today, or in the second, on a named date. If the last parameter is omitted, as in

>   at 2300

the commands to be executed are read from the standard input, the input being terminated by EOF.

The *at* command is more sophisticated than *cron* in many ways. It sets up the environment for the command correctly, setting the directory, the shell variables, and the UID and GID. The commands to be executed are entered in a file in the directory **/usr/spool/at**, and are preceded by commands to set the environment to the same as that when the command was issued. It requires that the command *atrun* be initiated regularly (usually every five minutes, activated by *cron*), which looks at the waiting scripts stored in **/usr/spool/at** to see if any are due for execution.

A security bug in *at* is that the run-time ownership of the program is taken from the ownership of the *at* file in the **/usr/spool/at** directory. To avoid possible breaches of security, the *at* command should be made SUID, with the above directory owned by the same user, and writable only by the owner, in a similar way to the earlier discussion of the *lpr* spooler.

Chapter 13   Some examples of
systems programs

In this chapter a number of programs are outlined. Some correspond to
existing Unix commands, others to possible additional commands. The programs are not the original code, and are in no way complete in all details.
They are intended merely to illustrate the way various typical activities are
handled. They are written for simplicity, not efficiency.

13.1 *init*

The *init* program controls the later stages of the booting procedure, and the
control of the logging-on and off of users when the system goes into multi-
user mode. The detailed purpose of, and functions performed by, *init* are
described in the chapters on booting-up and logging-in. The following program, an outline of *init* code, performs those functions, but includes none of
the extras such as, for example, responding correctly to the various 'kill'
signals.

```
/* declare NTTYS structs, with fields for
    pid, whether active, gettytype, linename */
struct {
    char active; /* 1 if active, 0 if inactive */
    char ttytype; /* a representation of the type of terminal */
    char *linename; /* the name of the line in /dev */
    int pid; /* the pid of the terminal process */
} line[NTTYS];

main()
{
    int i;
    system( "sh" ); /* initial super-user shell, and wait for it to finish */
    system( "/etc/rc" ); /* ready for multi-user, mount file-systems etc */

/* Store the information from the "/etc/ttys" file
    in the array of structs "line" declared above; */
    ... open file /etc/ttys ...
```

```
        for ( i=0; i<NTTYS; i++ )
        {
            ... read one line from /etc/ttys ...
        }
        ... close the file ...
```

```
    /* We need to put a getty on each line mentioned in /etc/ttys
       which starts with a 1 */
        for ( i=0; i<NTTYS; i++ )
            if ( line[i].active ) /* the .active field is 1 if the line is to
                   be active */
                startup( i ); /* see below for details of "startup" */
```

```
    /* Each process now has a getty, wait for deaths signifying a logout */
        for ( ; ; ) /* i.e. for ever */
        {
            p = wait(); /* p gives the number of the process which has died */
            ... lookup p in table of pids to find the number of the line; ...
            ... perform logging out accounting on that line; ...
            startup( i ); /* restart the login on that line */
        }
        ... exit! ...
    }
```

```
    startup( i ) int i;
    /* start up an appropriate getty on the i-th line in /etc/ttys */
    {
        line[i].pid = pid = fork();
        if ( pid>0 ) return; /* parent = init, no further action here */
        if ( pid<0 )
            { error( "Init fork failed" ); /* cannot fork, execute some error routine */
            ... }
```

```
    /* If we get this far, this is the new child of init,
       it must become a getty */
        divert stdin to the terminal line;
        divert stdout to the terminal line;
        divert stderr to the terminal line;
```

```
    /* exec to getty, pass the terminal type as parameter
       except that the parameter should be a null terminated string */
        execl( "getty", "/etc/getty", line[i].type, 0 );
    /* We only pass here if the "exec" failed */
        error ( "Init exec failed" );
    }
```

13.2 *getty*

The function of the example of *getty* given in the next program is to set the
properties of the line to which it is attached using the parameter given to it as

an indication of the terminal type. It then writes the 'Login:' message, and *exec*s to *login* when a reply has been received, with that reply as parameter.

```
#include <sgtty.h>

main( argc, argv) char *argv[];
{
   char message[16];
/* argv[1] gives the name of the terminal type;
   look-up argv[1] in /etc/ttytype to find which type of terminal,
   read all the characteristics into a local structure */

/* call ioctl with the required parameters to set the terminal properties
       */
   ioctl(0,...); /* channel 0 is the terminal;
      ioctl parameters are very system dependent */

/* print the installation heading */
   system( "cat /etc/logmessage" );
   printf( "Login: " );
   ... read chars from keyboard on stream 0 until a newline is encountered,
      store them null-terminated in the array message ... */
   execl( "login", "login", message, 0 );

/* error condition */
   error( "Getty exec failed" );
}
```

13.3 *login*

The detailed operations of *login* are described in an earlier chapter. The example below assumes various sensible names for the fields of the structure declared in the file **/usr/include/passwd.h**, but these would need to be checked in practice.

```
#include <passwd.h>

struct passwd *pwd;

main( .... )
{
/* get entry for this user from the /etc/passwd file */
   pwd = getpwent( argv[1] );
/* if the entry isn't found, we should exit */

/* if there is a password entry, check it */
   if ( *entry.passwd ) /* no entry if first char of string is null */
   {
      ... switch off echo by ioctl or system( "stty −echo" ) ...
      printf( "Type password: " );
      ... read the reply to end-of-line ...
```

```
    ... switch echo back on ...
    ... encrypt the user's reply ...
    ... compare it with the entry in the passwd record ...
    ... exit if they disagree ...
  }

/* print the message of the day */
  system( "cat /etc/motd" ); /* clumsy way to list a file */

/* print notification if you have mail */
  if ( access( "mailfile", 4 ) )
    printf( "You have mail.\n" );

/* set the user and group identifiers from root to their new value */
  setgid( entry.gid ); /* must be first! */
  setuid( entry.uid );

/* change to the user's home directory */
  chdir( entry.home );

/* exec to the required shell, default is /bin/sh */
  if ( *entry.sh )
    exec( entry.sh, "sh", ... ); /* user special */
  else
    exec(  "/bin/sh", "sh", ... ); /* default shell */

/* We shouldn't reach this point */
  error( "Login exec failed" );
}
```

13.4 A menu-driven shell

The shell outlined in the following program offers a simple menu-driven
system offering a very limited set of commands. The user either selects a
new filename, edits the default file, *nroff*s it to the screen, or to a printer, or
logs out. No other facilities are offered.

```
char filename[20], command[50];

while( 1 ) /* for ever */
{
    printf( "Do you want to\n\
a) choose a filename\n\
b) edit the current file\n\
c) view it on the screen\n\
d) print it\n\
e) logout\n\
Type a, b, c, d or e : " );
    ch = getchar();
```

```
    switch( ch )
    {
      case 'a' :
          printf( "File? "); ... read a string to end-of-line ...
          .... store in the array filename ....
          break;

      case 'b' :
          ... Use strcat to generate the string "ed filename"
            in the array command ...
          system( command );
          break;

      case 'c' :
          ... generate the string "nroff filename" in command ...
          system( command );
          break;

      case 'd' :
          ... generate the string "nroff filename | lpr" ....
          system( command );
          break;

      case 'e' :
          printf( "Finishing" );
          exit( 0 );

      default:
          printf( "Reply not understood %c\n", ch );
    }
}
```

It is intended only to illustrate that a shell for a particular use of the machine can be a very straightforward program.

13.5 cat

The simple version of the *cat* command in the next program illustrates the Unix convention in which a command reads from standard input if there are no parameters, and reads all its parameters otherwise.

```
#include <stdio.h>

int   fd, i;
char buffer[BUFSIZ]; /* the standard i/o buffer size */

process( fd ) integer fd; { process input from file descriptor fd }
{
    while ( ( n = read( fd, buffer, BUFSIZ ) ) > 0 )
      write( 1, buffer, n );
}
```

```
main( argc, argv ) int argc; char *argv[];
{
   if ( argc>1 ) /* read named parameters */
   {
      for ( i=1; i<argc; i++ ) /* for each argument */
      {
         fd = open( argv[i], 0 );
         if ( fd < 0 ) /* file open failed */

         {
            fprintf( stderr, "Can't open %s\n", argv[i] );
            exit( 1 ); { fail immediately }
         }
         /* file opened successfully, read it */
         process( fd );
         close( fd );
         }
      }
   }
/* if argc == 1, there are no parameters, read standard input */
   else
      process( 0 );
   exit( 0 );
}
```

Using pointers, the first part of the main program becomes as follows.

```
argc--; argv++;
if ( argc ) /* if there are parameters */
{
   while ( argc-- )
   {
      fd = open( *argv++, 0 );
      ...
   }
}
else ... /* no parameters */
```

13.6 *lpr* and *lpd*

A general output spooling system consists of two independent programs. One program (such as *lpr*) is called by the user as in

```
lpr file1 file2
```

or

```
grep "abcd" file1 file2 | sort | pr | lpr
```

and stores the output (the spooler's input) in a temporary file somewhere. The second program (such as *lpd*) independently lists to the printer output which earlier calls of *lpr* have stored, and removes the temporary files as soon as they are printed. If there are no further temporary files requiring printing, the program exits.

The second program must somehow be woken up if it has died, and a new temporary file becomes available from *lpr* ready for listing. To accomplish this, the first program, when it finishes (when the input from the user is complete) can look to see if the second program is active and, if not, initiate it. Alternatively, the first program can always initiate the second, and it is now the second program that checks to see whether another invocation of itself is active; if so, it exits immediately. Other considerations are mentioned in the chapter on file-systems, in relation to the use of 'suid' facilities.

A typical *lpr* program checks to see whether parameters have been given; if so, it has to copy the files given as parameters to the spool area, if not, it reads from its standard input. The temporary storage area for the spooler is typically the directory **/usr/spool/lpd**. If the input is from files named as parameters, these can be copied directly to the spool area. If there are no parameters, it reads input from its standard input to a temporary file, but the file in which this is stored must not be made available until the program supplying the input finishes (since there is no knowing how long the program will take to complete). The temporary file in this case must be distinguished from temporary files available to the spooling printer, so must either start with a different letter, or be a different directory, such as **/usr/spool/lpd/tmp**; on termination of standard input (the receipt of end-of-file), the file is transferred to **/usr/spool/lpd**. A crude version written as a Bourne shell script might be as follows.

```
dir=/usr/spool/lpd

if test -z "$1"
then # if no parameters, read standard input
    cat > $dir/tmp/lpr$$ # from standard input, wait for EOF
    mv $dir/tmp/lpr$$ $dir # when finished, move the file
else # parameters given, copy them all to spool area
    for i
    do
       echo ... newpage, header etc ... >> $dir/lpr$$
       cat $i >> $dir/lpr$$
    done
fi

lpd & # initiate the second program
exit 1
```

The second *lpd*-type of process has to check for locks, then *cat* and *rm* each file in turn, as sketched below.

```
LOCK="/tmp/lpdlock" # name of lock-file
cd /usr/spool/lpd
umask 777 /* to ensure that the lock file has no permissions */

if lock-file already exists
then exit 0
fi

> $LOCK /* create the lock-file with access mode 0;
      critical section problems occur here */

if ls > /dev/null # if files exist
then
    for i in *
    do
      echo ... form feed, heading ... > /dev/lp
      cat $i > /dev/lp; rm $i
    done
    rm $LOCK
    lpd & # more files may have appeared whilst these were being printed
else
    rm $LOCK
fi

exit 0
```

13.7 *chown*

The code in the next program sketches a version of the *chown* command which changes both the owner and group of named files to those of the user named as the first argument, as in

```
chown user file1 file2 file3
```

It differs from the traditional *chown* command in setting both the UID and GID of the named files, and in being executable by any user. (Note that the *chown* system call, as opposed to the command, does set both UID and GID.) To prevent file ownership being changed at random, it asks for the password of any user involved (the new owner of the files, and the previous owners of the files) if these are different from the user issuing the command. It does not, as given here, look at ownership of the directories in which the files reside; in practice, that would have to be considered also. The option flag '−g' asks that the group owner of the file be not changed. The command must be root-owned with SUID facilities to enable it to execute the system calls to *chown*.

```
#include <stdio.h>
#include <ctype.h>
#include <sys/types.h>
```

```
#include <sys/stat.h>
#include <filepwd.h>

struct  passwd  *usrpwd, *filepwd, *getpwnam();
struct  stat       stbuf;
int   newuid, usruid, okuid = −1;
int   status;
char    *namep;
int   gflag = 0, gid;

main( argc, argv ) char *argv[];
{
    register c;

    while ( argv[1][0] == '−' ) /* crude flags check */
    {
      if ( argv[1][1]=='g' )
          gflag++; /* don't set group */s
      else
          printf( "Flag not recognised %c\n", argv[1][1] );
      argc−−; argv++;
    }

    if ( argc < 3 )
    {
      printf( "Usage: chown newuid file ..." );
      exit( 4 );
    }

    usruid = getuid(); /* logged in users's UID */
    if ( isnumber( argv[1] ) )
    {
      newuid = atoi( argv[1] ); /* given numeric UID */
      if( ( filepwd=getpwuid( newuid ) ) == NULL ) /* get passwd entry */
      {
          printf( "Unknown uid: %d", argv[1] );
          exit( 4 );
      }
    }

    else if( ( filepwd=getpwnam( argv[1] ) ) == NULL ) /* given login name */
    {
      printf( "Unknown user: %s\n", argv[1] );
      exit( 4 );
    }

    else
      newuid = filepwd−>pw_uid; /* uid of new file owner */
/* check new owner isn't self, and self isn't root */
    if ( usruid && newuid!=usruid )
      checkpasswd( "New owner", newuid );
```

```
    for( c=2; c<argc; c++ )
    {
      stat( argv[c], &stbuf );
      if ( usruid && stbuf.st_uid!=usruid )
        checkpasswd( "Old owner", stbuf.st_uid );
      gid = ( gflag ? filepwd->pw_gid : stbuf.st_gid );
      if( chown( argv[c], newuid, gid ) < 0 )
      {
        printf( "Error can't chown\n" );
        status = 1;
      }
    }
    exit( status );
}
checkpasswd( s, uid ) char *s;
{
    if ( okuid==uid ) return; /* uid acceptable */
    usrpwd = getpwuid( uid );
    if (*usrpwd->pw_passwd)
    {
      printf( "%s is %s; ", s, usrpwd->pw_name );
      namep = crypt( getpass( "Password: "), usrpwd->pw_passwd );
      if (strcmp( namep, usrpwd->pw_passwd ) )
      {
        printf( "No permission!\n" );
        exit ( 4 );
      }
    }
    okuid = uid;
}
isnumber( s ) char *s;
{
    char c;
    while( c = *s++ )
      if( ! isdigit( c ) )
        return 0;
    return 1;
}
```

13.8 A possible *help* command

The shell script that follows outlines a possible *help* command. The command takes a word from the user, and suggests commands to which the user might look for further information. It does this by searching files based on the permuted index of the Unix Programmers Manual, and is similar to the BSD *apropos* command.

```
tocdir=/usr/man/man0

if test "$1"
then answer=$1
else
echo −n 'To find the manual entries relevant to a given word,
type the first few letters of the word:
(if you are interested in "remove", "removing", "removed" etc
type the letters "remov", for example ... but omit the quotes!)
Then for more information, execute the "man" command as indicated.
.*> '
read answer
echo This is a list of the manual entries containing words starting ."$answer\".
fi

while test $answer
do
    cd $tocdir
    ( cat .*<< ++++
.ll 79
.lt 79
.de xx
.br
.\\\\$1 : \\\\\$2
.br
.tl '''try "man \\\\\$3 \\\\\$1"'
..
++++
    for i in toc*
    do
      grep −y "[ˆa−z]$answer" $i
    done ) ˆ nroff ˆ sed "/ˆ$/d"

    if test "$1"
    then
      shift; answer=$1
    else
      echo −n "Want to try another keyword?"
      read answer

      case $answer
      in
        [nN]*) echo "Bye!"; exit;;
        *) ;;
      esac

      echo −n "What is the keyword?"
      read answer
    fi

done
```

The commands necessary to generate the files from which it works, **toc1** for section 1 of the manual, **toc2** for section2, and so on, are below.

```
tmp1=/tmp/tmp.1
tmp2=/tmp/tmp.2
tocdir=/usr/man/man0

for i in 1 2 3 4 5 6 7
do
    cd /usr/man/man$i
    ls > $tmp1

    /bin/ed − $tmp1 << ++++
      g/^\$/d
      g/^.\$/d
      g/^..\$/d
      g/intro.2/d
      1,\$s/.*/e &\\
      \/SH *NAME\/+1p/
      w
      q
++++

    /bin/ed − < $tmp1 > $tmp2
    echo "1,\$s/ *\\\\\\\\\\− */("$i") /" > $tmp1

    if [ $i = "2" ]
    then
      echo 0a >> $tmp1
      echo "intro(2) introduction to system calls" >> $tmp1
      echo . >> $tmp1
    fi

    echo w $tocdir/tocx$i >> $tmp1
    echo q >> $tmp1
    /bin/ed − $tmp2 < $tmp1
    rm $tmp1 $tmp2
    cd $tocdir
    sort −u tocx$i > toc$i
    rm tocx$i

    /bin/ed − toc$i << ++++
    1,\$s/(.) /" "/
    1,\$s/.*/.xx "&"/
    w
    q
++++

done
```

Appendix 1   A summary of the Bourne shell features

As noted in one of the introductory documents to Unix, the shell itself is quite a powerful programming language, although most users do not take full advantage of all its capabilities. It must be emphasised that this appendix is just a summary of some of the less straightforward aspects of the shell, and is geared to uses such as those of the system administrator.

A1.1 Control flow

While the basic shell commands are well known to most users, not many users make full use of the control-flow features during ordinary use at the terminal.

A1.1.1 for loops
The format is

```
for <variable> in <value list>
do
        <statements>
done
```

in which the variable is referred to with a '$' sign as usual in the statements. This construct takes a variable given as the first argument and repeats the given statements with that variable set in turn to each of the values given in the list. The value list can be explicit, or generated from filenames using pattern matching, or generated as the result of a command. Thus the command

```
for i in 'cat filelist'
do
        echo File $i; nroff $i; ....
done
```

allows commands to be executed for each file named in the file **filelist**.

If the list is missing as in

```
for i
```

then the variable is set to each of the arguments to the shell script $1, $2 ... in turn.

As another example, to print all files in the current directory which contain the string 'error', use

```
for i in * # the * is interpreted as all filenames in the current directory
do
      if grep −s 'error' $i
      then pr $i
      fi
done
```

In the Bourne shell, the output from a *for* loop can be redirected, as in

```
(cat introduction;
      for i in chapter*
      do
            cat format $i
      done ) | nroff −ms | lpr
```

which *nroff*s the **introduction** and **chapter*** files, separated by copies of the **format** file.

A1.1.2 case statements
The format is

```
case <chooser> in
string1 ) action1 ;;
string2 ) action2 ;;
esac
```

The *case* construct forms a multiway test, similar to the C switch. It checks the value of a 'chooser' (usually a shell variable) against various given options, where the matching is done using shell-type constructs for literals or patterns. As an example, to recognise option flags '−s' and '−t', use

```
case $1 in
−s ) sflag=yes ; shift;;
−t ) tflag=yes ; shift;;
−* ) echo "Flag not recognised \"$1\"" ; shift ;;
 * ) break;;
esac
```

Pattern strings are matched to the chooser as in the *ed* command, and strictly in order. Thus '−[ab]' matches '−a' or '−b', while '*' matches anything and must never occur except as the last pattern. The ';;' ends the actions to be taken for a given pattern which succeeded; several possible patterns separated by '|' can be given and all the shell metacharacters can also be used. The terminating *esac* (the word 'case' backwards) closes the *case* as in Algol68.

A1.1.3 if statements
The format is

```
if <statements>
then <statements>
else <statements>
fi
```

The statements following the *if* are executed, and the returned status of the last one of these is used to decide whether to execute the statements following the *then* (if the status was zero) or the *else* otherwise. Control then proceeds following the *fi*. Most commands return a status of some sort; *ls* can be tested to see if there are any files in a directory, and *grep* to see whether the given string appears in the text. The *grep* command has an additional flag '−s' so that it returns a status, but suppresses the actual output; we can then have a command such as

```
for i in chapter*
do
    if grep −s interesting $i
    then nroff $i
    else echo Chapter $i doesnt contain the word
    fi
done
```

to search for a given string in a number of files, and to act on only those files containing the string. The *test* command is often used in conjunction with *if*, and can be used to test for many conditions relating to string, variable values and file properties. To check whether a user has write access to the file **/etc/passwd**, for example, use

```
if test −w /etc/passwd
then ...
```

This facility is often available in a different form, the condition being enclosed in square brackets, as in

```
if [ −w /etc/passwd ]
then ..
```

A1.1.4 while loops

This is the most common looping command, and has the format

```
while <statements>
do
      <statements>
done
```

The first statements are executed, and the status of the last of them is used to decide whether to continue with the loop or not. Often used with *while* is the : command which has no effect, but which always returns true. To loop for ever, use

```
while
do
    who
    sleep 60
done
```

The colon can also be used to introduce a comment, since its parameters are ignored.

A1.1.5 The '.' command

This command (a single full stop or period character) will read in and execute a shell script file without forking, whereas the *sh* command forks a new shell. The '.' command thus allows shell scripts to alter the user's environment by returning results in shell variables, for example, or by changing the working directory of the current shell. This is how the *.profile* or *.login* file is read in at the initiation of the shell.

A1.1.6 Breaking out of loops

The *break* command breaks out of an enclosing loop, and if a number is given as parameter, it will then break out of that many enclosing loops. The *continue* command resumes processing at the start of the next iteration of an enclosing loop. To read and process all flag arguments to a shell script, i.e. all those arguments starting with a '−' until a real argument is found, a possible outline would be

```
while :
do
   case $1 in
      −a ) .... do this ....; shift;;
      −b ) .... do this ....; shift;;
      −* ) echo Unrecognised flag \"$1\"; shift;;
      * ) break;
   esac
done
```

A1.2 Special commands

The following commands are special in that, for some reason, they must be
executed within the shell, rather than by forking a child process.

cd
Although it is possible to write a binary program to do this, it will not achieve
the desired effect, since only the child will change directory. The parent (the
shell) would remain in its original directory. The command *cd* is therefore
detected as a special, and is executed within the shell itself. Early shells used
chdir for this function.

eval
This function takes arguments, works out any parameter substitution, and
then executes the resulting command. It will cope with several layers of
nested substitution.

exec
The command is given in the form

        exec command

and has the effect of executing the named command without invoking a fork.
The command named overlays the current shell, which cannot then return.
This is useful mainly for renaming commands. Suppose that it is desired to
rename the standard *ls* command for a particular user with the name *dir*. To
do this, create a executable file named **dir** containing the line

        exec ls $*

The object is now achieved, at the cost of one process rather than two
separate ones.

exit
This causes exit from a non-interactive shell. If a numeric parameter is
given, then that will be the exit status of the command.

export
The default shell as set up by the system for a user has a number of initialised
shell variables, such as HOME, PATH and PS1, whose values can be used by
calling $HOME, $PATH and $PS1. It may be desirable to alter these values,
or create and initialise additional variables, and for any of these variable
names and values to be automatically exported to any forked shells. The call

        export PATH

ensures that the PATH variable becomes available to any child process. The *export* command is called with the names of those variables which it is wished to export.

A call of *export* with no parameters displays the names of the variables which are currently marked for export.

login and newgrp

These commands are both executed directly by the shell, and cause the current shell to be overlaid by a new shell. The new shell has a new UID and GID following a *login* command, and just a new GID (with the original UID) following a *newgrp* command. Both command files must, of course, be SUID and root-owned, in order to have the privilege necessary to change the UID and/or the GID.

read

If this command is executed with one parameter, the parameter is assumed to be the name of a shell variable, and the command reads a line of text from standard input into that variable. If two parameters are given, the first word of the input (that is to say, input upto the first space or tab character) is put into the first variable and the rest of the line into the second. With n parameters, the first '$n-1$' words are put into the first '$n-1$' parameters, and the remainder of the line into the last variable. The command returns failure exit status on encountering EOF. As an example, to list the sizes of the files in the current directory, the command could be

```
ls −l | while read perms links user size junk
do
echo $size
done
```

readonly

This command sets a given shell variable to be 'readonly', i.e. ensures that its value cannot be changed at a later time. If no parameter is given, it will print out the names of all 'readonly' variables.

set

This command can be used to set the shell's own flags as in

```
set −v
```

to set the shell into verbose mode, or it can be used to set the shell parameter variables, as in

```
set hello world how are you
```

which would give the values

$1=hello $2=world $3=how $4=are $5=you

Without arguments it lists the current values of all variables.

shift
This command shifts up all the positional parameters one place, so that $2 becomes $1, $3 becomes $2, and so on. This is useful, for example, when taking account of flags in a command, as in

```
case $1 in
    −s) sflag=true; shift;;
    −t) tflag=true; shift;;
    −*) echo unknown flag $1;;
esac
```

which will leave the value of '$1' as the first non-flag parameter.

times
This command prints out the values of the accumulated user and system times for processes run so far in this shell.

trap
This command enables the trapping of incoming signals in a similar way to the *signal* call in C. The first parameter given is the command to be obeyed when any of the signals given by the following numeric parameters are received. The first parameter is null if the signal is to be turned off. Signals have their usual numeric values, with 0 for logout, 2 for interrupts, and so on. Since the signal received on logging out is 0, the execution of

```
trap .logout 0
```

early on during a logged-on session will cause the file **.logout** to be executed on logging out.† This command is often inserted in the **.profile** file under the Bourne shell, and can be combined with a **.logout** file to produce any required actions on logging out. The command

```
trap "" 1 2 3
```

has the effect of turning off keyboard interrupts.

Another illustration of the *trap* command relates to the use of the **.profile** file. If the following lines are included in the **.profile** file,

```
if test −r $HOME/.last
then cd `cat $HOME/.last`; echo working directory `pwd`
```

† The file name will be relative to the working directory at the time of logging-out. It would normally be specified as **$HOME/.logout**, for example.

```
fi
    trap "pwd > $HOME/.last" 0
```

then the current working directory at the time of logging out will be saved in the file **$HOME/.last**, and the next *login* will reset to the same directory.

umask

This command is again used frequently in **.profile** and **.login** files. It has the effect of prohibiting specified protection bits whenever files are created. A common value of the parameter is 002, which has the effect of prohibiting the 'public write' permission bit on all files subsequently created. Another possible setting is 077 for paranoids who require no access by anyone else to their files, and 222 to prevent any access to files being created. (See chapter 7 for comments on the value 222.)

wait

If a numeric parameter is given, which is the PID of a child process of the shell, this command waits for the given process to end. If no parameter is given, it waits for all children of the shell to finish. This enables a command to be started in the background with the & facility, and after various other actions, the shell can wait for it to complete before continuing.

A1.3 Command separators

The standard way of typing several commands on a line is to separate them by semicolons; the semicolon causes the actions to the left to be completed before the actions to the right are initiated.

Following a single command by an & will run the program 'forked off' or 'in the background', in which case the shell does not wait for it to finish before it prompts for more input. Using the symbol & as a separator causes all but the last command to be forked off, as in

```
comm1 & comm2 & comm3
```

The symbol && has a special significance in the Bourne shell. Typing a command such as

```
cc file.c && a.out
```

compiles the C program, and then if the compilation was successful, executes the second command (in this case, executes the compiled program). The command to the right of the && is executed only if the command to the left completes and delivers the result 'true'. Similarly the command

```
cc file.c || lint file.c
```

will execute the compilation first, but in this case will only continue to the second command if the first fails. In this example, the program source is fed to *lint* if the compilation fails, to obtain more diagnostics.

Command grouping with parentheses has already been mentioned; superficially parentheses cause grouping more or less according to the rules of algebra, but with some complications. In this way many processes can put output to one file or program, as in

```
(pr file.c; cat README; cd ..; cat hello) | lpr
```

It should be noted that a new shell is invoked for each set of parentheses, and in the above example, the *cd* command within the parentheses will have no effect on the initiating shell.

A1.4 Shell variables

Variables can exist and have values in a shell just as in a program. Shell variables all take string values, and their values are obtained by prefixing their name with a $ symbol. Their values are set in the Bourne shell by typing a command such as

```
variable=value
```

where there are no space characters adjoining the '=' symbol. The shell and the login command generally define several standard variables, which already exist on entry to the shell. Common ones are

```
HOME    your login directory
USER    your login name
PATH    your default search path
PS1     your primary prompt
PS2     your secondary prompt
MAIL    your mail directory
TERM    your terminal type
```

Other variables which may be set by the system or the user include SHELL, which defines the user's default shell, which is then the program called on shell escapes using '!' in editors and *write*, for example, and EDITOR, which defines the user's default editor, to be called whenever editing facilities are required, such as within a mail system. The latter may look for further variables to determine the user's particular profile for the editor.

These variables and their values may well differ considerably from system to system.

A1.5 Input/output redirection

The shell's capability to redirect I/O is one of its greatest features; with this feature, anything that can appear on the screen can either be captured in a file or sent as input to a further program.

The standard symbols $<$, $>$ and | are familiar to most people using Unix. However these are only special cases of more general commands. The symbols $<$ and $>$ can be made to work on any file descriptor, not just on the standard input and output. By default they work on file descriptors number 0 (the standard input $<$) and 1 (the standard output $>$). However, file descriptor 2 is intended for error messages, which normally are not redirected, so that they still appear on the terminal, to inform the user of errors in forked-off processes. This file descriptor also can be redirected, using the combined symbol $2>$, where the redirection symbol is immediately preceded by the file descriptor number. It is simple therefore to catch the standard output in one file and the error messages in another, using

```
make file > make.out 2> make.errors
```

Two file descriptors can be combined by redirecting one of them onto the other, as in

```
make file 2>&1 > make.out
```

which combines file descriptors 1 and 2 onto file descriptor 1, and redirects that output into a file. To report error messages in the shell, use

```
echo "Error in ...." 1>&2
```

to divert the standard output of *echo* onto the error file descriptor.

Output should normally be unchanged if it is redirected. However, some commands (including modern versions of *ls*) try to be clever, and produce multi-column output when working to a terminal, and single column output otherwise. Such commands make the testing of shell scripts more difficult.

Users writing shell scripts should be familiar with the use of '$<<$' to take input from the shell script file itself, as in

```
ed $i << ++
g/old/s//new/gp
w
q
++
```

to edit a chosen file using specific editing commands.

Appendix 2   Summary of the C shell features

The C shell is a development of the Version 6 shell, originally developed by Bill Joy at the University of California, Berkeley, with the intention of providing:

- A C-like syntax for shell programs.
- A more intelligent command interpreter, with more powerful in-line editing and full history substitutions.
- A better control over processes. This part was added by Jim Kulp at IIASA, Vienna, and required kernel modifications to provide extra signals. It is unfortunately not included in what are called C shell implementations on several of the small machine Unix systems which the author has used.
- A more efficient command accessing mechanism. The contents of all the directories in the command search path are used to create a hash index when the shell starts up; accessing individual commands is thereafter much faster.

The C shell accepts most of the normal syntax of the shell, so there are no fundamental differences when using the basic commands. The usual pipe and input/output redirection symbols retain their meaning, but the flow control structures are different.

A2.1 Simple Bourne – C equivalents

The following list gives some Bourne shell constructions and with the equivalent C shell commands.

BOURNE SHELL	C SHELL
for name in list	foreach name list
case word in	switch (word)
pattern) ... ;;	case pattern ... breaksw
esac	endsw
if expr then ... fi	if (expr) ...
if expr	if (expr)

then ...	then ...
elif ...	elseif (expr)
then ...	then ...
else ...	else ...
fi	endif
while expr	while (expr)
. file	source file
break [n]	break [break]
continue	continue
exit [expr]	exit [(expr)]
export	setenv
read	
readonly	
times	time
trap	onintr

A2.2 Some C shell commands

Some of the features unique to the C shell include the following:

alias   if string 'a' is aliased to string 'b', every occurrence of the string 'a' in a command is replaced by the string 'b'; one can thus alias 'ed' to 'vi', 'dir' to 'ls −l', and so on.

alloc   gives statistics on the amount of dynamic core currently being used.

bg   will put the current, or a specified process into the background.

default   provides an explicit C-like default in shell switches.

dirs   prints out the directory stack.

fg   will bring the current or designated process back into the foreground.

hashstat   tells you how well the internal hash table is doing at locating commands.

history   prints out your last *n* commands.

jobs   will list your active jobs. The whole handling of forked-off processes is much more user-oriented in the C shell.

kill   is also built into the C shell and can kill a specific process by reference to when it was started.

limit   sets a limit on the resources a command can use, i.e. amount of CPU-time, largest file it can create, the greatest core it can dump etc.

notify   will cause the user to be notified of the termination of asynchronous (forked-off) processes.

popd
pushd } help maintain the directory stack.

rehash	will reform the internal hash table.
repeat count command	repeats the specified command count times.
stop	will stop a given process which is currently executing in the background.
unalias	will get rid of specified aliased commands.
unhash	will refrain from using the hash table search for commands.
unlimit	will cancel specified limits.
unset	is the inverse of set.

A2.3 C shell variables

C shell variables are assigned values by the *set* command as in

    set a=hello

The environment variables generally have names in lower case, where those in the Bourne shell are in upper case. There are also certain variables set up distinct from those in the Bourne shell, including the following:

argv	is equivalent to $1, $2 etc in B-shell scripts, used as $argv[1], $argv[2] etc.
cdpath	gives a set of directories to try when doing a cd, i.e.

    cd fred

will try fred in the local directory first, then fred in the directories in cdpath.

cwd	is set to the current working directory.
echo	is set when the $-x$ flag is set.
histchars	is set to a string of characters that are used in history substitutions.
history	is set to the number of commands you wish to keep.
home	is equivalent to HOME.
ignoreeof	is set if the shell is to ignore end of file characters, thus preventing accidental logouts.
mail	is similar to MAIL.
noclobber	is set if the shell is to check if files exist before writing on them.
nonomatch	is set if the shell is to complain when metacharacter expansions fail to find a match.
notify	is set by notify above.
path	is equivalent to PATH.
prompt	is equivalent to PS1.
shell	is the file in which the shell exists.
status	is the returned status of the last command.
time	if set will print out timing statistics about processes.
verbose	is set by the $-v$ option to C shell.

A2.4 Command editing

The C shell allows various forms of command line editing. The easiest one to use is the history substitution.

The C shell maintains a history of your most recently typed commands, and these are repeatable. The easiest form is

!!

which just repeats the last command. However something like

!11

or

!−2

will repeat your eleventh command or your second last command, respectively. Also possible are non-ambiguous stems to historic commands, such as

!wri

which will pick out some previous command such as

write ef

As well as this it is possible to pick certain parts out of previous commands such as:

!−2:0−4

which will pick out words up to the fourth of the second last command.
Also possible are:

removal of trailing pathname components
removal of . suffices
removal of all but . suffices
substitution as in ed
removal of leading pathname components
global changes

A2.5 Process control

This part of the C shell allows processes to be started and stopped, to be attached, disconnected, and reattached to the terminal.

This is achieved through having an extra set of signals, so involves changes to the kernel. With these it is possible to send a suspend signal to a process which will then sit around waiting to be restarted, or to move running commands between background and foreground. This means that a process can be started, then via a signal told to stop and then restarted in the background. If later you wish to bring it into the foreground, to run it interactively, you can do so. The C shell notifies you when background processes terminate or when new mail arrives, before the next command prompt.

Appendix 3 Summary of commands

All commands mentioned in the text are summarised below. Ordinary user commands are either ignored or are summarised very briefly; commands related to management functions have a more full description. Commands described more fully elsewhere in the book refer the reader to the appropriate chapter. For full details of any command, see the standard Unix manual.

ac
This command is for summarising login/logout accounting, using information recorded in the file **/usr/adm/wtmp** by the login process; see the chapter on logging in and out for details of **wtmp**, and the chapter on performance for details of the *ac* command.

adb
The name stands for 'Another DeBugger', following the original *db* (debugger) and then *cdb* (C debugger) on Version 6, to say nothing of *sdb* (more recent) and *od* (octal debugger). The command is intended to assist in program debugging by enabling the core image of a program to be inspected in conjunction with its relocation tables. A core image is usually dumped to a file named **core** when a program receives certain signals. The specific signals causing core dumps are listed in the on-line manual entry for the *signal* system call. The *adb* command assumes by default a core image of the program in a file **core**, and an executable program in a file named **a.out**. Other names can be specified for both of these files if required. The **a.out** file must still contain the relocation tables of identifiers and addresses, i.e. it must not have been stripped (by the *strip* command or the '−s' flag to the compiler or loader).

The *adb* command allows many complex operations to be performed by those familiar with the binary layout of executable programs, such as printing out the values of variables, the state of the stack, or interpreting program code as assembler instructions. The details of the format of executable programs and machine instructions will vary between systems; some details will be found in the 'a.out' entry in section 5 of the manual.

However, the most frequent use is to find the stack history of a C program which has failed, to give the point in the program at which the error occurred, and the values of active variables. To give this information, after *adb* has been called, the command to *adb* is

      $C

which gives a list of outstanding subroutine calls, with parameter values in octal, and with selected values of variables local to those subroutines. An additional command

      $r

to *adb* prints the register values, very machine dependent, and of interest to few. To leave *adb* when you have obtained enough information, type 'EOF' (end-of-file, usually 'control-d').

The more recent command *sdb* is intended to be more helpful to ordinary mortals, and used in conjunction with C programs gives line numbers, variable values, and allows the program to be executed one instruction at a time.

ar

The command *ar* is for maintaining archive and library files. To create a new archive file or library from a number of '.o' files in the current directory, type

      ar r libname *.o

where **libname** is the name of the library file. For fuller details, see the section on libraries in chapter 3.

The archiver can also be used to combine a number of small files into one larger one, where the files are not necessarily object code. Typically it may be easier to send information which consists of a large number of small files to another site by first combining them into a single file with the archiver, and splitting them up again into separate files at the receiving end.

at

A command for the scheduling of one-off processes. It uses the directory **/usr/spool/at** to store a file for each waiting process. A program *atrun* is started every 5 minutes by *cron* to see if any processes now need to be started. See the chapter on major commands for details.

awk

The *awk* language gives a very convenient way of obtaining information from 'one-line = one-record' files or output, such as the file **/etc/passwd** or output from

      ls −l

It essentially allows lines to be chosen or ignored by means of tests on the whole line, or on individual fields within the line; it then allows a C-like language to pick up information from fields within each chosen line, process them as required, and print a summary at the end. See the chapter on major commands for details.

basename
This command is useful in writing system shell scripts. The call

```
basename filename suffix
```

returns the part of the filename obtained by ignoring any directory names up to and including any last of any '/' symbols in the name, and stripping off the given suffix from the name. Thus to get from a filename ending '.c' to one ending '.o', use

```
oname=`basename $file .c`.o
```

Any leading directory names in the filename will be deleted, ensuring that the result is a local name.

calendar
This is a crude but useful start to a diary system. The basic *calendar* command looks through a file containing information where each line includes a date and a message, selects those lines containing today's or tomorrow's date in American form (month followed by day-of-month), and extracts that line. Normally a central file **/usr/lib/calendar** is used to provide information for the message-of-the-day, and per-user files such as **$HOME/calendar** are used (perhaps via a mail system) to send messages to individual users. The command */bin/calendar* is a shell script which calls a program in **/usr/bin/calendar** to produce an edit capable of selecting today's and tomorrow's dates, and the */bin/calendar* shell script passes the information to an appropriate message system. The daily run of this program is normally initiated by *cron* before users login in the morning.

cb
The command *cb* is for the 'beautification' of C programs. The call

```
cb < prog.c > new.c
```

produces a new version of the program in **prog.c**, and puts the result in **new.c**. The chosen format may not be liked by some; everyone has their own ideas on how programs should be laid out. However, the command does give a way of producing programs formatted to a single standard, which is useful for an installation manager. For more individualised formats, a post-processor for *cb* output can be easily be written to transfer it to variant formats, since *cb* has produced a known style. The *cb* command is particularly bad at handling long comments.

cc

This command invokes the various passes of the C compiler. Much of the compiler is rewritten in versions for different processors, and although some features may be irrelevant on some processors (such as the need for separate instruction and data space) most of the following flags should be effective on all systems. It is however known that a number of the non-Bell compilers are incomplete in a number of ways.

Flags which should be available include:

$-s$	remove relocation bits (a loader flag).
$-l<letters>$	search named library (a loader flag).
$-Ddef$	equivalent to '#define def' for use with '#ifdef' statements to the preprocessor.
$-Dname=val$	equivalent to '#define name val' in the preprocessor.
$-Uname$	to 'undefine' the name.
$-I<directory>$	specifies the directory in which '#include' files are to be found.
$-o$	store the loadable program in the file whose name is given by the next parameter; good compilers default to the name of the program source file without the '.c' suffix.
$-O$	optimise (a mythical flag on many non-Bell compilers).
$-p$	profiling: allow run-time profiling of the program's execution, an essential to quality program debugging.
$-S$	produce an assembler listing in a file with '.s' suffix.
$-P$	run only the pre-processor stage, leave the output in a '.i' file. This comes as a '$-E$' option on some modern compilers.

cd

Change current working directory. This is not an ordinary command, since it has to be performed within the shell. It used to be called 'chdir' (as the C system call still is), and is still available also under that name on most shells.

chgrp

Change the group ownership of a file or list of files; 'su' only. The format is either

        chgrp <group number> files

or

        chgrp <group name> files

If the group is given as a name rather than a number, its number is looked up in the **/etc/group** file. This command is normally used in conjunction with *chown* below.

chmod

Change the access modes to a file; the format is either

>   chmod <octal-mode> files

or

>   chmod <ugo><+-><rwx> files

The flag to set the SUID bit (see the chapter on files) is

>   chmod u+s <files>

and to add the SGID bit is

>   chmod g+s files

For the sticky bit (see the chapter on performance), use

>   chmod +t files

chown

The command to change the user ownership of a file or files; it can be executed only in 'su' on most systems. It can be given in either of the forms

>   chown <login name> files

or

>   chown <numeric uid> files

It does not change to group ownership to the group of the named user, and should normally be used in conjunction with *chgrp*. Better versions, instead of requiring the user to be super-user, require that the user know the passwords of the present owner of the file, of the new owner, and of the owner of the parent directory. If the logged-in user is either of these, then that password need not be requested.

clri

To clear the information in an 'inode' in an emergency. This command is **very** dangerous; it can, of course, be executed only by a user with write access to the raw disc device. The device must be quiescent, unmounted if possible. After use, the command *fsck* must be used to tidy up the free space list on the disc.

cmp

The command compares two files, and reports whether they are identical. For text files, it is not as useful as *diff*, q.v. For comparing binaries, *diff* cannot be used, so *cmp* is essential.

comm

Print the lines common to two files, or the lines occurring in one file and not another, or vice-versa. Both files must be sorted. This command is useful in, for example, commands such as *spell* to determine words used which do not occur in the standard dictionary. In the production of the index for this book, the output for the indices (which are computer generated) is fed through a command

        ... | comm −23 − ignore-list | ...

where the file **ignore-list** contains a list of the entries which the system generates, but which are not required, the parameter '−23' requests that words in the second and third columns of the full output are to be omitted (leaving only the first column, the words occurring only in the first file) and the second parameter, '−', indicates that the first input stream comes from standard input.

cpio

This is another command for combining a number of files into a single output stream, perhaps comparable with *tar* in some respects. The command

        cpio −o

takes the names of the files to be combined from its standard input, and produces the combined output on its standard output. This can be put, for example, to a file, or a magnetic tape, or sent over a network. The names of the files are included in the output. The inverse operation is performed by

        cpio −i patterns

where a pattern selecting the files to be extracted is given as an argument to the command, and the main text is read from the standard input.

cron

A program to initiate regularly scheduled processes. It uses information from the file **/usr/lib/crontab**. Unlike the *at* command, it is reasonably efficient, in that it initiates one process, determines from **/usr/lib/crontab** when the next process will need to be started, then sleeps until that event is due. It must, of course, be woken up if a new entry is added to the table, which may occur before the next existing scheduled event. See the chapter on major commands for more details.

crypt

The same command is used for encrypting and decrypting files. A typical call is

        crypt < old > new

The password will be requested on-line; see the chapter on security for further discussion.

date

The normal user uses this command to give the current time and date. It is used only by super-user for setting the machine's time and date. The call is

date 03120930

to set the date to month 3, day 12, time 0930 hrs. In that case it generates two extra entries in the file **/usr/adm/wtmp**, one giving the time understood by the machine before the change, the other the time after the change. The difference must be taken into account when computing the logged-on time of a user who was logged on while the time-change took place. The logged time is the difference between the times of logging-in and logging-out less any time advances which occurred during the logged-in period. If the **wtmp** file does not exist (typically because the **/usr** disc is not yet mounted) no record of the time change is made.

dd

Device to device copying program; for further details, see the section on dumping the filestore.

deroff

For removing 'nroff' commands in text files. A particularly useful option is

deroff −w

which removes nroff commands, and splits the text to obtain output in the form of one word per line.

df

Enquire the number of blocks free on a file-system device. If no parameter is given, all devices are included; if a parameter is given, then just that device is inspected. This command is often now combined with the *mount* list, so that the output for each file-system device gives the mounted directory, the size, and the number of free blocks.

diff

The command *cmp* mentioned earlier merely compares two files, and reports whether they differ. The *diff* command reports the differences, and can give them in a form appropriate for editing one of the files into a copy of the other. It is particularly useful in comparing different versions of, for example, the source of a program, to see what modifications have been done.

It also provides an economy if two nearly identical files are to be stored on a system. It saves considerable space in that case to store one file, and a *diff* output which can be used to edit it to obtain the other version. The *diff* output will be considerably smaller than the complete second file would be, and the second version can then easily be generated when required, at the cost of an edit.

du

For summarising the 'disc usage' under a directory. Flag '−s' for total only, '−a' for all files. Files linked within the sub-tree are counted only once. Files linked outside the sub-tree are counted once.

dump

The command to dump the file-system to, for example, a magnetic tape or cartridge. See the chapter on dumping for details.

dumpdir

This command reads a magnetic tape or cartridge produced by *dump*, and list the names of all the files on it. See the chapter on dumping for details.

ed

This command is the standard Bell editor, and is used mainly for its compatibility across Unix systems, and to implement edit scripts produced by, for example, the *diff* command. Most installations use a different screen editor (such as *vi* or *unipad*) for normal editing. The Bell editor is reasonably (but sadly not completely) compatible in its use of regular expressions with *sed* and *grep*. It uses temporary workspace under **/tmp**.

For high security work, the Bell editor has an encryption mode introduced by the '−x' flag, which is compatible with the *crypt* command (i.e. files produced using *crypt* can be edited using 'ed −x file', and vice-versa). However, the editor's temporary files are not well encrypted with the standard version of the editor. A more secure version should be obtained if the problem is serious.

expr

This command evaluates expressions and delivers the result; it is particularly useful in complex shell scripts. For example, to print out a decreasing number of minutes left until a particular event (typically a system shutdown), the following commands (in the Bourne shell) could be used:

```
mins=5
while test $mins != 0
do
    echo "$mins minutes left"
    mins=`expr $mins − 1`
    sleep 60
done
```

The C shell has a number of arithmetic operations built-in.

f77

Many versions are now available on different processors. Like any compiler, they are very processor dependent. The standard *f77* compiler has all the flags of the C compiler (including '−D', '−I', etc), and in addition accepts as parameters the names of source files ending in '.c' (and passes them to the C compiler), in '.s' (and passes them to the assembler), and in '.o' (and passes then directly to the loader), as well as Fortran 77 files (ending in '.f'). It is thus effectively a general-purpose 'compile' command.

file

A useful command when exploring a new system, this command suggests the type of file whose name is given as parameter. It's not always right! Try

        file /bin/*

for example, to find which of the commands in **/bin** are shell scripts. It is useful to the system manager in checking that all command programs are stripped and optimised.

find

This command searches that part of the filestore under a given directory, performs tests on each file found, and can execute commands selectively on those files. It is particularly useful in system work. For example, the command

        find /usr −name "*junk*" −exec rm −f {} ";"

will search the filestore below the directory **/usr**, and delete any files with the string 'junk' in their name. The command

        find /tmp −atime +6 −exec rm −f {} ";"

will remove files from **/tmp** which have been unaccessed for 6 or more days. Such commands can be run regularly on an overnight or weekly basis to tidy the filestore.

getty

Part of the logging-on process. See the chapter on logging-in for details. The program actually resides in */etc/getty*.

grep

Useful for, for example, searching source code to find the occurrences of a given identifier. In a shell script, to test whether a given string or pattern occurs in a file, just the exit status of *grep* is required (true if at least one occurrence is found), use the flag '−s' as in the Bourne shell example

```
if
        grep -s pattern files
then
        echo "Pattern found ..."
fi
```

The command also has a '−y' flag on some systems, '−i' on others, which causes upper- and lower-case letters to be treated as equivalent.

init

The systems program which is activated as the last part of the booting-up process. The program actually resides in */etc/init*. See the chapter on booting-up for details of its functions, and the chapter of example programs for a summary.

iostat

The command for monitoring input/output statistics. It is fully described in the chapter on performance.

kill

Sends a signal to a process, e.g.

```
kill -2 1234
```

sends signal 2 to process 1234. Except for super-user, the process being signalled must be owned by the user sending the signal. The super-user should beware of sending signals to process number 1 (which happens to be *init*), since these can drastically reconfigure the system. Super-user can send signals to any process. The specification of default actions to be taken on the receipt of signals is shell dependent; see the appropriate shell documentation.

ld

The loader *ld* has the job of collecting '.o' modules produced by compilers, searching for required modules from libraries, and linking them together into an executable program (default name **a.out**). Many flags ('−o', '−l' and others) given in a call of the compiler *cc* are passed directly to the loader. Flags of particular interest include:

$-o$ Put the output into the file named as the next parameter rather than into the file **a.out**.

$-l$**<lib>**   Search the named library (**/usr/lib.<lib>**) for unsatisfied identifiers.

$-s$ Strip the relocation tables from the program.

learn

The *learn* command controls an instructional process for a user, using pages of information stored under **/usr/lib/learn**. An updated version of the program is now marketed as 'Instructional Workbench'.

lint

The *lint* command performs a number of checks on C program source, and comments on suspicious or unlikely constructions. It is particularly useful (or even essential) in view of the poor compile time checking done by most C compilers.

To check the modes of parameters and results of library subroutines, it relies on mode summaries of all library subroutines. These are stored in **/usr/lib**, under names such as **llib−lc** for the subroutines in the library **libc.a**, **llib−lm** for the subroutines in **libm.a**, and so on.

ln

To create a new link or name to a file. Several related commands can often be combined into one, linked to several names, and the particular action determined by the name by which the command was called rather than by a flag. Typically in the Bourne shell the command would be

```
case $0 in
    name1 ) AFLAG=yes; action for name1;;
    name2 ) BFLAG=yes; action for name2;;
    * )    echo "help";;
esac
```

since the parameter '$0' is the name of the command. In a C program there would be code to look at the string pointed at by *argv[0]* as in

```
if ( strcmp( argv[0], "name1" ) == 0 ) { ... }
else if ( strcmp( argv[0], "name2" ) == 0 ) { .. }
else { ... }
```

Directories cannot be linked (otherwise circular routes in the filestore could be generated), but devices can, on occasions, be usefully linked to more than one name.

login

Described extensively in the chapter on logging-in and out. It is normally a root-owned SUID file with access only to its owner.

lookbib

Part of the support for *refer* command, q.v.

lorder
Necessary to order semi-compiled modules in a library, to ensure that there are no problems with lost references. Given a set of '.o' files in the current library, use

```
ar cr libname 'lorder *.o | tsort'
```

to build the library in the correct order. See the chapter on the tour of the filestore for more details.

lpr (and lpd)
The two programs between them form the 'line-printer' † spooling system. The *lpr* program collects a user's output from its standard input or from files given as parameters, and stores the information in the spool area **/usr/spool/lpd**. It works in conjunction with *lpd*, the daemon which actually prints the saved files, and then erases them. See the section on SUID bits in the chapter on file-systems and the chapter of example programs for more discussion.

ls
There are many variants of this simple command now around. Managers should be particularly aware of the flag '−i' to print the inode numbers of each file, and of '−lg' to give the group owner of the files instead of their owners. Some versions of *ls* confusingly produce multi-column output when the output comes to the terminal, but single column (more useful for post processing) when the output is sent to a file or pipe.

mail
This is the simple electronic mail command that comes as standard on Unix. At many sites it has been enhanced to offer better facilities for handling mail, offering its own filing facilities for mail in different subject areas, or from different users. A simple

```
mail user
```

facility must be available for networking purposes.

make
See the chapter on major commands for a full discussion.

man
The *man* command for printing entries from the manual is discussed during the tour of the filestore.

---

† This is wrongly named since most printers are serial nowadays!

mesg

For reasons discussed in the chapter on security, it may be desirable to prevent public write permission on a terminal. The call

      mesg n

prevents further messages, the call

      mesg y

permits them, while

      mesg

reverses the current state, whatever it is. See the chapter on security for reasons why it may be desirable to do this.

mkconf

Used for reconfiguration in the system generation phase.

mkdir

The command *mkdir* is for making directories, and must be root-owned and SUID. It creates the new directory, makes the '.' and '..' entries in it (pointers to itself and its parent directory), and makes the new entry in the parent directory.

mkfs

To make a new file-system on a block-structured device; it completely overwrites any information already on a disc, and must be used before a disc can be mounted as a file-system. The disc must be unmounted at the time. For details, see the chapter on devices.

mknod

To create a 'special' file, normally a file for a new device. Details are given in the chapter on devices.

mount

The command

      /etc/mount /dev/disc1 /usr/guest

will mount the file-system on the device **/dev/disc1** under the directory **/usr/guest**. An additional parameter '−r' causes it to be mounted (software) read-only. The owner of the new directory **/usr/guest** is determined by the ownership of the directory at the head of the new file-system, and may be changed by performing a *chown* on **/usr/guest** after the system has been mounted. The permissions can similarly be changed by performing a *chmod* on the mounted directory. After the disc has been unmounted, the original ownership and permissions reappear on the directory.

Files under the original directory **/usr/guest** become inaccessible while the new directory is mounted, but are available again after the disc has been unmounted. It is unmounted by

```
/etc/umount /dev/disc1
```

the directory name being unnecessary. The command

```
/etc/mount
```

with no parameters will give a list of the device and directory for each mounted file-system. (This is kept in **/etc/mtab**, and must be cleared on boot-up; see the appropriate chapter for details.)

mv
This command affects only directory entries if the old and new names are on the same file-system, but involves the copying of files if the old and new names are on different file-systems. It can be used by root to move directories within a file-system.

ncheck
A call of *ncheck* applied to a raw file-system device as in

```
ncheck /dev/rdisc
```

gives the names and inode numbers of all files on that device. The call

```
ncheck −i 10 11 12 13 /dev/rdisc
```

gives the names of the files with the given inode numbers on that device. The call

```
ncheck −s /dev/rdisc
```

gives just the files with SUID modes, useful for checking security. It can be used to find quickly who owns which files.

newgrp
This call logs the user into a new group; it does this by *execing* to a new shell with the same UID as the old one, but with a new GID. The new gid is looked up in the file **/etc/group**. It is not analogous to *login*, in that

(a) it changes only the GID, where *login* changes both UID and GID;
(b) it does not execute any **.profile** or **.cshrc** file;

(c) it does not carry any environment across.

There should be a *newusr* command analogous to *newgrp*.

nice
The command

    nice command arg1 arg2 ...

executes the command 'command arg1 arg2 ...' at a lower-than-usual priority. In Unix numerically high priority number for a process (as would appear from a 'ps −l' command) represent low priority activity. The highest effective priorities are shown as negative numbers, and are available only to super-user. The command

    nice −10 command

executes the given command, dropping the effective priority by 10 (to a numerically larger value). Only the super-user may increase priorities by using

    nice −−10 ...

to increase the effective priority by 10, subtracting 10 from the numeric priority.

nm
This command is used for listing the relocation addresses of identifiers within a program. It can be used only on un-stripped programs. The *ps* command can work by, for example, looking up the location of the process table in the Unix kernel by using *nm* output from the file /**unix**, and then knowing where to look in the core image for the required information. Various flags are available, to specify, for example, whether the output is to be ordered by core address, or by identifier. The command, since it relates closely to loadable programs, will of course vary considerably on different processors.

nroff
This is the main text formatting program for use with character printers under the Unix system. For full details, see the companion volume by Barron and Rees.

od
This command is still available on some systems, and is the 'octal debugger', now superseded by the command *adb*.

passwd
Changes a user's password; the new password must be typed twice for safety, a rule which should (but does not) also apply in *crypt*. The new password

should contain a mixture of upper- and lower-case letters, digits, and other symbols to be reasonably secure. The super-user is not asked for the old password; an ordinary user is.

The command must be root-owned and SUID to enable it to access the file **/etc/passwd** and modify it. It sets a lock-file to avoid simultaneous modification by two users.

prof

For use in profiling; it displays the results from the file **mon.out** produced when a program has been run after compiling with the '−p' option. The '−p' flag to the compiler produces additional code in the program which causes line execution counts to be put into the file **mon.out** when the program is run. The command *prof* then combines the relocation information in **a.out** and the counts in **mon.out** and produces a summary of, for example, the total execution times and number of calls of subroutines which occurred when the program executed. This sort of information is essential for a professional approach to program development and testing.

ps

Gives (in no particularly useful order) the details of processes running on the machine,

    ps

for just the user's own processes in terse lack of detail,

    ps l

for a more detailed version of the same,

    ps a

for all processes. There are many much more helpful variations available which can give information for only those processes related to a given terminal or user, and can relate entries by preserving the 'child–parent' hierarchy, and giving details of 'child' processes following details of the 'parent' process. The *ps* command obtains its information for the kernel tables, found from **/dev/kmem**.

pstat

The purpose of *pstat* is to display values from various of the tables of information held by the system. Like *ps*, it uses the namelist from **/unix**, and reads the memory tables from **/dev/kmem** so must be root-owned and SUID. The options are numerous, relating to process and file activity; details should be sought in the manual.

ptx

For use in generating the permuted index at the front of the manual. It produces output from its standard input by taking each line, copying it and rotating it cyclically so that each word appears at the beginning of the line in turn, and then orders the complete set of output lexically. Thus each line will appear several times, with different words at the start of the line. Lines starting with simple words ('a', 'the' and so on) are not generated. The output is finally put in the form

        .xx ....

so that the user can supply any formatting (*nroff*) macro named *.xx* appropriate to the required output. The index at the front of the Unix manual is produced using this command.

pubindex

For use in conjunction with the *refer* command, q.v.

quot

The call

        quot

gives the quotas of disc space used by each user in the complete filestore. Parameters allow the command to be restricted to a particular file-system, or the usage for a particular user to be specified; otherwise the whole filestore and set of users is summarised.

ranlib

Used in converting general archive files into a form suitable for use as libraries. This command has appeared and vanished on different Unix versions. It is in Version 7, vanished in System III, and reappeared in System V. It essentially looks at the external references required by each of the modules in a library, and inserts a header at the top of the library so that the loader can pick up all the modules it will require in a single pass. It is an alternative to (and better than) the use of the commands *lorder* and *tsort*.

refer

This is the *nroff* preprocessor for inserting references automatically into text, and is part of the general additional *nroff* support. It requires a macro library (such as 'ms') which supports the macro calls which it generates, and the appropriate file of references. The inverted index to the references to speed access is generated by *indxbib* on some systems, *runinv* on others. See also *pubindex* and *lookbib*.

restor

For restoring file-systems or individual files from output produced by the *dump* command. See the chapter on dumping.

sa

The command for analysing the shell accounting information. See the chapter on performance for more details.

sdb

This is a recent variant of the debugger *adb*, compared with which it is easier to use, and more helpful to ordinary users.

sed

The stream editor, particularly useful acting as a genuine filter editing information passing down a pipe. Typically output from commands such as *nm* or *ncheck* can be of considerable quantity, and required information may be better selected by the use of *sed* if *grep* is not powerful enough.

Since the standard Bell editor has a severe limit on the size of files it can edit, this command can also be useful to edit arbitrarily large files. This use vanishes if one of the newer screen editors is in use, with no serious limits on the number of lines or on the length of lines. As an example (which could be done better in other simpler ways), the output from a simple *ls* command can be edited into a set of commands, and passed to the shell as in

```
ls | sed "s/^/command /" | sh
```

sh and csh

The basic common shell programs. The shell is terminated by an EOF character.

The name of the default shell (the program called by the '!' escape in *ed* and *write*, for example) should be part of the environment, given by the value of the variable 'SHELL'.

When in the editor, for example, it may be useful to execute the command

```
!sh
```

to allow the user to execute several commands, change directory, etc before returning to the editor by logging-out from the temporary shell.

size

Gives the sizes of the different parts of a loadable program. The output will obviously be different for different processors (particularly those with virtual memory), but will typically include the size of the text (the program code), data (the initialised data area) and bss (the non-initialised data area such as the stack for local variables) segments.

sleep

This command causes a shell script to suspend itself for a given number of seconds. If it is required to execute some command repeatedly, pausing in between for one minute, a possible Bourne shell construction is

```
while true
do
        command
        sleep 60
done
```

A *sleep* is woken up by a standard interrupt signal (SIGINT), usually 'delete' or control-c.

sort

This command is useful in many shell scripts, since commands such as *comm* and *word* require that their input be ordered. The command gives the impression that it holds the record for the greatest profusion of possible flags! It is sufficiently complex for reference to the full manual to be recommended.

spell

The *spell* command is for spelling checking; it effectively looks through the source text for words not occurring in the standard system dictionary **/usr/dict/words**, and reports them. It does this essentially by splitting the text into single words, sorting them into alphabetic order, removing duplicates, and then executing a *diff −23* command between this output and the **words** file. Varied beginnings and endings are taken into account. The flag '−b' specifies British spelling (it should be the default in the UK), and '−a' for American. These are managed by extra files of British-only and American-only words, kept in raw form under **/usr/src/cmd/spell**, and in hashed form under **/usr/dict** in files such as **hlist.b** for the British-only words. Lastly there are two extra wordlists, one for 'stopped' words (words which may look acceptable but are not), and one for 'local' words.

strip

This takes an **a.out** type of file, and strips out the relocation tables needed by commands such as *adb* and *nm*. The same effect is produced by using the flag '−s' in the *cc* compiler or the *ld* loader. The command *file* reports on whether or not a program has been stripped. If a file has been stripped, its size is significantly reduced.

stty

Used without any parameter, this command reports on the current mode settings of the current terminal. The terminal line to be referred to is determined from the standard output of the command, so that if its standard output is redirected, it can be made to refer to another line, as in stty > /dev/tty23

When called with parameters, it attempts to set the line modes to those specified. Typically parameters will set baud rates, switch echo on or off, switch to upper-case-only mode, set parity, set screen height, and set tab settings. There may be variations for different teletype drivers. See also *tset*.

su
This is most frequently used in the simple form

        su

which (after checking a password) creates a new super-user shell. On logging out from the *su* command, the user returns to the original shell, which has been suspended in the interim. It can also be used to create a temporary shell in any name, as in

        su guest

to create a new shell in the name of *guest* (both UID and GID being looked up in **/etc/passwd** and set). The command *su* must be root-owned and SUID. Logging out from the *su* shell returns the user to the original shell.

sync
This command is essential before taking a system down, to flush the buffers, and update the super-block. See the chapter on taking the machine down for details.

tar
The tape archiver; see the chapter on dumping.

tbl
Part of the *nroff* support, this one for laying out tabulated information. Again, it needs the support of a macro package such as 'ms'.

time
The command line

        time

gives the time used by the current shell so far, while

        time command arg1 arg2 ...

will run the name command and arguments, and on termination will report on the processor times used by the user and the system, and the elapsed time used by the command. It produces slightly different information in the Bourne shell and C shell.

touch
To set the modification date of a file to the current time; if the file does not exist, it will be created (empty). Thus no space is required other than that for the directory entry. Useful for markers in the *make* command.

tr
The *tr* command is straightforward to use, and has uses in, for example, converting upper-case to lower-case by

```
tr [A-Z] [a-z]
```

It must be used as a filter (i.e. reading from standard input, output to standard output always, not with files named as parameters) as in

```
deroff −w text | tr [A-Z] [a-z] | sort
```

The parameters to *tr* should in general be quoted, since expressions such as '[A-Z]' as above would be wrongly interpreted by the shell if files with names consisting of a single upper-case letter existed in the current directory.

troff
A photo-typesetting version of *nroff*.

tset
This takes as parameter a mnemonic for a type of terminal, as used in **termcaps**, and sets all the parameters necessary for that type of terminal. Its use saves a number of calls to *stty*.

tsort
Intended for use with *lorder* in the creation of ordered libraries. See the section on making libraries.

umount
See *mount*.

uniq
This command is primarily for removing adjacent duplicate lines in a file, for which reason the input is normally in sorted form. Typically the file may be a text file changed to one word per line (such as by *droff −w*) and sorted into alphabetic order, and the removal of duplicates will then give a list of all distinct words in the file. This is such a common requirement that the *sort* command has a flag '−u' which will remove duplicate lines in its sorted output.

update
Run regularly by the system to flush memory buffers to disc. See *sync*.

uucp and uux
Unix to Unix communication and execution. An inter-machine system, useful in linking machines over simple serial or dial-up lines, and essential for inter-machine mail. It has been augmented by much other user software, and by better networking, by which time it becomes a very major item of software.

wait
In the shell (not to be confused with the system call from programs) the command *wait* waits for all children to finish. Thus

```
command1 & command2 & command3 &
wait
```

will wait for all three children to finish. Beware that the *wait* command waits only for children of the current shell to finish; more complicated commands such as

```
one | ( two1 & two2 ) | three &
wait
```

may not wait for all of the subsidiary processes to terminate.

wall
To send messages to all logged-in users; this is not a sensible command to which to allow free public access. In some installations it is restricted to super-user, but a lesser restriction (such as availability to group 'bin') can avoid unnecessary use of the *su* command. Typically a call might be

```
echo "System going down in 5 minutes" | /etc/wall
```

who
A popular command for ordinary users, especially beginners! It interprets the data in the file **/etc/utmp**. The variant

```
who am i
```

just gives the entry for the user typing the command. A call with a single parameter assumes that the parameter is the name of a file to be read instead of **/etc/utmp**, typically **/usr/adm/wtmp**.

Appendix 4 **Summary of the C preprocessor**

The initial stage of C compilations is performed by a text preprocessor, which is normally a completely separate free-standing program. It is usually stored in **/lib** or **/usr/lib** under a name such as **cpp**. The preprocessor executes a number of modifications to the program source before it is passed to the compiler proper, and its operations should not be confused with those of the compiler. The preprocessor also has other applications than C, being usable as a first pass to other compilers, and as a simple text processor in its own right.

All preprocessor commands occur on lines starting with the '#' symbol. Most are one line definitions, but can stretch over several lines if necessary by escaping the internal newlines with a backslash.

```
#define WEIGHT  (net_weight * 10 * mass / 30 + \
          9.81 * gross_weight * 60 )
```

A4.1 #define

There are two quite distinct uses of the *#define* feature. One is for the 'macro-expansion' of text, so that in the simplest case the definition

```
#define TAX 0.15
```

then causes each occurrence of the text string

```
TAX
```

anywhere in the source to be replaced (before the compiler sees the source) by the string '0.15'. This is straight substitution; the source string '2*TAX' will be replaced wherever it occurs by the string '2*0.15', which will cause re-evaluation of the multiplication each time it is encountered unless the compiler performs sophisticated optimisations.

A more complicated use of *#define* involves calls with parameters, as in the macro expansion

```
#define MAX(X,Y) (X>Y?X:Y)
```

This causes any character string such as

```
MAX(i,'a'+j)
```

to be replaced by the text

```
(i>'a'+j?i:'a'+j)
```

These may be used for clarity (the meaning of 'MAX(...,...)' if more obvious than that of the full conditional expression) or efficiency (very simple functions are more efficiently executed by in-line code than by function calls with their attendant parameter passing and stack handling; the corresponding penalty is that in-line code involves the substitution of the code of the function at every call, and may take up more space for complicated functions).

As well as the user-defined constants and macros, the preprocessor has some built-in definitions, such as

```
__FILE__ : the current filename
__LINE__ : the current line number
```

Another quite distinct use of '#define' which should not be confused with the above relates to definitions which are either present or absent, but do not represent any particular character string expansions; they control the inclusion or omission of text at compile time. Any sections of code enclosed between lines

```
#ifdef Z80
---
#endif
```

are ignored unless a statement

```
#define Z80
```

has been encountered earlier in the preprocessor pass. The condition is false if the statement has not yet occurred, or if the statement

```
#undef Z80
```

has subsequently been encountered. Thus if slightly differing versions of a source are to be kept, such as two versions for two different processors, processor dependent code can be included in some compilations and not others by including a single *#define* ... line at the top.

Lines of source can be excluded rather than included by

```
#ifndef Z80
---
#endif
```

Further combinations are possible, as in

```
#ifdef Z80
---
#else
---
#endif
```

where code before the 'else' is included if 'Z80' has been defined, that after the 'else' is included if 'Z80' is undefined; and as in

```
#ifdef Z80
---
#elif pdp
---
#else
---
#endif
```

where the 'elif' is equivalent to 'else if', and the code following will be executed in this case if 'Z80' is undefined, but 'pdp' is defined. In addition, 'ifdefs' can be nested as required.

Also possible are logical operations on defined strings such as

```
#if Z80 && lint
```

for the logical 'and' (both 'Z80' and 'lint' must be defined), or

```
#if pdp || Z80
```

for the logical 'or' (either 'pdp' or 'Z80' or both must be defined).

This facility is also available on good compilers as a parameter to the compiler command. The parameter '−Ddef' is equivalent to a line

```
#define def
```

at the top of the program, and the parameter '−DLBUF=2048' is equivalent to a line

```
#define LBUF 2048
```

Thus in a *make* file, one could include

```
cc −DZ80 −o prog.com prog.c
cc −DZ80 −o prog.exe prog.c
```

to make two versions of the object program and store them in appropriately named output files.

The compiler preprocessors on different machines should have '#defines' such as 'unix', 'vax', 'pdp11', 'mert' and 'tso' already built-in and set up as appropriate.

A4.2 #include

There are two variants of this facility for the inclusion of named source files at an appropriate point in the text. The first takes the form

```
#include "file"
```

in which the preprocessor searches for the named file first in the current directory, then in a standard directory, usually **/usr/include**. When the file is found it is included completely and the text in the file inserted at the current point. The preprocessor itself reads the text of the included file thus allowing further '#defines' and '#includes' in the included file, and so on. The second form is

```
#include <file>
```

and will look only in the standard include directory, and complain if the file is not there. This form is used generally for the standard header system files that are referred to in the manuals, such as **/usr/include/stdio.h** for the standard input/output library, inserted by the line

```
#include <stdio.h>
```

Since the first form includes the second form (they would differ only if there was a name in the local directory of the same name as one in the standard 'include' directory), the second form is now dropping out of usage.

By convention the included files generally end with a '.h' suffix (for header) if they cause no code generation, but with '.c' if they include C code. Alternative directories for 'include' files can be named at compile time with the '−I' argument, as in

```
cc file.c −I.. −I. −I/usr/bill/h
```

which will search the three named include directories in order for any included files.

A4.3 Some examples of the use of #define

When developing a program it is often useful to have print statements in it which are purely for debugging, and are not required once the program is fully developed. Here again the preprocessor can provide a solution to the problem with the declarations

```
#ifdef DEBUG
#undef DEBUG
#define DEBUG(args)    printf args
#else
#define DEBUG(x)
#endif
```

Then lines such as

```
DEBUG(('reached line %d in file %s\n',__LINE__,__FILE__));
```

can be used for debugging. If DEBUG is currently defined, the DEBUG statements will be turned into printf statements; otherwise the DEBUGs will be converted to NULL statements and ignored. The use of extra brackets should be noted; the DEBUG macro itself must have a fixed number of parameters, where *printf* has a variable number. To overcome this, the *printf* parameters and their containing brackets are given as a single parameter to the macro.

Another non-trivial example of the use of defines is to handle the inconvenience when running the *lint* type-checking program on a C-program. Many 'spurious' messages may be generated by calls to, for example, the *system* subroutine, when the returned value is not used. In order to keep *lint* happy, one way around this is to declare functions of which the returned value is not required specifically in the following way.

```
#ifdef lint
#define VOID _VOID_ = (int)
int _VOID_
#else
#define VOID
#endif
```

To lint it appears that you are always assigning to the variable _VOID_ the returned results of functions. However when compiled with the C compiler, this code will be left out. With newer C compilers there is actually a type VOID for this purpose.

Appendix 5 **Proposed syntax standard for Unix commands**

In most Unix installations, the manager will add new commands to the system from time to time, which are particularly appropriate to that installation. These commands should conform as far as possible to the Unix philosophy, and a set of proposed standards is listed below. These arose at a Unix meeting, and represent the general views of users as to what 'the Unix command interface' really is.

(a)   Command names must be between 2 and 9 characters inclusive; straightforward, but a number of (non-Bell) Unix distributions already include several one-letter commands.

(b)   Command names must include lower-case letters and digits only.

(c)   Option names must be a single character in length.

(d)   All options must be delimited by '−'.

(e)   Options with no arguments may be grouped behind one delimiter. There are two distinct styles in existing commands, demonstrated by the *ls* command, in which all the options follow a single '−', as in

>   ls −lgt

and the *cc* command, in which the options are shown separately, as in

>   cc −s −O file.c

(f)   The first option-argument following an option must be preceded by white space. Thus an option '−f' allowing a nominated file must be used as in

>   dump −f /dev/device

and not as in

>   dump −f/dev/device

209

Presumably this rule implies that, for example, *nroff* macro packages should be selected as in

```
nroff −m s
```

and not as in the current practice of

```
nroff −ms
```

(g) Option arguments cannot be optional. This rule is broken in the '−o' option to the standard Version 7 *cc* command, in which

```
cc −o file prog.c
```

causes the output to be stored in the named file, but

```
cc −o prog.c
```

defaults the binary program to the file **prog**.

(h) Groups of option-arguments following an option must be separated by commas or separated by white space and quoted.

(i) All options precede operands on the command line.

(j) The string '−−' may be used to delimit the end of the options.

(k) The order of options relative to one another should not matter.

(l) The order of operands may matter and position-related interpretations should be determined on a command-specific basis.

(m) The string '−' preceded and followed by white space should be used only to mean standard input or standard output.

Index